<u>Strategy:</u> A Roadmap to Value
A Novel/Guide to Developing a Strategic Plan

BY: Michael P. Gendron

ISBN-13: 978-0-9798257-5-0

Preface

This book will introduce the readers to a new way of thinking about their business, growth & profitability. The book is focused on three different companies… entrepreneurial; mid-market – mid-size; and mid-market – moderate size.

The businesses are fictional, but the examples and events are those actually encountered during the years.

Throughout the book, three business owners meet periodically. I've identified these executives as the 'Three Amigos.' The 3rd generation owner has historically been a mentor to the younger owners.

Each segment of the book includes action steps that the reader can take to immediately improve company value. For example, in the section labeled 'Meeting with VP-Sales', there are examples of how to improve a sales organization's performance.

There are many references to "Lean Business" since Lean Business principles can improve every process, in any company… any size … anywhere in the world.

Strategy Introduction

Fifteen executives, seated at long conference tables, were anxious for the seminar to conclude. Several were busy taking notes of the speaker's final highlights; some were scanning emails, while others were scanning the clouds outside the tinted windows.

Jackson, the conference leader, flipped to his final slide, understanding that the audience was predictably anxious to finish the 1-day seminar. It was always difficult to be the last speaker – the one between tired executives and cocktails at the seminar's conclusion.

Jackson continued. "There are 8 steps that can be used to develop a strategic plan:
1. Assess the competitive environment.
2. Identify competitive priorities.
3. Self-assess the Company.
4. Define strategic goals.
5. Identify a strategic growth strategy.
6. If an organic growth strategy, determine if it is based on cost, product differentiation or technology.
7. If an M&A strategy, determine if it will be a platform or bolt-on M&A strategy.
8. Define actions and begin execution.

So let's just leave you with a final thought. No matter the size of the company, the industry - profit or non-profit organization – if you don't have a strategic plan, you will not get the greatest benefits from your invested resources. Questions?"

Patricia, the 30-something blue-eyed blonde, looked up from her journal, and raised her hand. "Jackson thanks for the discussion. I'm a small business – less than $10 million of annual revenue – and I've heard you repeat several times, 'get the senior staff together to develop the strategy.' So basically, I'm the senior staff. Suggestions?"

Jackson knew Patricia was a hi-potential entrepreneur from her mannerisms, attire and professionalism. She was one of three in the audience who frequently took notes, and peppered Jackson with questions to clarify a strategic concept.

"Great question, Patricia. When I describe the Senior Staff, I mean anyone in the Company that can contribute to the development of a meaningful strategic plan. While you may not have a team of VP's to work with, I'm guessing that there are a few essential people that are critical to your business. You may have a Manager of Operations who can give you insight about how the day-to-day activities can be improved or streamlined… maybe hears rumors about the market, or perhaps can do some grass-roots recruiting for you."

"Yes, there are a few key people, but they really don't think strategically. They are fully committed to daily deliverables."

"I understand, but without their tactical knowledge, you'd be out of business. That's where the strategic plan leadership is valuable. I like your questions, Patricia. If you have more questions, let's pick this up at the reception."

"Other questions?"

Doug, the elder statesman in the audience looked very thoughtful, as if reliving the past years' activities. "Jackson, I've been in my business for quite a few years – maybe I should say decades. I've never considered a need for a strategic plan, since I'm the owner and responsible only to myself. I've got a good feel for what's happening in the industry, so why take my staff 'off-line' for a warm and fluffy, feel-good, blue-sky brainstorming session?"

"Simply put, Doug, you shouldn't"

Doug's puzzled look demanded clarification. "If you take your staff for – what did you call it – 'a feel-good, fuzzy, brainstorming session,' you've wasted your time. The strategic plan session is real work. Folks have responsibilities throughout the session. Participants should be creative and focused on the future. There are concrete deliverables - not just pretty words that make you feel good. When a proper planning session is complete, you'll have broad guidelines for your future, specific timelines and measurable commitments from your team.

When done right, they'll feel a sense of ownership and personal commitment that they may have never felt before. An effective planning session may have some team building, but the session shouldn't be a group hug and a rope climb exercise. The team will discuss real issues… historical facts… competition … and your Company's strengths & weaknesses. And if you – as the owner – aren't ready to hear their opinion – well, the session will be a waste of time."

"So you're saying I shouldn't have a strategy?"

"No, you shouldn't have an undisciplined, fluffy discussion without goals and objectives."

"Jackson, I want to pick your brain a bit – maybe with a cold beer in my hand."

"Deal – if no other questions, let's break for some refreshments."

Most of the participants immediately adjourned to the bar for cocktails.

Patricia, Doug and one other middle-aged gentleman huddled informally. Jackson overheard some of the discussion.

Doug, who asked the last question, was a tall silver haired exec in a traditional blue blazer, button-down white shirt with open collar.

Jackson observed the group dynamics. The two younger executives deferred to his status as if he were an informal leader.

John, the third member of the group, leaned forward into the group. "Thoughts Doug?"

"I really liked the session because Jackson made me think a bit differently. I've got to step back and look at the landscape a bit more. Lately I've become entrapped in the day-to-day activity, and I really haven't paid attention to the macro environment. I guess my problem is that the business has been very successful for the past 28 years and I haven't felt the need for a documented strategy. I know what we can do in our operation, and quite simply, taking the staff to an offsite sounds like it could be a bit expensive. So, I guess I'll just spend a few extra hours of think-time and scratch out my plan – no need to burden the team."

Patricia's thoughtful look showed that she considered preparing a formal plan might be excessive. "John, what are you going to do?"

"I'm going to invest in a few cold drinks and maybe a long lunch with Jackson. Like Doug, the planning concepts seem to be on target, but I'm not convinced I need an offsite. I'll put some heat on Jackson and see what happens. Patricia, you've got the reputation of being on the front of the curve. I'm a bit surprised that you're not jumping at strategy?"

"I'm all in for strategy. I just want to be sure that I use a reasonable process. Hey, they've started to serve – let's get some refreshments."

It was clear that these three have some kind of informal relationship. Doug was perhaps the most successful and senior of the business owners. Perhaps he also owned the largest Company of the three.

Jackson was at the bar, encouraging attendees to order a cocktail, while shaking hands and thanking them for their attendance. The group buzzed with casual chatter about sports, the weather and the upcoming Bengals season.

Patricia strolled to the bar, ordered a glass of Chablis, and moved closer to the large group. As with many casual discussions, when the group saw the attractive blond on their informal boundary, one of the group invited Patricia into the conversation. Although not a football fan, she didn't interrupt the conversation with business, and smiled in agreement with the Bengals roster discussion.

After a few moments, she made eye contact with Jackson, and said, "Can we talk about strategy in my company?"

"Sure, let's go over to that high-top so that we don't distract these folks." He touched her elbow, guiding her to the table. "So what shall we talk about?"

"Jackson, I'm a small Company with 30 employees. We're driven by customer demands, daily deliverables and things go wrong. We've grown from my living room *assembly line*, to leased space with production and warehousing. It's a simple business, in a simple market. I'm committed to reinvesting in the operations, but I don't see a direct link between a multi-day expensive offsite and improving the day-to-day business."

"I understand your concerns, and based on your questions during the seminar, I know that you are committed to success. A strategy meeting doesn't need to be offsite. I use that term mainly to emphasize that the team needs to be isolated from daily activity so they can look beyond the horizon. Many times, the offsite is in the Company conference room, with a 'Do Not Disturb' sign on the door.

The real key to the strategy meeting is for the leader – that's you – to be aware of what is possible, and not be constrained by history. So let's say during the past 5 years you've grown at – shall we say 20% annually?"

"Not a bad guess…"

"And you want to continue to grow at 20%. Would you be happy with that rate?"

"Sure – over the long term, that's a wonderful goal."

"Well, why be conservative when you're developing the strategy? What if you asked yourself, 'How do I grow at 40% a year?"

Her broad smile and wide eyes signaled amazement. "I wouldn't dare think like that."

"I understand your conservatism, but when you're in the strategic planning mode, rather than just plan sequentially, think differently. Have you considered an expanded product line? Perhaps outsourcing some new designs? Maybe acquiring a competitor? And your distribution is now limited to - what, generally within about 100 miles of Cincinnati? What would it take to get into Chicago?

When you think distribution, how about through major retail channels like Macy's or Target?"

Patricia laughed. "… Absolutely never considered those things… I don't have the resources or the brand for that kind of expansion."

"Then how about bringing in an equity partner? Just some quick math… if you could triple your business in the next 4 years, and only had to give up 40% of your business, is that a good thing?"

"OK – I get it, Jackson. Maybe we should get together to talk more about planning. I'm not saying I'll do it, but I want to understand the next step. I'll drop you an email."

Jackson was pleased with the discussion. He recognized for many years that entrepreneurs are extraordinary people – no barriers too big to overcome. But they often don't have the broad based experience to explore new avenues – like distribution or outsourcing arrangements.

John introduced himself and said, "Jackson, it seems that you and Patricia got into a deep discussion. I wanted to spend a minute with you to talk about my company and what you think we should do to rapidly build value."

"OK – let's spend a minute. Let's move over there," gesturing to a table near the window. They both refreshed their cocktails.

"Talk to me, John. What's on your mind?"

"Well, I've got this company with about $30 million of sales. I'm in my mid-40's, and know it's time for me to start thinking about transition. The kids have no interest, so it looks like I'll have to sell the place. I've got plenty of runway left – no urgency - but I'd like to pretty up the place a bit, just in case timing is right. Any suggestions?"

"As I mentioned in the seminar, there is never a bad time to start strategic planning. It sounds like this may be an ideal time for you. If you'd like, I can stop over to your office and we can discuss specifics.

In general, I can coach you and your team through the strategic planning exercise in 10-15 days of my time over a period of 3+- weeks. I never go beyond 4 weeks elapsed time, because you folks have a business to run. Also, if it gets to be 4 weeks, we lose the energy required to make things happen.

Shall we talk about this next week?"

After referring to his calendar, Jackson said, "I'm open all day Wednesday?"

John confirmed that he had 2 hours open Wednesday, and the meeting was set for 8 AM.

Doug, the elder statesman of the informal pod, tapped Jackson's shoulder to get his attention.

"Hey, how about we have breakfast next week. I'd like to pick your brain about strategy. Are you open next Tuesday, 7:30 at First Watch?"

Referring to his calendar, Jackson confirmed his availability, and the meeting was set.

Jackson moved among the other attendees to informally ask if there were any questions. The remaining executives asked several general questions, more to be polite than being interested in the answers. They then quickly shifted the discussion to the sports' teams.

Jackson moved to the sidelines to jot some notes in his journal, ensuring that his upcoming meetings with Patricia and John would reflect today's discussion.

Jackson always arrived early so that he could review his notes. At exactly 7:30, Doug arrived. With purposeful, long strides he walked to Jackson and greeted him with a broad smile and firm handshake.

"Great that you could meet with me this morning, Jackson. Have you had a chance to look at the menu?" Doug was always direct and to-the-point - always seeming to be under time pressure.

"Sure, they have great specials here, and I'm set to go whenever you are."

Christopher, the server, greeted Doug as Mr. Green, and asked if he would have his usual oatmeal. Doug confirmed the order, and Jackson ordered the special.

As Christopher poured the coffee, Doug started the conversation. "That was an excellent seminar that you gave last week. I liked all the ideas that you tossed – very useful stuff. But I'm not convinced that I need to do a strategic plan. I'm thinking that I'll just use the concepts and drive through the strategic planning exercise myself. Anybody ever try that?"

"Certainly – and some can do a very effective job. It's a matter of self-examination, candor, getting the team to buy-in, and prioritization of activities."

"Well, that's what I thought, and over the weekend, I decided to develop a plan – perhaps not as thorough as one that you might develop, but it should do well for my Company. I've been running the place for almost 30 years, and we've made it through every recession so far - and with flying colors."

He pulled a one-page bullet point summary from his inside jacket pocket.

"I knew you wouldn't mind if we discussed this briefly – especially since you created the incentive for me to do this."

Jackson had been through similar meetings after many of his seminars. "Glad to discuss… but I've got another meeting at 10, so I'll have to be out of here by 9:30."

Jackson was comfortable reviewing some of the high level concepts with executives that attended his seminars. He found it curious that some business owners were uncomfortable completing a thorough strategic planning exercise.

"I pushed some numbers together, a list of strengths and weaknesses, and wanted to share them with you, confidentially of course."

John Davidson Enterprises, Inc.

	Act			Budget	Strategic Plan			
	2015	**2016**	**2017**	**2018**	**2019**	**2020**	**2021**	**2022**
Sales	89.0	86.0	91.0	93.0	97.0	101.0	104.0	109.0
Gross Margin	44.5	32.7	41.0	46.5	48.5	60.6	57.2	60.0
SG&A	12.0	16.5	13.2	13.5	13.3	14.0	14.5	15.0
Pretax	32.5	16.2	27.8	33.0	35.2	46.6	42.7	45.0

Strengths
- Hard driver
- Great reputation
- Quality workforce

Weaknesses
- No successor
- Limited resources
- Weak IT systems

"I can have a heck of a business as I look out a few years. Check out that growth rate. I'm guessing that I can achieve that – we'll probably pick up another product line or two within the next few years. Maybe even buy a local competitor – you never know."

"That is a very reasonable growth rate. And I especially like the profitability. May I say that the strengths and weaknesses look a bit slim? Are you comfortable that you've carefully assessed strengths and weaknesses?"

"Jackson, I've thought about these things a lot during the past few years. With your seminar, I knew that I had to put things on paper. We're a tight ship and we don't have many weaknesses."

Jackson continued the discussion as he enjoyed the frittata.

"Doug, what do you think the market growth rate would be in your industry? Perhaps 3-4% overall."

"That's about right."

"So you're planning to grow at market rate? Will any of your competitors drop out of the market? Are you expecting any new competitors?"

"I think some of my products will lose share to competitors, so I've built in an acquisition. M&A is a great way to grow."

"Ever done an acquisition before?"

"No, but I'm not overly concerned. I'll just buy the assets. I attended a seminar a few months ago, and the attorney mentioned that an asset acquisition was often the least risky method to acquire a company. When I thought it through– well sure, I agree."

"I don't have a calculator, but it looks like your gross margin rate is improving. Anything in particular"

"Absolutely. This isn't pie-in-the-sky. I've been reading about 'lean manufacturing' and the likely results from the program. We'll implement lean, and improve the margins. I've heard some stories, and the returns from such an effort are enormous. I've only put a 5% margin improvement in the plan."

"And your SG&A looks like the percent to sales is dropping. Any thoughts?"

"Absolutely – leverage Jackson. Leverage off the fixed base. While I haven't gotten into the details, I think we can grow this business without a lot of incremental SG&A."

"But you've noted that you have a weak IT system. How will you resolve that?"

"The cloud is the thing these days. Folks have told me that a company can be up on the cloud in a matter of weeks. Several folks in the Rotary Club told me they converted from their stand-alone system to the cloud in just a few weeks."

"Was their system the same software, but just a different host – not their hardware, but the software developers cloud."

"Yes – good guess. It was a snap – so they said."

The conversation wandered among topics such as competitors, a more in-depth discussion of strengths and weaknesses, and how the Company would both capture market share and acquire companies and/or product lines.

At about 9:20, Jackson summarized their discussion.

"Doug, you've put a lot of thought into this plan, but I'm not sure that you've effectively engaged your management team. I don't know your business, and I haven't met any of your team, but do you think that they could add more depth to your analysis?"

"I can understand your question, Jackson. If I weren't so familiar with the business and the team, I'd seriously ask that exact question. But I'm out there every day, sometimes working side-by-side with them. I know how they think."

"OK – and how about the *team engagement* part of the plan?"

"The guys are just like family. If I tell them to do something, they'll run with it and deliver it on time, every time. We're a very tightly managed organization."

"Well, I guess that you've done the deed. Hey, it's almost 9:30. Have we accomplished what you wanted to accomplish?"

"Yes… I just wanted to review the strat plan with you to get some feedback."

"OK – let me give you a quick summary. I like the way you've considered many of the topics… expanded product line, acquisitions, strengths & weaknesses, and financial projections to get some accountability. I think that you might be light in the strengths & weaknesses, and your creative engagement of your team may also be … well, you may have an opportunity to get more value if you toss the strategic planning challenge to them, but you're in charge.

Your expectation of fairly simple M&A through asset purchase is certainly possible, but my gut tells me it might be high risk to assume the complexity away.

Also, may I suggest that you dig down another layer on your spending and gross margins? They seem to be a bit aggressive.

Great to see you, Doug, and keep in touch. I'd like to hear how things turn out."

With that, a handshake and Jackson snatched the check and quick-stepped to the cashier.

As he walked to the car he wondered if he had been candid enough about the superficial strategic plan Doug prepared. When he got to his car, he jotted a note to follow up with Doug in 6 months.

Intro Meeting with Patricia

Patricia's office was in Over-The-Rhine (OTR) – a converted brewery completely renovated into a modern, open architecture office. The OTR location allowed her to have the light assembly facility adjacent to the offices. The office was decorated with bright, colorful murals that cheerfully contrasted with the aged brick walls.

The décor reflected her personality – lean, functional and proper. An array of plants carefully distributed among the low-level workstations provided some privacy, while not intruding on the open-office theme.

Glass-walled conference rooms with sheer drapes provided privacy without disrupting the openness.

Patricia's *office* was a conference table in the open area - a tempered glass plate resting on stainless steel stanchions. A selection of sharpies, a Mont Blanc fountain pen, and the Apple iPhone adorned the top. A lightly filled In-Box, and a full Out-box covered the front right corner of the surface.

When she saw Jackson enter the office, her smile brightened, and she quickly greeted him, while directing him to the conference room.

"Great to see you Jackson. Glad you could fit the meeting into your schedule. Coffee? Water?"

"A water would be great."

Opening the fridge, she selected two, chilled Fiji waters.

"I'm certainly glad that you could fit me into the schedule, Jackson. Your schedule must be very hectic, given your ideal client of 'middle-market'. Based on what I've read, the term 'strategic plan' is not often used in that size company, giving you an unlimited supply of clients. And, truthfully, I'm one that hasn't used the term. Your brief seminar piqued my interest, and I'd enjoy hearing more."

"Patricia, I was impressed by your participation in the conference. You're the type attendee that keeps me on target, and a little bit stressed with your questions. And that's a good thing. What shall we talk about?"

"Excellent – let's get to it. I've put together some information that might help you understand our Company. As I mentioned, I think that I'm a bit too small for strategic planning, but since you know our size and you fit me in the schedule, I'm guessing that I'm not. Now you've got to convince me. Let's take a look at the information."

Fashion Clicks LLC

Incorporated	1/1/08
Current Staffing	
Owner	1
Manager	3
Associates	35
Controller	1
Total	40

P&L

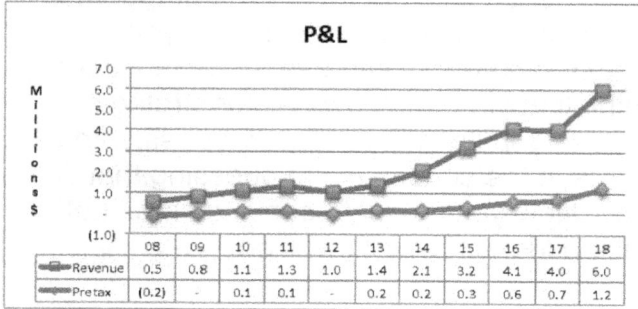

P&L

	08	09	10	11	12	13	14	15	16	17	18
Revenue	0.5	0.8	1.1	1.3	1.0	1.4	2.1	3.2	4.1	4.0	6.0
Pretax	(0.2)	-	0.1	0.1	-	0.2	0.2	0.3	0.6	0.7	1.2

Primary Productds:
Fashion accessories (Locally Sourced)
Fashion Accessories (Foreign Sourced)
Distribution
Primarily local (within 500 miles)
Very Limited - Internet
Marketing
Primarliy Direct Sales to Boutique Retail

"Jackson, I've never talked about strategic planning with anyone before, but I thought this might be useful to acquaint you with the business. Any thoughts?"

"My first reaction is 'wow'. The last few years have been excellent. What's happened with the revenue?"

"I think that '14-'16 we were just getting distribution and becoming better known in the area. Our '18 sales are projected, but we're on track. We added a few products to our line – more soft goods. Profits are up because we've held margins and so far haven't had any inventory problems. We're just starting to look at a better website that will give us a more national – maybe even an international – reach."

"And have you seen much change in your headcount during the past 2-3 years?"

"Well, our last major change was in '12 when we had some serious inventory control problems... we terminated the warehouse manager."

"I guess my first impression is that you've come a long way in a short time. If you could scratch out some longer term goals – say maybe through 2021 – what do you see?"

Right now, without any serious thinking, I'd like to see revenue of about $7 million – let's say a 5% growth rate."

With that, Jackson and Patricia discussed many of her personal goals for the business. Some goals were less financial than cultural. She was concerned about the well being of her employees and that included career growth for each of them. She wanted to provide childcare, college tuition assistance, performance bonuses... so many benefits. She also wanted to be financially secured within the business, and grow the operation with modest risk.

During the discussion, Jackson scratched out the rough organization chart.

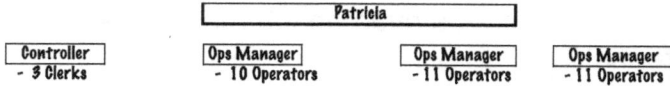

Patricia			
Controller - 3 Clerks	Ops Manager - 10 Operators	Ops Manager - 11 Operators	Ops Manager - 11 Operators

"Patricia, it looks like if you were to assemble a team of folks to develop a strat plan, you might include the 3 managers and the controller. Are there any critical folks in the operators?"

"Not an operator but the op's manager who designs many of the products and understands the supply chain is essential to the organization."

"OK- she should definitely be on the planning team. As I think through your operation, it's lean and compact. I'd suggest that you have a half-day *offsite* – and that could be here in your office, but without interruptions.

The agenda would focus on some history, your personal goals for the business and maybe some aggressive financial targets. We could talk about the competitive landscape – maybe get into specific competitors – and highlight some of Fashion Click's strengths and weaknesses.

Before that meeting, I'd suggest that I spend a couple of hours with you to better understand your expectations, and 1-2 hours with each attendee. I can get some insight from them about what they consider to be possible. So let's say 2 days of preparation, half-day in the meeting itself, and 1-1.5 days review and summarizing the plan to the team.

Here's my commitment – this whole process could be done in 5-7-business days elapsed time, which allows your team to continue day-to-day activity. It'll take about 3-5 days of my time. With that minimal investment, you'll have a plan to reach your goals, and we will establish performance targets that you can measure periodically.

This won't be a 30-page plan – maybe 5-7 pages - but since it's your first, you'll have a roadmap to guide you through the next years.

Thoughts?"

"So when can we start?"

They researched their calendars and set the schedule to begin next week.

"Great, Patricia. I'll let you introduce the planning concept to your team, and we will meet with the controller next week to develop the historical information. From there, I'll meet with your ops managers to get background information about the business."

Intro Meeting with John

John's $30 million revenue business, established in 1975, was more mature than Patricia's. The facility was a post-war, non-descript brick building in Oakley. When

Jackson arrived, he passed the 12 spaces reserved for John and, most likely, his senior staff. The 4 spaces closest to the entrance were marked 'Visitor'.

The dark wood receptionist desk dominated the entry, and 6 deep cushioned leather chairs were available for visitors. The dim lighting would likely be enhanced by the early morning sun, but otherwise was too dark to read small print.

The mid-40's receptionist, surrounded by mounds of paper, appeared to be processing invoices. When the door squeaked open, she immediately looked up, smiled and welcomed Jackson.

After asking for his business card, she announced Jackson's arrival to John through the paging system.

A few minutes later, John arrived and escorted him through the paneled hall to his personal conference room.

"Jackson, I must admit that I attended the seminar as more of a curiosity than a serious business discussion. But your examples – well, they made perfect sense. Focusing beyond the horizon – great concept that I've been doing for years, but without the full engagement of the team.

You also dispelled my idea of a strategic plan that we often joked about - a task that takes months to prepare and becomes a block of paper on the shelf. When you said that a plan could be completed in 3+- weeks… well, I want you to explain just how that can be done."

"Sounds like I have a challenge. So how shall I proceed?"

"It's your show. You know my concerns. I've put some background information together. Let's spend a minute to acquaint you with the business."

Here's our organization.

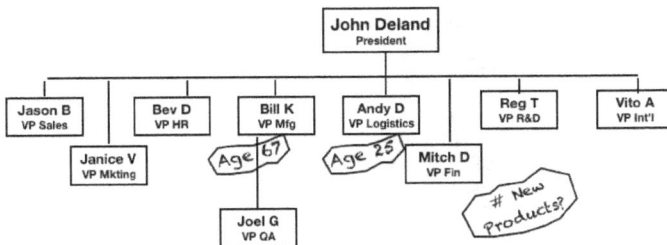

"We've evolved this organization over the years to adapt to changing conditions. I like what we've done so far… what do you think?

"As background, I've heard that current theory is to have up to a dozen direct reports – a flatter organization… And to be honest, the international folks don't all need to report to me. It's more of an ego thing for Vito. And if I was honest about it, the marketing function is more of a customer service."

John shared the financials and commented about several notable facts.

Millions US $	2016		2017		2018	
	Amt	%	Amt	%	Amt	%
Sales:						
Metal Fab	11,450.0	43.3%	11,750.0	42.3%	11,550.0	38.6%
Casting	7,805.0	29.5%	8,055.0	29.0%	8,350.0	27.9%
Resale	4,355.0	16.5%	4,555.0	16.4%	3,500.0	11.7%
International	2,775.0	10.5%	2,955.0	10.6%	5,915.0	19.7%
Other	65.0	0.2%	455.0	1.6%	635.0	2.1%
Total	**26,450.0**	**100.0%**	**27,770.0**	**100.0%**	**29,950.0**	**100.0%**
Gross Margin						
Metal Fab	4,580.0	40.0%	4,700.0	40.0%	5,197.5	45.0%
Casting	2,341.5	30.0%	3,222.0	40.0%	3,340.0	40.0%
Resale	1,088.8	25.0%	1,138.8	25.0%	875.0	25.0%
International	1,526.3	55.0%	1,625.3	55.0%	3,549.0	60.0%
Other	19.5	30.0%	113.8	25.0%	127.0	20.0%
Total	**9,556.0**	**36.1%**	**10,799.8**	**38.9%**	**13,088.5**	**43.7%**
SG&A						
Selling	2,645.0	10.0%	3,332.4	12.0%	4,492.5	15.0%
Marketing	1,587.0	6.0%	1,666.2	6.0%	1,797.0	6.0%
R&D	793.5	3.0%	1,388.5	5.0%	1,497.5	5.0%
Financa	661.3	2.5%	694.3	2.5%	748.8	2.5%
IT	529.0	2.0%	555.4	2.0%	599.0	2.0%
Legal	529.0	2.0%	555.4	2.0%	599.0	2.0%
HR	396.8	1.5%	416.6	1.5%	449.3	1.5%
Other	-	0.0%	-	0.0%	-	0.0%
Total	**7,141.5**	**27.0%**	**8,608.7**	**31.0%**	**10,183.0**	**34.0%**
PBT	**2,414.50**	**9.1%**	**2,191.05**	**7.9%**	**2,905.50**	**9.7%**
Headcount						
Operations	65		55		48	
Sales/Mkting	17		18		20	
Admin	6		6		7	
Total	**88**		**79**		**75**	

Doug reviewed the product sales summary.

New Product			
Engine Cast	400.0	950.0	2,100.0
Custom Fab & Eng		350.0	750.0
Other			
Total	**400.0**	**1,300.0**	**2,850.0**

Jackson observed, "That is great growth in the Precision Cast sales. Anything interesting happening?"

"We've had great success in the European market. For some reason they really like the quality and service that we provide for them. We've been trying to exploit that at home, but haven't been able to land anything big here in the US."

"You said Europe, but it isn't in the International sales."

"That's something that we need to clean up. It seems that it grew so fast, and we knew what it was, we just didn't change the reporting."

Jackson explained the typical strategic plan process includes the executive staff and other key personnel identified by the owner. Once the owner's goals are clear, Jackson and John will explore opportunities for growth and profitability. Jackson will then interview the staff, always sensitive to the owner's goals. Candid staff interviews are the foundation of the planning process.

The process is straightforward – understand goals … brainstorm alternatives … understand resources and constraints… facilitate the planning process ensuring full engagement by the team… summarize the results and develop metrics that can be used to monitor performance.

Jackson explained that no more than 1-2 hours per executive interview session would keep the discussion focused and creative, minimizing the impact on the daily activities. Jackson will summarize the discussion for each executive interviewed to use as planning background.

After these confidential interviews, Jackson will meet with the owner to discuss how the business can reach – or perhaps exceed - his goals.

Jackson and John will then develop an agenda for the offsite, define the background information to be used at the meeting, and schedule the executive interviews.

The preliminary executive meetings will be the foundation of the offsite, but during the offsite the team interaction may identify unforeseen opportunities and obstacles. The successful facilitation will ensure executive engagement and commitment to the plan.

The plan will include an executive summary; Visions/Mission statement, competitive analysis, strengths & weaknesses, financials and a project plan with names, task dates and deliverables that will achieve the Company's goals.

John observed, "That sounds like a lot of work in a short time. My initial response is – WOW. But let's step back a bit. We can't afford market research and a lot of competitive analysis. If we don't get independent analysis, how will we ever complete such a plan?"

"Excellent question, John. Let me ask this, do you and your team understand the market and competitive products?"

"Well, we have a pretty good understanding of the market, but that's not in-depth like you'll need."

"John, I don't need anything – it is you folks that have the need. As we get into the active discussion about competitors, it's my job to keep a quick pace, push you and your team within certain time constraints to identify issues. As we discuss these items, we could very well determine that in certain areas we don't know enough about the business. At that point, we establish a task for one of your team to fill that knowledge gap. Remember how I said earlier that this wouldn't be a perfect plan, but one that moves you down the path to better business. A combination of experience, knowledge, and resources of time and capital available will achieve your goals. Our goal is to continuously improve your business. If we were to try to make an absolutely perfect plan, we'd still be working on it in 6 months. That's of no value to you or your team."

"I'm starting to appreciate how you do this planning. So we're talking about minimal intrusion on the day-to-day job, mining our current knowledge, understanding my goals, and developing a plan that the entire team *owns*. And you say in 10-15 days of your time, I'll have a plan?"

"Correct."

"OK – normally I don't make a decision this quickly, but it seems that my risk is minimal, and the upside is a plan that the team develops. Can you put a firm proposal together? I'll evaluate it and get back to you within 24 hours. Agreed?"

"You'll have a proposal this afternoon."

The Three Amigos #1

One week after the seminar John, Doug and Patricia – informally named *The Three Amigos* - met briefly after the monthly Chamber of Commerce meeting.

"John – Patricia – how about a coffee? I want to pick your brain."

Doug was still thinking about his strategic plan – the one-page document that he shared confidentially with Jackson.

"I wanted to share a bit of my experience with you. Do you remember that 'Strategic Planning Seminar' we attended a week ago? Well, I couldn't let that Jackson guy off the hook, so I invited him to breakfast to hear more about his *planning* process."

Doug was very animated and quickly continued, not giving anyone time to respond.

"Over the weekend before I met with Jackson, I put a strategy together for my Company and decided to test Jackson... you know, find out if he had any substance, or was he just a consultant that delivered BS and a large bill. We talked for an hour or so, and it seems that he's a guy that comes into a business, asks a few questions that we answer, and then he reports to us what we already told him. Maybe he's not a total jerk, but I decided that he's not so good… I wanted to share my experience so you don't have to waste your time."

Patricia cleared her throat, and said somewhat nervously, "Doug, I'm glad that you cornered me today. I spent some time with Jackson. I'll agree that his process seems far too simple, and that he asks questions, we answer the questions and then he summarizes our answers. I met with Jackson, and he asked me several questions. I didn't have the answers.

Doug, he asked questions that I should have been able to answer. His questions weren't about 'today' but about tomorrow and how would I achieve my goals. When I considered a few days of his cost and what I might learn – not from myself but from his questions – I saw a slight upside. He assured me that a plan wouldn't require weeks of his time. My target is no more than 5 days of his time.

I signed with him. We're doing a plan."

"Ouch – are you serious?" Doug was surprised given her tight expense control and what seemed to be a frivolous cost.

John leaned into the conversation.

"Doug, I also met with Jackson. After a couple hours of discussion, I signed up with him as well. And until Patricia just mentioned it, I didn't realize exactly why. Now I realize it is because of the questions that he asked. I think his years of experience are the key to his planning method. He doesn't know about my business… my industry. He relies on my team's knowledge of the business.

He knows the questions, not the answers. His facilitation process is tight and well controlled so that we don't wander across months of planning. Doug, if my team can spend 5-10% of our time across 2-3 weeks and focus on the future, my downside risk – the cost - is insignificant if we align the Company to my personal goals.

And Patricia, how did you get him to commit to 5 days when I need 10-15?"

"Smaller company. He'll be interviewing – what – 10+ people in your shop? For me, he'll talk with 3-4 of us. Simple math." She smiled broadly.

Doug leaned back in his chair, unconvinced, sipping his coffee. "Glad you folks can afford a *consultant*. I'm going to stick with my two-pager and launch into the future. Say, do you mind if we meet occasionally just to get a progress report on Jackson? Since you folks are spending the time and money, I'll let you be my test case."

Both agreed.

Patricia now felt a bit concerned about spending the money, but she had made the commitment… buyer's remorse settled in.

Doug was fully confident in his decision –
especially when he considered the minimal
cost in his $30 million business.

Jackson Initial Meeting With Patricia

Patricia was concerned about the amount of preparation work required. She wanted this to be an outstanding planning session without many hours of prep work. Surprisingly, Jackson asked for the last 4 quarters financial statements, the previous 2 year-end statements, and a headcount summary for each period.

"Jackson, we don't prepare quarterly financials."

Jackson responded, "OK then – just the y-t-d statements for March, June, September and December, and the year-end statements for 2017 and 2018 if they're easily available."

"Jackson, our statements are pretty simple. You're not going to see much detail. And would you mind if I just had simple headcount summaries like the one I showed you a few days ago?"

"That's ok – I just want to see how you're managing the business today. There's no right or wrong – just how you're managing today. And for headcount, I'll take anything you've got... shouldn't spend 30 minutes summarizing – directional number of people is fine. No need to analyze payroll or do anything special for me."

The next day Patricia sent the statements by email. She included:

	2012	2013	2014	2015	2016	2017
Sales						
Basic	923,112	957,794	1,895,688	2,149,292	3,059,668	4,295,884
New Products	33,551	418,983	194,088	1,050,850	980,007	1,661,064
Total	956,663	1,376,777	2,089,776	3,200,142	4,039,675	5,956,948
Cost of Sales						
Basic	535,405	641,722	1,118,456	1,547,490	2,080,574	2,749,366
New Products	26,505	213,681	75,694	620,002	695,805	1,046,470
Total Cost	561,910	855,403	1,194,150	2,167,492	2,776,379	3,795,836
Gross Margin						
Basic	387,707	316,072	777,232	601,802	979,094	1,546,518
New Products	7,046	205,302	118,394	430,849	284,202	614,594
Total	394,753	521,374	895,626	1,032,650	1,263,296	2,161,112
GM %	41.3%	37.9%	42.9%	32.3%	31.3%	36.3%
Expenses						
Assembly Labor	255,456	224,545	365,665	211,234	212,334	544,676
Marketing						
Gen'l	4,566	2,887	12,544	25,877	37,456	29,800
Web	7,343	2,332	14,788	27,556	37,556	42,332
Commission	28,998	57,668	98,807	101,344	199,780	257,668
All Other						
Admin	44,556	54,522	52,234	66,545	68,565	77,998
All Other	30,611	1,964	156,012	22,196	4,059	18,861
Total Spending	371,531	343,918	700,050	454,752	559,750	971,335
SG%A %	66.1%	40.2%	58.6%	21.0%	20.2%	25.6%
Pretax	23,222	177,456	195,576	577,898	703,546	1,189,777
% of Sales	2.4%	12.9%	9.4%	18.1%	17.4%	20.0%
Product Line GM						
Basic GM%	42.0%	33.0%	41.0%	28.0%	32.0%	36.0%
New Prod GM%	21.0%	49.0%	61.0%	41.0%	29.0%	37.0%
Labor as % of Sale:	26.7%	16.3%	17.5%	6.6%	5.3%	9.1%
Marketing % of Sak	1.2%	0.4%	1.3%	1.7%	1.9%	1.2%
Commission % of S	3.0%	4.2%	4.7%	3.2%	4.9%	4.3%
Admin % of Sales	7.9%	4.1%	10.0%	2.8%	1.8%	1.6%
New Prod % Total	3.6%	43.7%	10.2%	48.9%	32.0%	38.7%
Sales (000's $)	956.7	1,376.8	2,089.8	3,200.1	4,039.7	5,956.9
Basic	923.1	957.8	1,895.7	2,149.3	3,059.7	4,295.9
New Prod	33.6	419.0	194.1	1,050.9	980.0	1,661.1
Admin + Other	75.2	56.5	208.2	88.7	72.6	96.9
Headcount	22.0	27.0	29.0	30.0	35.0	40.0
000's $Sales/H/C	43.5	51.0	72.1	106.7	115.4	148.9

Jackson mused, '*Frequently entrepreneurs look at raw numbers, and concentrate their efforts on satisfying customers and managing the daily operations. Since their time is extremely limited, they tend to compare current year performance to prior years. It is sometimes difficult for entrepreneurs to step back from the transactional activity and strategically review the competitive environment, the Company's strengths and*

*weaknesses, and identify business
opportunities.'*

Although Jackson was unfamiliar with Patricia's
retail segment, he analyzed the raw data and
summarized the information using graphs to
identify unusual trends.

Jackson arrived at Patricia's office 10 minutes
early, hoping to observe some of the office
activity before their formal meeting. One of the
office staff greeted Jackson, asking if he'd like
a bottle of water. She quickly passed chilled
spring water to Jackson, while guiding him to
the reception seating.

There was a very positive vibe as folks
attended to phone calls and on-line activity.
The young staffs' casual/business casual dress
complemented the office architecture. The
quick office tempo resembled a metronome
pacing a Sousa march. Smiles prevailed.

Yes, Patricia has cultivated a very positive
environment. If she can now focus this energy
on the proper strategy, she has a winner.

After a few minutes, Patricia greeted him.
"Jackson, great to have you for our first official
planning meeting. I can't tell you how excited I
am about strategic planning. I'm not sure what
to expect, but I'm all in, and I trust your
judgment."

At a quick pace, she escorted Jackson to the conference room. Sheer drapes drawn, but both still visible to the curious staff.

"I announced our strategic plan goal to the staff yesterday. They were very curious, to say the least. Jackson, did you notice that most of the folks are millenials?"

"Sure did. They seem like a very motivated group of employees."

"Associates, Jackson. I'll share a secret with you. Some of them saw you here last week, and wondered how someone your age could help such a young organization. I could only laugh, and mentioned that age is in the mind, and I hoped they had as active an imagination as you. You won't disappoint me, will you?"

Jackson leaned back in his chair and smiled broadly smiled, "Not my intention to disappoint, Patricia. But I'll let you be the judge of that. So let's get to it.

First of all, tell me how you got started in this business, and some points of excitement – good or bad – that are highlights from the past few years."

For the next half-hour, Patricia reveled in her accomplishments – not in a boastful way, but rather as one who overcame insurmountable challenge through hard work, high credit card balances, and some 100-hour workweek's.

Her eyes flashed with excitement as she carefully described some of the worst times, and how through sheer force of will, she overcame impossible challenges. Yes, she was the ultimate entrepreneur who was now ready to graduate to the next stage of business. A business that plans rather than reacts… a business that measures future risk and opportunity and thinks beyond the horizon.

"That's a great summary of the history of this Company, Patricia. So now, let me show you a few different ways to look at the Company's performance. I've taken your numbers and graphed a few specific items. I like graphs so that I can better understand trends – I'm not so much interested in an individual year's results."

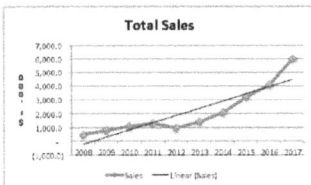

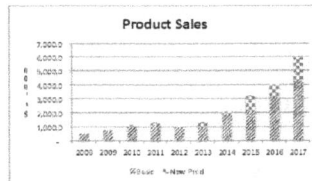

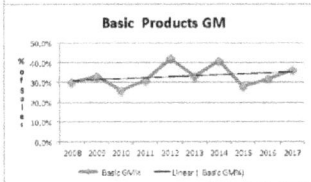

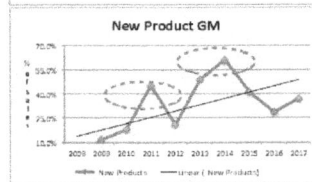

Commission % Sales

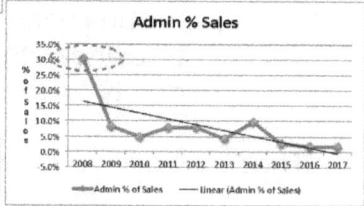

Admin % Sales

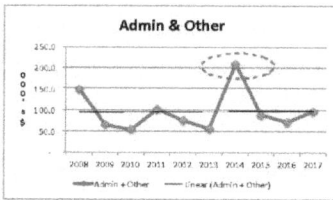

Admin & Other

With that brief introduction, they reviewed the charts. By focusing on trends, peaks and troughs in the annual results, they identified several decisions – and failures – that Patricia recognized.

Several of the major, and very successful decisions made include:

- Three years ago, Patricia started to broaden her product line with new products, resulting with higher gross margins.
- She outsourced more of the light assembly work to the manufacturing source. This improved growth without additional headcount.
- Her key business development person started in 2015, and has slowly improved the new product launch cycle.

- By using the web, she has expanded distribution without major investment.
- She expanded her commission sales force and increased commission rates.

As Jackson reviewed the charts, Patricia was initially surprised at the patterns she observed. When Jackson questioned several of the peaks and troughs in the discussion, she again relived some of her entrepreneur conquests – and failures.

It wasn't easy being a thirty-something entrepreneur, but she seemed to thrive in the environment.

Jackson then reviewed the charts of select items. In 2018, new product sales were clearly saving the Company. Sales peaks occurred seasonally around Mother's Day, and were ramping up in the 4th quarter in anticipation of the holiday season.

Patricia explained that Natalie was the new product specialist, and while she had been employed for the past 3 years, she only recently spent many hours of overtime sourcing new products.

Assembly labor tracked favorably with sales, since some of the new products were sourced complete. Natalie prepared a simple financial analysis that showed it was cheaper to have the manufacturer assemble the products than have them shipped to Cincinnati for final assembly. This allowed them to keep assembly labor costs low, while increasing sales.

"So what do all those assembly people do now that many complete products are outsourced?"

"We keep them busy on many other tasks in the business. There aren't any associates standing around doing nothing."

"OK – that sounds good. I'm curious. Is it possible that there may be more value added activities they can perform rather than just keeping busy?"

Patricia frowned – she flashed a bit of defensiveness. In a measured sentence, she responded, "I suppose there may be."

Jackson immediately recognized the sensitivity. "One thing I've done throughout my career is challenge what I'm doing. Heck, I try to pay attention to my daily activities, and occasionally I stumble… get in a rut and don't realize it. By constantly looking for a better way, I discover the treasure of time.

So let's talk about new product development. How many months does it take to develop a new product?"

"Not an easy answer. It really depends on how much time Natalie and I have to concentrate on NPD. So it can range from – oh, let's say 8-10 weeks when we're focused to as much as 6 months."

Jackson nodded. "And when I look at the graphs, I notice that the sales spikes coincide with new product introductions. Do I also see that gross margins increase with a new product?"

"Of course. New designs equal greater profit."

"So, if you examine exactly how many hours it takes to develop a new product, what would you guess?"

"We don't keep track of it that way, Jackson. It just happens – hopefully so that we catch the seasonal peaks."

"Well, could it take 50 hours to develop a new product?" Jackson could see her frustration, and probed again. "Could it be as much as 200 hours?"

"OK, Jackson, I know your job is to poke at our business to help me manage better, but I don't have that kind of information."

"OK – if I said it takes 200 hours of research, investigation, preparing prototypes, drawings etc. to create a new product, would that be a stupid number?"

"Probably not stupid, but I really don't know."

"So theoretically, if you and Natalie spent the next 2.5 weeks exclusively on new product development, you could have a new, hot fashion, high margin product ready for market."

"Well, I suppose, but that doesn't count the time to qualify an offshore resource, transfer the product specs, and allow for 8 weeks transit. Jackson, it's just not as simple as you portray."

"OK – I tend to oversimplify. Hey, let's grab a water and stroll around the operation."
Jackson knew it was time to change the venue, and Patricia was ready to explode with frustration.

Jackson neatly stacked his papers, allowing some cooling-off time. After a few moments, he smiled, stood and strolled to the refrigerator. "I'm buying," as he extended a bottle of spring water.

Patricia laughed at his exorbitant generosity.

"C'mon, let me show you the operation."

For the next 30 minutes, Patricia proudly displayed her operation, greeting employees by their first names. As they viewed the various operations, Jackson sprinkled the discussion with operating questions.

As they returned to the conference room, Jackson asked one more question before they were seated. "So why do you think you need a couple of months to arrange supply from China?"

By now, Patricia became accustomed to his Colombo style of innocent questions that will ultimately lead to an enlightening conclusion.

"OK, Jackson, let me ask you a question. Why do think it could take less time for an offshore supplier?"

"Maybe that's not the right question to be asked. Are we really looking for a quick turn, inexpensive offshore supply? Or are we looking for a product that is hot fashion, with high gross margins that we can immediately launch, and over the product life generate healthy profits?"

"I surrender. I don't get it."

"Well, when I think of your fashion products, speed is valuable – greater margins and higher sales. Over the long term, an offshore supplier may be the perfect low cost producer, but how much are you giving up in high selling price by a delayed delivery. Compare that to how much premium to manufacture introductory lots produced here in the US.

I also think about a high fashion product that you'll have to buy by the container-load – or at least at high volume.

Without getting into firm numbers, I'd like to whiteboard some alternatives – shorten the development cycle time by months, so that you can have potentially many new products and not just a few.

Now whatever we do today, it isn't necessarily something that you want to execute, but when we scratch some concepts on the whiteboard, we're not changing schedules, buying container-loads of product, signing long-term contracts etc. All the things that can add up to very expensive decisions."

With that, Jackson grabbed a marker and started to explore ideas with Patricia.

He first focused on routine activities performed by Patricia and Natalie.

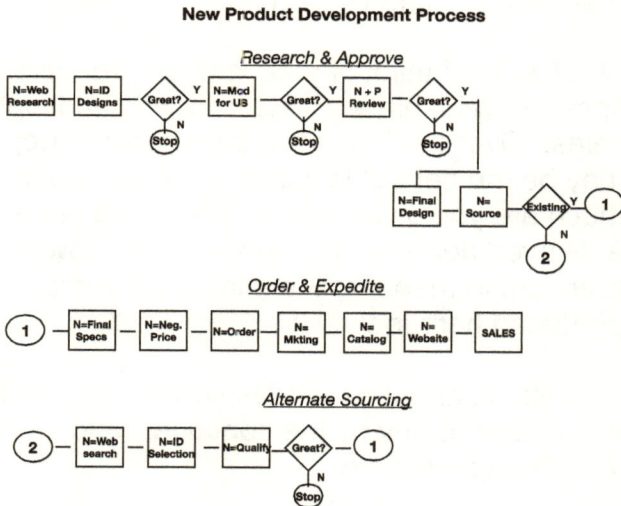

New Product Development Process

Research & Approve

Order & Expedite

Alternate Sourcing

"Now we have the shape of NPD - not fixed and firm – but big chunks of time. But let's scratch out some more concepts. In round numbers, in an average month, what percent of time do you spend on new product development?"

"That varies. Could be as much as 20% of my time, but depending on the time of year, it could be as little as 5%."

"OK, so let's look at the annual calendar. Let's assemble a best guess about Natalie's normal workweek. We've put the seasonal development in – and look at the overtime required. If our goal is to get new products launched without Natalie's burnout, we need to offload some of her daily routine."

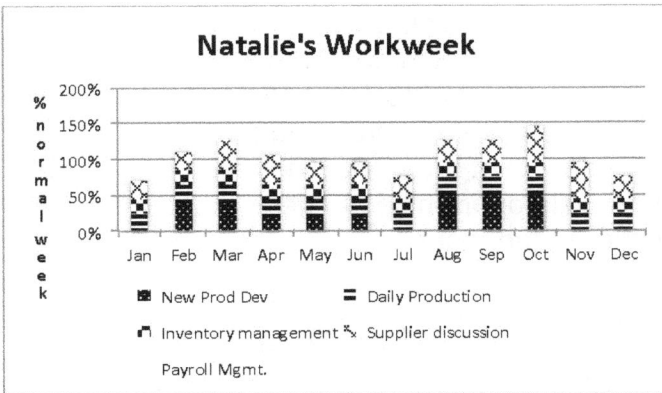

Patricia scratched some notes on her pad. "Jackson, I agree that would be ideal. How do we do that?"

"That's a later discussion. For now, let's just concentrate on NPD." He then created a new graph.

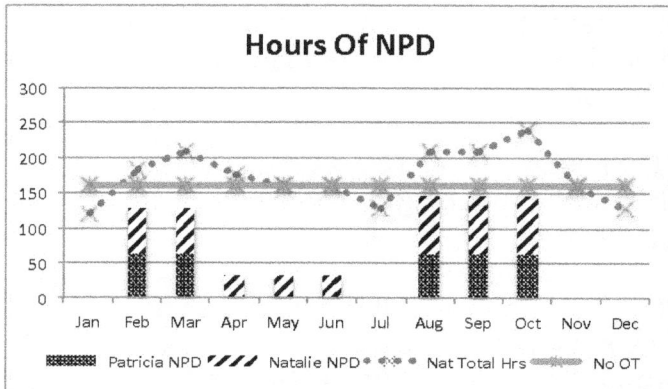

Hours Of NPD

Jackson drew a line with 12 marks indicating months. In a quick-paced brainstorming session, they estimated both Natalie and Patricia's approximate schedule of new product development and developed a rough graph of the time spent on NPD. They also identified potential opportunities to delegate some lesser value-added tasks to other non-critical people.

"Let' say, for example, it takes 200 hours to develop a new product. If we assume that we have seasonal demand for new products, and decide that we won't have Natalie working nights and weekends to perform this critical task, here's what a work schedule may look like."

Patricia walked to the whiteboard, carefully considered the chart.

Once they completed the annual development schedule, Jackson concentrated on the development task itself. New product development was highly dependent on Natalie's drawings that were often modified in a brainstorming session with Patricia. The next step was to engage an independent technician who converted the concept drawings to formal product specifications, including sizes when appropriate.

Patricia observed that the technician's time was usually a bottleneck. "How can we fix that resource?" she mused.

"It's only a question of time and money, Patricia. Do you think that there is only one resource that can do the work in today's global, wired economy? Heck the University of Cincinnati has a DAP program… many graduates and many potential interns. You never know until you explore the web-universe."

"I'm going to jot that as a to-do task."

"Great. Now let's talk about sourcing."

Again, the white-board filled with scribbles, diagrams, and a final list of issues.

"OK, Patricia, we've spent a couple of hours. Not exactly what I intended, but this is great stuff." His broad smile conveyed a sense of extreme satisfaction.

Open issues

- Natalie's time
  - Delegation
- Bottleneck - tech time
  - Tech resources
- New product sourcing
  - new materials
    - tech mat'l
    - leather
  - reliable local sourcing
- DAP interns

Patricia was pleased… she never experienced such an enthusiastic session that focused on breaking down barriers and concepts.

"Patricia, I'll pretty this up a bit – you know, maybe a PowerPoint – so that we can look at this again tomorrow."

As Jackson took pictures of the whiteboard for this afternoon's work, he was very pleased to introduce Patricia to the Theory of *Constraints*– a technique explored by Eli Goldratt in his book "The Goal."

"Patricia, this was an excellent session. Shall we get together at 8 AM tomorrow? Or what do you suggest?" Jackson always liked to keep a tight schedule, telegraphing to the client that quick turnarounds and tight schedules help accelerate change.

As Jackson left the building, Patricia reviewed her notes from the session. Her assessment... *'Amazing how much we covered in just a couple of hours. What's even better, Jackson didn't dictate to me, he just asked questions. He never once told me what to do, but pursued answers until I was confident in my statements. Clever... very clever.'*

That evening, Jackson examined the pictures of the whiteboard. Some of his notes were so rough that he may not get the information transcribed accurately. That is exactly why he labels notes as *draft,* and he encourages clients to review and adjust information as necessary. It ensures that all parties have consistent thoughts.

The next morning arriving at 8:00 AM, Jackson brought several hardcopies of the summary so adjustments could be made. He linked his computer to the LCD projector. Meanwhile Patricia was wrapping up a meeting with her staff.

When she arrived at the conference room, Jackson greeted her with, "Big time emergency?" baiting her with a question so that he better understood her operating environment.

"Not at all, Jackson. We have a daily huddle to establish priorities and share what's happening in the business."

"Now, that's a great idea."

"One of the tips I picked up in a management book. Works great because we're all aligned on Company deliverables for the day. I'm anxious to understand some longer range strategic deliverables, so let's get at it."

Patricia's businesslike approach was part of a winning formula for strategic planning. She seldom displayed a defensive tone.

After a brief review and a few adjustments of the slides, Jackson redirected the conversation to the executive team.

"So Let's talk about your team. I'm most interested in hearing about the top tier, but I'd like to get a better understanding of whatever you think is important about your organization."

"OK – got it. Let's start with Natalie. After yesterday, you know that she is the creative engine, right?"

Jackson nodded agreement.

"Well, it's not because she graduated from DAP – you know, the UC program. It's because she has boundless energy, and is totally committed to the success of the business. She has done more personal research on fashion trends, materials, customer needs, competitors etc. than I could ever pay her for. And it's not just her creative talent, but also her virtually relentless attention to detail. Saying she is my right hand is a gross understatement."

"So let's hear about it."

With that, Patricia shared a half-dozen stories about what seemed to be either superhuman effort, or an awareness of market trends that no one else recognized. Natalie did this, and somehow kept up with the daily requirements.

"So you mentioned that there is no way to ever compensate her for her efforts. Why do you say that?"

"I guess it's more of an unknown. She must spend many personal hours doing her research, but she never asks for overtime."

"And is she hourly, or salary – maybe with a bonus?"

"Hourly."

"And why is that?"

"I guess it's just a carryover from when she was first hired. She came in as an hourly worker, and I just never considered anything other than that. To be honest, until the last year, I really couldn't afford anything else."

"And now? Or let me ask this another way, …could you afford to lose her?"

"I'll exaggerate a bit, but 'lock the doors!' Heck no, I'd be dead without her in this Company."

"So let's develop a task that says you will carefully evaluate her value to the Company, and create a compensation plan that reflects her critical nature, is within your financial constraints, gives her the satisfaction of your acknowledging her value, and let's the rest of the team know that you are recognizing value to the Company."

"OK – I'll accept the task – but I'm not sure how much I can afford."

"Compare that potential cost to losing her as a resource. Who else should we talk about? Anyone else critical to the business?"

"On the leadership team, I've got 2 other operations' managers and the controller. The operations' managers manage production, and one manages all the logistics and warehousing."

"Considering the Company size, sounds like a good distribution of workload. So talk to me about the managers. I'm thinking current performance, technical and managerial skills, and growth potential. You know, who is a star, potential star, someone that needs a lot of work… just a summary of your current impressions."

"OK… let's start with Jason. He's been with me for about 2.5 years. Good guy. Keeps close tabs on everything in the production areas. Production is really assembly of outsourced product to fill an order. He's goal driven, but unfortunately not the most creative problem solver. Needs a bit of oversight, and hope to gosh something doesn't get to be non-standard. He goes off the reservation when things aren't perfect."

"So is he trainable? Or has he maxed out in that role? Let me say it another way. If the Company grows at – let's be a bit crazy – 20-25% a year, can he handle the growth… be trained to deal with that kind of growth?"

"That's a good question – and I'm not prepared to answer."

"OK, let's not get bogged down and rush an assessment. You just got another assignment, Patricia."

For the next hour, they discussed the other manager and the controller. Patricia received several more assignments focusing on specific criteria:
- Assess key associate's current performance.
- If performance is at an average level, are they trainable?
- If trainable, how much will training cost, and how long will it take to get to above average performance.

- Are they capable of growing to that required by a Company with x% growth?

"And remember, Patricia, if the individual can't reach the expected performance level, that doesn't mean you should necessarily coach them out of the Company, since if you grow at an exceptional rate, there may be a role within their capability. The decisions are yours to make."

"I understand, but this discussion is torturous. I guess that's the responsibility when you're the boss."

"Patricia, what's your vision and mission for this Company? What is your culture at Fashion Clicks? Who do we serve? What are your operating philosophies? Growth expectations? Product lines? How will we reach them?"

"Whoa. Why so many questions, Jackson?"

"Because until we figure out your vision and mission, we can't get you there. Let's start with your culture. It seems that you are a high-quality organization. Respect the employees, customers and suppliers. Is that a fair statement?"

"Yes. If we can't behave in a responsible manner, we shouldn't be in business."

"Will you be able to grow to your financial goals thinking like that?"

"I'll repeat, if I can't be first class ethical, I shouldn't be in business."

"I understand your commitment and I believe that's the only way to successfully build a company. Today you're a high-quality ladies fashion accessory Company. Is that all there is? Will you reach your economic goals as ladies fashion accessory?"

"It's definitely possible."

"Possible or probable?"

"It would be a stretch."

"Let's talk about who you are. You are a fashion accessory Company – maybe that's in research or maybe you do the design. You focus on accessories, generally selling for less than $100. Does that sound right?"

"And we concentrate on women's fashions."

"Right. But your skills are in research and design of textiles for women with a selling price of less than $100. Is that the limit of your market?"

"I suppose that we could expand into men's and children's products... seems to fit the research and design skill set. And when I think about our product line, why limit it to textiles... mostly natural fibers. So we could also include perhaps leather goods, and during the past few years, high-tech fabrics have surfaced as 'in demand."

"If you were to expand your product line to other materials, and fashion accessories for men and children, would that increase the probability of reaching the $10 million goal?"

"For sure. And as I think about our processes, it seems to fall in nicely. We now have a working process for design research and sourcing, receiving, packaging and shipping accessory products. Seems like it's a reasonable step to take."

"If you expand your product line, will you have to change any of your distribution channels?"

"Not change them, but if we have a broader product line, we may be able to expand distribution beyond the boutiques into some of the big-box stores – Macy's, Nordstrom's. But that would be a stretch."

"Today you have annual sales of about $6 million. Where would you like to be in 3-5 years?"

"Ideally, I'd like to be a nice round $10 million of sales, and have a pretax of $2 million in 3 years." As she spoke it was clear that she wasn't confident about the numbers. It seemed to be more of a wish rather than an achievable target.

"Now that would be nice, Patricia. Let's figure out how to get there.

Your mission is to sell high-quality women's, men's and children's fashion merchandise, in the traditional boutique channel, but also expand to the big-box, and on the web. You'll maintain the highest ethical standards when working with employees, customers and suppliers. …That about right?"

"Dead-on."

With that, they broadly analyzed the financial goal. Jackson used the term, 'Let's chunk this out.'

For the next two hours they listed and ranked topics ranging from low to high probability. Topics included:
- Inflation assumptions
- Pricing flexibility
- Market channels
- Geography (regional, national, international)
- Competitor actions
- New products
- New product lines
- Regulations

"Jackson, this has been fun, and you've challenged my imagination and gotten me to a point where I almost believe this is possible. But don't we have to be more realistic in this process?"

"Absolutely. But why don't you think this is possible?"

"Well for one, this rough model suggests that we need to launch – what is it – 3+ new products a year, and we're challenged to get out one new product a year. Isn't this plan a bit aggressive?"

"Excellent question. Earlier we also broadly defined that about 200 hours of direct activity to develop and launch a new product – over a 6-month period. You mentioned that Natalie is critical to new product development. So tell me, is Natalie working exclusively on new products and product lines today?"

"C'mon Jackson, I told you earlier that she is working on many different areas. Give me some slack, will you?"

"So what other tasks is she doing that are more important than new product development?"

Jackson let the question hang, got up and walked to the refrigerator to grab 2 waters. Without probing any further, he tossed a bottle to Patricia, and didn't speak another word.

Patricia glared at the white board, motionless. After a few moments, she started doodling in her notebook.

"Jackson, I'm not happy about this. We went through this yesterday. You charted it, and Natalie has several other responsibilities.

You're hitting me with some very difficult questions, and I'm not happy."

"Just as I intended, Patricia. From this point to $10 million with 20% pretax, you've got to think differently. Now let's look at what we just did. In broad terms we framed how you can achieve your goal. It requires managing the business differently. To reach your goals, you're going to make decisions that make you very uncomfortable.

The beauty of a strategic plan is that we'll scratch out the concepts on the whiteboard without actually spending any money, without changing any careers. We're brainstorming and testing ideas to see if they fit the real world.

At this point we don't have input from your staff – trying to conceptualize what is possible. I'll guarantee that you cannot accomplish these goals without buy-in from your staff. But that's why you and I are somewhat shaping the strategy to consider what may be reasonable – without the staff input.

When we get to the offsite, we'll talk about the stretch goals, and listen – yes listen – to the input from those folks critical to achieving the goals. If I facilitate properly, we'll identify strengths and weaknesses we've never considered... we'll hear about competitive issues never identified before... we'll identify insurmountable obstacles that will cause us to change our expectations. But by engaging your staff in the process, we'll get the creativity of those that actually do the work to identify the solutions.

The reason that we're meeting now is to – on a macro basis – understand what we believe to be reasonable goals and a reasonable way to achieve them."

Patricia stared at the white board, thumb and index finger pinching her chin in deep thought.

"Jackson, I'm going to have to sleep on this. I'm nervous about the process – not that I don't trust you, but I'm very uncomfortable."

"Understood. Let's wrap this up for now. I'll put some notes together tonight, and let's meet tomorrow to talk about our progress. I won't move forward with anything if you are *too* uncomfortable, but I will tell you that if we plan properly, the steps we take won't be a bet-the-Company, but rather each separate step will be a comfortable risk for you to take.

You'll see when I put the notes together. Deal?"

"8:30 tomorrow? But I've got a 9:30 with an outside vendor."

"Tell you what. I'll get the notes to you by 9 PM tonight so that you can review the concepts in better form before the meeting."

"9 PM tonight. Agreed."

Jackson took pictures of the last whiteboard segment, and packed his notes.

"Patricia, you've done great today. It may not feel like we've accomplished a lot, but when you look at the results, I think that you'll be pleasantly surprised. This will be in your mailbox by 9 tonight."

After Jackson left, Patricia was exhausted and uncomfortable about today's session. She looked at the white board thinking, 'Jackson has such a positive attitude, but he just doesn't understand my business. He has wished away many of the obstacles. He seems to know what he is doing, but growing by more than 50% in the next 3 years – wow, it would be great, but is it even possible. Guess I'll wait and see...'

That evening, Jackson assembled the notes and started to develop some financial guesstimates about the future. There were some serious challenges that Patricia must overcome, but it certainly seemed possible to grow by 50% if she takes all the right steps.

Jackson sent the summary to Patricia at 8:45 that night.

Millions US $	2017	2018	2019	2020	2021	2022
Inflation		2.0%	2.0%	2.0%	2.0%	2.0%
Price Increases		2.0%	2.0%	2.0%	2.0%	2.0%
Baseline	6.0					
Pricing Impact		6.1	6.2	6.4	6.5	6.6
New products						
Soft Goods		0.6	1.2	1.2	1.8	2.2
New product lines						
Sport			0.3	0.6	1.0	1.5
Hard Goods				0.2	0.2	0.2
	6.0	6.7	7.7	8.4	9.5	10.5
Market channels						
Baseline	6.0	4.5	4.5	4.4	4.3	4.5
Mass Market		1.5	1.0	1.3	1.7	2.0
Web (US)		0.5	1.3	1.9	2.4	2.5
International		0.2	0.5	0.8	1.1	1.5
Total	6.0	6.7	7.7	8.4	9.5	10.5
Geography						
National	6.0	6.5	6.8	7.6	8.4	9.0
International		0.2	0.5	0.8	1.1	1.5
Total	6.0	6.7	7.3	8.4	9.5	10.5
Gross Margin		4.0	4.4	5.0	5.7	6.3
SG&A		3.0	3.3	3.5	3.8	4.2
Pretax		1.0	1.1	1.5	1.9	2.1
Pretax % Sales		15%	15%	18%	20%	20%
GM %		60%	60%	60%	60%	60%
SG&A % Sales		45%	45%	42%	40%	40%

As she reviewed the summary, she focused on new products, market channels and the geography displayed.

She had never before considered a more rapid new product introduction schedule since Natalie was maxed-out. … Add a sport line…men's and children… why not?

Jackson must have something specific in mind when he outlined the 'web' sales. Sipping a glass of cabernet, she wondered aloud, 'Is it possible?'

Jackson arrived at 8:30 the next morning. They sat in the conference room and discussed the financials.

"Jackson, I'd love to have these results. But they scare me a bit. Can you talk me off this ledge?"

"Patricia, when I looked at your historical performance, you had a baseline of $600-800k of new product launches each of the past few years. We've got to increase that to get to your target of $10 million of sales. One solution to $10 million of sales is to introduce 3 new products a year. This is a decision that you get to make. If you dedicate Natalie to new product development, you've solved that constraint to growth."

"But if I do that, who will do Natalie's job?"

"Well, if new product development is a critical skill, and Natalie has that skill, should we ask her to do things of lesser value? It seems that scheduling and production – while complex and real time - may be difficult. But someone can be more easily trained in scheduling than new product development. You've said that you have 100% confidence in Natalie's judgment. And remember, we're just scratching out ideas to help guide us during the offsite meeting.

We may discover other obstacles during the offsite, but we'll have key employees to help us sort out obstacles and solutions."

"OK, Jackson. I'm way out there on the trust meter. I'm uncomfortable, but if you say so, let's continue."

During the next hour, they discussed the challenges of Mass Market, Web and International sales growth. Jackson listened to her concerns as she reviewed the sales expectations. "I hear the issues. I agree that we just can't wish them away, but with the right resources, do you think that we can accomplish the goals?"

Patricia's answer was always the same. "Yes, of course with the right resources, we can do it. But where will those resources come from?"

And with each objection, Jackson responded with, "Let's let the team address that challenge."

After nearly an hour, Patricia was more at ease, but still concerned about the overall direction.

In the next few minutes, Jackson and Patricia roughed out the schedule for the individual meetings and the offsite agenda.

At the conclusion of the meeting, Jackson summarized. "Remember, we're just in the brainstorming mode. We haven't spent any money yet... we haven't reorganized your business... we haven't abandoned any customers. We're just planning. If at the conclusion of the plan, your financial goals are not achievable, we'll change the plan."

"Thanks Jackson."

Three Amigos #2

The next morning, Doug, John and Patricia met for their informal monthly meeting. Doug and John knew that Patricia had started the planning process, and were very interested in the initial results.

After Doug sipped his steaming cup of coffee, he leaned forward, staring at Patricia. "How did your early meetings go with Jackson? You've already met with him once, right?"

"I've had two meetings with him so far. The guy definitely has a positive can-do attitude, but his pace is a bit frightening. He's moving through concepts that I've never explored, and he has repeatedly mentioned, '… no worries, because we're not spending money, we're just planning'.

I know it's just planning, but the implication of some of the things that we've explored is really out there. He's got me working the international markets… introducing 3 new products a year."

"Whoa, Patricia. Three new products a year? How's that possible? Have you ever done three before?"

"Never. And sometimes we've been stressed with just one per year. And new product introductions are one of the keys to the sales and profit growth.

But here's the thing. He knows how important Natalie is to the process, and he just says, '…fully dedicate her to new product development…' Easy for him to say. He makes it sound so simple, but I'll have to shift her other tasks to someone else on the staff."

John leaned forward. "So, Natalie is critical to the new product development task. What is her magic?"

"She knows fashion – sort of a hobby for her. She's a bit of a nut, trolling across so many message boards and fashion websites – it's pretty amazing how she digests all the worldwide trends, and then POP – up comes a new design or product idea."

"And what else does she do? Is it scheduling, managing the logistics and a few other jobs? How easy is it to replace those skills with another employee?"

"Yes to all those tasks, and that's exactly what Jackson said. He and I brainstormed for a couple of hours shaping out how things might proceed, but he said the real key will be to get the feedback from the staff about how we can move forward."

After a few more minutes of discussion Doug challenged Patricia. "So have you concluded that you're wasting your time yet? And how much money is he costing you? I'm telling you, shut it down now and skip the fantasy land."

"Doug, it was a tough decision for me to launch this, and I really don't appreciate your criticism."

"OK, Patricia. I'm out of line. But I've been in business for more than 30 years, and it's easy for me to spot an empty suit. The guy says a lot of nice things, but hang onto your wallet. I'll shut up for now.

John, anything magic at your end?"

"Same old, Doug. I'll be starting with Jackson this week. A heads up for you – don't start bashing me on my decision. I know it's a risk, but for a few dollars, I'd like to understand how I might use some advanced principles to raise the value of the business."

"Gotcha… and I'll just sit in the weeds as you folks wander down the path. Good luck folks."

For the next 30 minutes they discussed city politics, and a few major local business transactions that were announced.

Breakfast concluded, and Patricia walked thoughtfully to her car thinking, 'I wish Doug would lay off the criticism… just shut up. I could just as well call him a dinosaur that couldn't spell the word strategy, but that wouldn't accomplish anything except fracture the relationship… and he does often provide some excellent mentoring.'

Jackson Meeting With John

A week ago, John, Doug and Patricia met in their routine informal monthly meeting. Although John was offended by Doug's comments about his decision to engage Jackson for strategic planning, it didn't change his resolve to complete a project.

John expected Jackson at 9 this morning for their initial meeting. Since Patricia explained the content of their meeting, he was prepared to discuss some broad goals.

Jackson arrived at the facility at 8:45, and parked in one of two remaining visitor spots.

As he entered the lobby, he noticed that one wall held a selection of brochures – another with reading material that included Flying magazine, Road & Track and numerous business and industry publications. Materials were geared to the middle-aged male, and industrial executives- male or female.

The receptionist peeked up from her desk when she heard Jackson enter. "Welcome sir. May I help you?"

"Yes please, my name is Jackson and I'm here to meet with John."

She punched a few numbers on her phone, and after a brief conversation, hung up the phone. "John will be with you shortly."

While waiting, Jackson strolled to the literature displayed on the wall. Upon closer look, he noticed that, in addition to hobby and business publications, the Company included some literature that shared some of their recent accomplishments.

Jackson was surprised at the extent of the Company's local community support. Honorary photos displayed John receiving community service awards, Company team photos of Habitat for Humanity participants, and various employees playing Santa, super-heroes, and the Easter Bunny at Children's Hospital.

The narrative described the Company's exceptional commitment to local charity.

While examining the literature, he felt a tap on his elbow. "Jackson, great that you could join me this morning. Have you had a chance to look at our 'bragging' wall? These employees are amazing. They do so much for the community, I just can't keep up with them."

"Looks to me like you support the community as well. Very nice, John."

John guided Jackson to the well-appointed conference room.

"Jackson, I'm really excited to talk about the future. Coffee or water?"

They both settled in at the conference table with spring water.

"So John, have you had a chance to talk with Patricia?"

"Yes – I had a great conversation with Patricia, and I'm anxious to start thinking differently. She mentioned that you asked some great questions – and while I probably don't know the answers, I'd like to be stressed a bit. She also mentioned that as you asked some of your questions she felt very self-conscious since she didn't know the answers. So, I'm prepared to feel a bit insecure. How would you like to start?"

"Let's just spend a few minutes talking about where you'd like this business to be in 3-5 years. Once we frame your expectations, let's talk about how you manage your business. Things like what kind of reporting – how often and what does it look like – who gets the reports – just some general information. Also, I'd like to understand your management meetings – who attends and how do you run them…"

John scratched a list of the items.

"And to scale this for you, let's spend about 20-30 minutes on those topics. Then we'll move on from there."

John passed one of the two files on the table to Jackson. "I thought that you might want to talk about some of these things."

"We have a reputation for being a highly ethical business. My goal is to concentrate on high value add, complex products that can't easily be duplicated by competitors. And I especially like leading edge tech. I've been thinking about a sales target in 3 years of a nice round $50 million. It's got a nice ring to it."

Jackson jotted the number in his journal, looked up and said, "Any deep science to that number?"

Smiling, John replied, "Well, it's nice and round, but I've also thought about selling price if I decided to sell the Company. I've talked to some of the folks in the industry, and they've said that most businesses in the industry sell for about 5-7 times earnings. I'd like to continue with about a 10% return on sales – that would be about $5 million, so that multiple would give me a comfortable $25 million pretax launch into retirement."

"Great – you've done some research. So when you hear that 5-times multiple, is that after-tax income?"

"No - EBITDA for earnings. I'm guessing that's similar to my pretax number."

"…Just a couple of points to consider. First, earning's multiples are good guidelines when selling a business, but not the only pricing factor. The EBITDA term is a compilation of pretax earnings plus interest expense, depreciation and amortization. It's a quick-and-dirty approximation of cash flow.

The real value of a company to a buyer is future cash flow, so at best historical EBITDA is a credibility factor, but that is not how a buyer values a business. And the calculation is before interest since a buyer chooses how to finance the business – equity or debt - so results shouldn't be impacted by the debt structure. Depreciation and amortization are non-cash expenses.

But let me dig a bit deeper. You mentioned average valuation. That means that some sell for a higher multiple, and some for a lower multiple. Do you intend to be average in 3 years?"

John laughed, as he reached for the water. "Not a chance in this lifetime. I run one of the best businesses in the industry – simply put, I'd be mad-as-hell if I was only worth average."

"OK- I like the way you think. As we work through the strategic plan, knowing that you want to excel and be above average, I'm going to push you a bit about investing in this Company. Agreed?"

"Sure. And if I don't like what I hear, I can ignore your words." With that, a big grin consumed his expression.

"I like your style, John - because that is exactly what I expect. This is your Company – not mine – so I can only suggest ways to help you achieve your goals.

So, let's pick apart your goal of $50 million in - let's call it 3 years. No need to be too conservative as we start. That doesn't mean we can reach $50 million in three years, but if we don't even try, we'll never get there."

For the next half-hour they talked about market conditions, competitors, keys to success and Company strengths and weaknesses.

They reviewed the current organization chart, and focused on several functional areas.

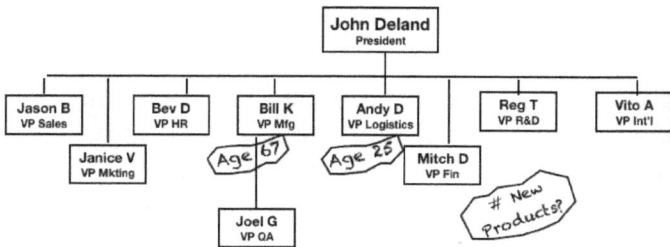

John Deland
President

| Jason B VP Sales | Bev D VP HR | Bill K VP Mfg | Andy D VP Logistics | Reg T VP R&D | Vito A VP Int'l |

Janice V VP Mkting

Age 67   Age 25   Mitch D VP Fin

New Products?

Joel G VP QA

"OK, John. That's a great overview of the organization. Just a couple of questions. First off, let's talk about Andy D… relative?"

"Yes, that's my step-son. Recent graduate of Purdue. Great kid – excellent record at Purdue, and he's worked here for three summers as an intern before we hired him full-time."

"Excellent. Tell me about his role in the Company."

"We brought him in as a VP to give him some immediate recognition for his degrees – up to a Masters in Global Logistics. The kid worked hard at the university, and, well, I'm proud of him. His work during the summers opened our eyes in several areas that helped us cut back on some inventories."

"Good sign – reduced inventories. Can you describe his responsibilities… maybe talk about the staff that report to him?"

"He doesn't have any direct reports. We've structured his role as one of special projects. He basically reviews the logistics operations, discovers a potential opportunity, does some analysis, and works with the team to implement change."

"Does he have any broad Company goals – for example, reduce inventory by 10%, or maybe reduce freight costs by 5%. Any macro goals, or pretty much ad hoc analysis?"

"No overall goals – just continuous progress."

"OK – how about Bill K, the Manufacturing VP. You mentioned he's 67. What's the future look like for him?"

"Bill's a great guy. He has kept us ahead of the curve for more than 2 decades. He's not the most energetic guy in the building – maybe he's lost a bit of his fire – but when we need some minor miracles in the manufacturing ops, he comes through every time."

"Great to hear. What kind of minor miracles does he power through?"

"We've had some major contracts with the likes of GE. Big projects. Somehow they've gotten off schedule, and we had to pull all the stops to get the orders out the door."

"Talk with me about off schedule."

"A couple of times this year, we've had some quality problems with the manufacturing process. It seems that some of the 'Bills of Material' have been out of phase with the latest approved schematics. When that happened, we discovered that we didn't have exactly the right materials to get the job out on time. Bill called in a few chips from some of the suppliers, and they expedited delivery for some of the materials.

The freight expense was a killer, but we ultimately met the contract delivery requirements."

"Great that Bill has those kind of relationships. Were you able to do any *root-cause analysis* to discover the source of the problem?"

"Historically we've had a kind of *peg-board scheduling process* for these special orders. Bill says that process gives us the flexibility to adjust schedules so that we never miss a deadline. Turns out that for this one shipment, we didn't have enough inventory."

"And did your perpetual inventory show that you had sufficient stock?"

"Yes – just an anomaly that we missed on this one."

"OK. Do you have any other inventory anomalies?"

"We have the occasional breakdown. The good news is that our inventory shrink is now down to less than a half-million dollars. Bill has really focused on inventory for the past few years. He's now got us up to nearly 2 turns per year."

"OK. AT 67, what's Bill outlook? Will he be retiring any time soon? Any concerns?"

"I've talked with Bill about this several times. He plans to die with his boots on. If I were to guess, he'll be here for another 3+- years."

"Is that good or bad, John?"

"Well, as long as he doesn't lose his edge, I'm ok with that."

"OK. Let's talks about Reg in R&D. Any thoughts?"

"Again, Reg is a *go-to* guy – someone I can depend on. We have new products every couple of years, once Reg identifies the need. So this year, for example, Reg spotted one of our competitors launching a pilot project. He had one of his engineers scrounge around to get one of the early prototypes, and they reverse engineered the product, and had a prototype out within 90 days of the competitors launch."

"Successful?"

"Well, as with every new product or innovation, we had some start-up problems – nothing that couldn't be fixed in a few months – but yes, there were a few bugs to resolve."

"Any impact on the customers?"

"Yes - the early adopters were mad-as-hell about the problems. The good news is that I made a few phone calls – took the big customers to the Precinct for dinner, and things smoothed out a bit. It's happened a few times before, so the customers don't stay angry for long. I think that they look forward to the Precinct dinners when it hits the fan."

"Are you comfortable with that kind of product launching snafu?"

"We're used to it – so I guess I'm ok with it."

"So let me ask you a question. If you could eliminate the production problems on the big accounts – e.g. GE – and you could launch maybe 2-3 new products a year, before your competitors, and without product performance problems, would that be a good thing?"

"Sure that would be great, but I don't think it could happen."

"So let's pretend that Santa Claus comes to town, waves a magic wand, and you could fix the processes. Good or bad?"

"Again, that would be great, but we've been working this business for many years, and we haven't been able to master the issues."

"OK – I won't press on this just yet, but I want you to think LEAN business."

"Jackson, I'm not interested in layoffs. So that's probably off the table for this business."

"Common misconception. LEAN doesn't necessarily mean layoffs. In it's finest form, it simply means eliminating non-value processes and activities. And if it's done well, you might even find that your earnings increase once things get cleaned up. Let's say in a lean shop, you might find that you never have shortages – think the GE order.

And you just might find that because you've managed the inventory properly, your inventory turns accelerate to – let's say 3-4 a year."
"You can't be serious about the inventory turns. That would be worth several million dollars of cash flow."

"Yes – and you could also avoid those expensive air freight charges. And how would your customers feel about getting new products in their hands that really work – first time, every time?"

John looked very serious after these last statements. He rubbed his temple briefly with a concerned look. "Are you serious?"

"Yes – let's not get ahead of ourselves – but you might ne surprised at the results that can be achieved with LEAN business practices."

"But if that's possible, does that mean we've been screwing things up for years?"

"Don't look at it that way, John. Think of it as an opportunity going forward."

John leaned into the conference table and the conversation continued about what could be – often to his surprise.

After a few more minutes of discussion, Jackson walked to the white board.

"Let's scratch out some rough financials. Something that you'd like to have in the next 3 years. I'll poke at you a bit – maybe suggest a more aggressive approach – but I'll never let you get out over your skis."

For the next hour, they drafted broad financials including new products, reduced inventories, improved gross margins, and some run-rate SG&A spending.

000's $	2018 Amt	%	2019 Amt	%	2020 Amt	%	2021 Amt	%
Sales:								
Metal Fab	11,550.0	38.6%	14,550.0	41.8%	17,200.0	41.6%	20,500.0	41.0%
Casting	8,350.0	27.9%	9,150.0	26.3%	10,450.0	25.3%	14,550.0	29.1%
Resale	3,500.0	11.7%	3,900.0	11.2%	4,200.0	10.2%	4,700.0	9.4%
International	5,915.0	19.7%	7,050.0	20.3%	8,700.0	21.1%	9,400.0	18.8%
Other	635.0	2.1%	150.0	0.4%	750.0	1.8%	870.0	1.7%
Total	29,950.0	100.0%	34,800.0	100.0%	41,300.0	###	50,020.0	100.0%
Gross Margin								
Metal Fab	5,197.5	45.0%	6,547.5	45.0%	8,235.0	47.9%	10,134.0	49.4%
Casting	3,340.0	40.0%	3,297.5	36.0%	4,180.0	40.0%	5,820.0	40.0%
Resale	875.0	25.0%	975.0	25.0%	1,050.0	25.0%	1,175.0	25.0%
International	3,549.0	60.0%	4,230.0	60.0%	5,220.0	60.0%	5,640.0	60.0%
Other	127.0	20.0%	30.0	20.0%	150.0	20.0%	174.0	20.0%
Total	####	43.7%	15,080.0	43.3%	18,835.0	45.6%	22,943.0	45.9%
SG&A								
Selling	4,492.5	15.0%	5,370.0	15.4%	6,850.0	16.6%	8,350.0	16.7%
Marketing	1,797.0	6.0%	2,100.0	6.0%	2,650.0	6.4%	3,456.0	6.9%
R&D	1,497.5	5.0%	1,750.0	5.0%	2,100.0	5.1%	2,750.0	5.5%
Finance	748.8	2.5%	800.0	2.3%	850.0	2.1%	900.0	1.8%
IT	599.0	2.0%	650.0	1.9%	700.0	1.7%	750.0	1.5%
Legal	599.0	2.0%	550.0	1.6%	650.0	1.6%	700.0	1.4%
HR	449.3	1.5%	550.0	1.6%	800.0	1.9%	900.0	1.8%
Other	-	0.0%		0.0%		0.0%		0.0%
Total	####	34.0%	11,770.0	0.0%	14,600.0	0.0%	17,806.0	0.0%
PBT	2,905.50	9.7%	3,310.0	9.5%	4,235.0	10.3%	5,137.0	10.3%
Headcount	75		78		90		110	

"OK- I'll clean these statements up a bit and get them back to you tomorrow. Now let's spend some time on what needs to be done to reach these goals."

Jackson discussed each functional area, asking questions about how the organization would function with the improved performance.

"John, I think there are a few things that we need to focus on:

- The manufacturing area needs to tone up – maybe try a pilot project in lean manufacturing. If you were to fully implement it, you should have 3-4 inventory turns a year. Your shrinkage would likely be no more than $100k – just a guess - and scrap will be reduced.
- Bill should develop a standard method to launch new projects. Your informal processes result with excessive spending – overtime, freight costs, and just general heartache throughout the manufacturing process.
- Reg needs to tighten up the new product development process – from understanding the market needs, to executing new product launches in a routine and systematic way. You'll want to lead the industry, not panic and follow your competitors with poor quality products.
- Your logistics are not competitive. Andy sounds like a good guy, but he needs some mentoring – maybe some outside coaching – and he needs goals that will benefit the entire organization. Heck, before you're done, you may be expanding to some offshore sourcing, and logistics will be a critical function once that starts.

And there's more, but we've eaten the entire 2 hours.

I would like to meet with each of your direct reports – not to review what we've just discussed – but just *listen* to them describe their operations within the Company.

No more than two hours each. When I've finished with your staff, I'll summarize and review some concepts with you. From there, we'll launch the offsite meeting."

"So let me understand this. You're going to spend time with them, and then give me some feedback?"

"It works, John. I've got to build trust with them, and encourage them to speak up about what they're seeing. Don't worry – I work for you – and I'll be sure that we discuss anything that's critical."

Jackson finished the discussion, packaged the papers, and took pictures of the whiteboard.

John's concerned look was customary. He'd just experienced a conceptual breakthrough that would be essential to move forward. It was good to be skeptical this early in the process.

Jackson asked Camille, John's assistant, to schedule the meetings with John's staff during the next few days, since the offsite was scheduled in less than two weeks.

Jackson arrived at Jason's office, and Jason immediately stood and walked around his desk to greet him. With a firm handshake and a salesman's smile, Jason greeted him. "Great to meet you Jackson. John has told me about the overall plan, and I'm very excited about strategic planning. We haven't done a strategic plan in the past, and I'm anxious to hear about your methods. C'mon over to the conference table. How would you like to proceed?"

Jason was a Penn State graduate with a concentration in marketing. His 12 years of overall experience, and three years with John's Company made him a good candidate to start the planning process.

"Well, I'd just like to hear about your sales process and how you think we should grow in the next few years. John and I have set some targets that I can share with you later in the discussion. So, for now, how do you manage your operations?"

With that Jason slid a packet of information across the table.

"OK. I've included some basic information in the packet. I've got the organization chart, with a brief bio of each rep, a description of our overall sales approach, commission and bonus plan, and some meeting minutes from our last few sales meetings. We have a weekly call to check the status of current and prospect customers, a quarterly meeting that aligns to special programs – you know, sales promotions, new product introductions etc."

For the next 30 minutes, Jackson quickly reviewed the documentation, postponing a detailed review until back at his office.

"Jason, tell me about your sales process."

Jason moved quickly to the whiteboard and summarized their sales budgeting method.

		Amount
Prior Year		28,000.0
Plus		
New Product 1	3,500.0	
New Product 2	2,000.0	
Total New Products		5,500.0
Organic Growth @ 5%		1,400.0
New Customers		1,350.0
Current Year's Budget		36,250.0

After a few minutes of discussion, Jackson asked, "It seems that a key to growth will be the timely introduction of new products. How's that going?"

"Not exactly as planned. We've had some engineering and manufacturing delays. Definitely leaves us with a gap."

"Any contingency plans built into the budget for new product delays?"

"We've always talked about a contingency plan, but given our desire for growth, we like to project an upbeat budget to the team – we don't prepare contingency plans."

"And you've identified a combined $2.8 million in organic growth, and new customers. How did you identify those targets?"

"Based on input form the sales team, we believe that the market will grow by 5%. In that number, we've included a 2% average price increase, and we expect to have better penetration in existing customers.

The new customer sales targets are from the sales team. They've each considered their territories, thought about their potential customers, and each rep signed up individually for the 'new customer' targets."

"Understood. Have you given them any guidance about how to develop the new customer targets? And how you might get new customers using all of your marketing resources?"

"No, we've left the sales planning to each rep. As long as they get to the desired sales budget total, we pretty much leave them alone."

"OK. I understand. Can I play with a few concepts on the board?"

Jackson always enjoyed sharing new concepts with eager young executives.

Selecting a black marker, he quickly drew a matrix with several columns, and 10 rows. Scratching out some headings for the rows & columns, he questioned Jason.

"So let's say this is your business. I saw from your materials that you have about a $3.2 million sales/marketing budget. When I think of sales, I think of actual customers and potential customers. I also think about all the sales and marketing resources that are available to compete. I've listed a few standard items. Any thoughts?"

	A		B		C		Total Spend
	Act	Pot	Act	Pot	Act	Pot	
Reps							
Base							
SPIFS							
Inside Sales							
Travel							
Advertising							
Collateral							
Trade Shows							
Website							
Promotions							
Other							
Total	-	-	-	-	-	-	-

"Sure – I think I know where you're going, but this looks like a lot of detail work. ... Not sure if I can complete the matrix."

"I understand your concerns, but let's not think of this as an accounting exercise. Let's just brainstorm some things. For example, how much does a rep earn?"

"Each rep has a different base – depending on how long they've been with us. And, in some territories – well, the commission plans differ because John has some favorites that he likes to take care of."

"Examples?"

"I've got 8 reps covering all the territories. Some have a minimal base – about $40k – with a generous commission plan. Several of the reps have a high base - $90k – with a more modest commission plan. All of them have a potential for an extra bonus if they accomplish certain objectives. So, they're all different."

"What was it - $1.2 million with 8 reps? How much off are we if we just said $150k each? Remember, we're not writing checks, but just trying to get an estimated cost."

"OK, let's play with $150k. What's next?"

"How much of your sales resource do you want to dedicate to new customers?"

"We're looking for about 5% of sales from new customers. So how about 5% of a reps time dedicated to prospecting?"

" ...5%. Does that mean new customers are not very important to you? Are you comfortable with that statement?"

"I think about customers as an annuity – a lifetime customer that I never want to lose. Once I get them, I want to keep them, so I'll dedicate a lot of resource to retention."

"Sure – but if you don't have new customers, and natural attrition occurs, you're sales will decline. Are you telling me that the success of your business relies virtually all on retention?"

"No, that would not be realistic. I guess that we do need new customers, which means I should probably dedicate more resource to them. Maybe up to 25% of my resources."

"On the grand scale that might be the right number. But there are many ways to retain a customer, and many ways to acquire a customer. Let's take a look at your sales/marketing resources." Jackson filled in the matrix with dollar values – a rough recollection of the budget that he saw earlier.

	Total
Reps	
Base	1,200.0
SPIFS	200.0
Travel	200.0
Advertising	500.0
Collateral	400.0
Trade Shows	200.0
Website	50.0
Promotions	300.0
Other	150.0
Total	3,200.0

"Now we have total resources available. And we want to split the resources between Actual and Potential customers. Are all customers of equal value?"

"All customers are not the same. I'd love to have a dozen new customers that spend at least $100,000 with us... better yet, $250,000."

"Where does that number come from? Let me ask the question in a different way. If you ran a high-low listing of last year's customer sales, what would you consider an 'A' customer?"

"What's an 'A' customer?"

"An 'A' is one of your largest customers. Can you run a high-low customer list?"

"Our system is great – I can run that right now."

Jason walked to his computer, input several criteria, and created the listing. Looking at the list, Jackson asked, "So where do you think the break for an 'A' should be?"

"There seems to be a great divide at about $500,000. Then the customers tally up in the $250,000 range."

"OK, then $500,000 and above is an 'A' customer. Let's scan down the listing." After a few minutes reviewing the listing, Jackson said, "And customers below $50,000 will be 'C' customers. Everyone between $50,000 and $250,000 is a 'B' customer. So let's continue with the exercise.

When I think of sales and marketing, I like to consider every touch-point that I can have with a customer – whether actual or potential. A few minutes ago, we listed the elements of your marketing mix. We included every type of contact with the customers, ranging from the personal touch – a sales rep calling on a customer – to a more remote touch, such as the website.

Ideally we want to balance the investment with the potential value of the customer to the Company. So for example, would we have a rep that costs us $150k a year, call on a "C" customer?"

"Jackson, some "C's" might have "A" potential."

"Great point. I'm glad that you clarified that. So when we think of potential "A's" they may be current customers who buy very little from us. Excellent point.

Would we have a rep call on a "C" actual & potential? Probably not. But we don't want to skip them altogether, do we?"

"Is that where the website, and trade shows enter the picture?"

"Seems like a great place to make that touch. And we'll provide collateral material to get the sale."

"Right. Now when I mention website, will our current website encourage the "C's" to buy? And another question – will it help "A's" continue to buy from us?"

"Hmmm. So there may be a dual purpose for the website. I should check to be sure that it serves the purpose."

"Let's skip to another spending category. Advertising. What is it and where do we do it? Again, I want to think about our multiple targets – A, B, C – and actual and potential customers."

"Jackson, I'm sure that we haven't developed our advertising to focus on particular targets. I think it's fair to say that I have some thinking to do."

"Jason, let's spend a few minutes and just scratch some things on the board."

Jason and Jackson enthusiastically started brainstorming the sales process and how best to allocate sales/marketing resources. After about 30 minutes, they had created a matrix that allocated resources among "A-B-C" customer classifications, and actual and potential customers.

	A		B		C		Total Spend
	Act	Pot	Act	Pot	Act	Pot	
Reps							
Base	500.0	300.0	200.0	150.0	25.0	25.0	1,200.0
SPIFS	50.0	100.0		50.0			200.0
Inside Sales	50.0	25.0	100.0		75.0		250.0
Travel	50.0	50.0	75.0	25.0			200.0
Advertising	350.0		100.0		50.0		500.0
Collateral	100.0	100.0	50.0	100.0	50.0		400.0
Trade Shows	75.0	25.0	50.0	50.0			200.0
Website		25.0	25.0	25.0	25.0		100.0
Promotions	150.0		100.0		50.0		300.0
Other	50.0		50.0		50.0		150.0
Total	1,375.0	625.0	750.0	400.0	325.0	25.0	3,500.0

Jason was surprised at how simple it was to allocate resources among the categories. There was nothing precise about the allocations, but in general the values represented a good guess about the importance of the customer segments. About 60% of the Company's resources were allocated to 'A' accounts, and of that amount about 30% would be dedicated to potential customers.

About one-third of the resources would be dedicated to 'B' accounts, while the remainder would be invested in 'C' accounts. Using this thought process, it was clear that we didn't want to invest high-cost reps in 'C' accounts, but we would handle them with the less costly Call Center, promotional material, electronic promotions, and the website.

Jackson stepped back from the board. "I'd say that's a heck of a job, Jason. One more thing just occurred to me. Is it the same kind of rep that sells to a new customer as one who manages an account? Is one a hunter, and one a farmer?"

"The two types of reps have a different DNA. We've tried to create a universal sales rep that can do both, and so far, we've done all right."

"So when you think of increasing sales by – let's say 50% - during the next 3 years, will your current sales force get the job done?"

"I don't know. I really haven't considered differentiating the reps, because we've never had such aggressive sales targets. I'll have to consider sales force composition in the plan if we're going to reach those sales levels.

Did we just finish a strategic plan for sales & marketing?"

Jackson laughed, and put his hand on Jason's shoulder. "If only it were that easy, Jason. This might – just might be – the first layer of thinking. You've got the process down, but I want you to think through at least one more layer down, and project out a few years.

When I say one more layer, we've differentiated among actual and potential customers, and we identified 3 different customer classes. When you consider each of the potential resources, the next question is 'how will we prepare for the sale?" For example, collateral material and sales scripts might be different for an 'A' compared to a 'C' customer. And compensation plans may vary a lot when considering an 'A' versus a 'C'. So there is still a lot of work to do.

Do you think that your current method of just letting the reps define their target customers is the right way to go?"

"I guess that I've been too trusting in the past. Maybe I should spend more time with the reps developing and approving a master list of targets. I think as a sales team, we need to be more thoughtful about how we manage the sales process."

"Do you have the right kind of sales reporting in the business?"

"Sure, I get sales reports daily – minute by minute if I'd like. Everything that I need is in the system."

"Well, that's one kind of sales reporting, but what about sales rep call reporting – you know, where they tell you what's happening in the market. And do you get any kind of margin reporting – perhaps by customer or type of customer?"

"Now that we've gone through this exercise, I'm going to think about how reporting might change to give us better information about the business."

"Jason, when we started this conversation, you also mentioned launching new products. How has that gone in the past?"

"It's been at best OK. We've had some issues releasing new products on time. And worse yet, it seems that we're a me-too builder – never an innovator, but always a follower."

"Are you satisfied with that performance? And if not, what are we doing about new product development and launches?"

"Not a whole lot that we can do. Everything comes from Reg's shop. He has some great engineers, but maybe they are perfectionists. I need new products, not absolutely perfect products."

"Interesting. You mentioned everything comes from Reg's shop. Is that good or bad?"

"Well, my sales folks are in the market every day listening to the customers. Sometimes they hear rumors about our competitors – you know, new products or services. Whenever I can, I bring the information to Reg – give him a head's up – but we don't have any formal process for new product development."

"Do customers ever ask for specific product enhancements?"

"Absolutely, but most times the engineers just humor us by listening. They have their own pet projects that they work on. Techy things mostly. Far too complex for our customers, but really 21st century things."

"Any thoughts?"

"If we're going to hit 50% growth, seems like we should formalize the market information so that R&D does something with it."

"Sounds like a plan. Will that be in your deliverables to work with Reg on new product development?"

"Youbetcha."

They spent a few more minutes discussing new product development. Jackson used more than 2 hours, but was very satisfied with the impact on Jason. As he wrapped up the discussion, he shook Jason's hand, smiled and said, "This was an exceptionally useful discussion about your operations. Just a quick heads-up, John is looking to grow to $50 million in the next 3 years. When you look at your sales operations, put that number in the mix, and think about how we can get there, and don't be overly concerned about today's constraints.

So, for example, you'll need new products. How many... what kind of expected sales from each ... when will the products be launched to get some pipeline as well as sell-through volume. Think about some targets, and how we can overcome the obstacles that you envision. In the past, I've noticed that time and money will solve most problems, if the right problems are identified.

This was a great discussion, Jason."

Jackson adjourned to his temporary office. He opened his journal and jotted some notes:
- Sales force management & CRM
- Sales training
- Improved sales activity reporting
- New product development process – needs work
- New products essential... licensing...M&A ... JV's?
- Sales force assessment & hunter/farmer evaluation
- Review advertising and collateral material; target customers

Meeting with Bill – VP Manufacturing

Bill's office was a stereotype VP manufacturing. Shelves were lined with prototypes and engineering gadgets. His thoroughly organized desk had few loose papers – most were stacked in neat piles. One wall displayed several photos of him and other executives – some with the regional politicians, others with prominent customers.

Bill was in his mid-60's, smiling and affable during the brief introductions.

"John gave me a bit of background. How would you like to proceed?"

Jackson leaned back in his chair, legs crossed at the ankles, fully relaxed. "Just tell me a bit about how you manage the manufacturing operations. What kind of reports do you get, communications style, and where you think we have the greatest opportunities to profitably grow the Company."

Jason prepared Bill for the questions, and Bill was ready to share information with Jackson.

He slid a manila folder across the table and flipped open the cover. "I thought that you might be asking about our operations."

He included an index with the numerous papers and reports. Jackson quickly scanned the index and focused on three areas:
- Performance Reporting
- New Product Introductions
- Inventory Management

After some small talk about operations, Jackson asked, "So talk to me about performance reporting. What does it look like, how do you measure performance, and how often and with whom do you meet?"

"Now that's a mouthful. Let's start with some of the management reports."

Bill pulled Section I from the file. This section, included several subsections:
- Daily
- Weekly
- Monthly
- Quarterly

Bill shuffled among the reports describing how they were often the foundation of staff meetings. Reports presented many of the key metrics necessary to manage the manufacturing operations.

Jackson focused on areas where he customarily finds opportunity.

"Looking at your monthly reporting, it seems that your scrap and rework costs are buried in the overall results. Can you discuss those briefly?"

"Brief discussion for sure. Overall we have a scrap run rate of about $400,000 per year. On the grand scale, that represents about .2% of sales and is well within averages for our industry."

"Sure – I can see the math. Let's focus on rework for a moment. How do you manage the rework?"

"We don't actually track the rework costs. It falls out through the manufacturing variances, and again, manufacturing variances are well within the averages for the industry. Total manufacturing variances net to less than .5% of sales."

"Ah, yes, netting to a half-percent of sales. Have you peeled that apart to check on what makes up the number?"

"I leave that detail to the floor managers. I have access to the detail if I want it, but if the department managers don't have a problem with the numbers, I'm ok with their judgment."

"So can we take a quick look at the detail?"

Bill moved to his computer, tapped a few keys and printed out the current month variance report.

	Month		YTD	
	Current Year	Prior Year	Current Year	Prior Year
Manufacturing Var:				
Labor Usage Var	19,566.0	11,354.0	97,789.0	65,776.0
Labot Rate Var	6,577.0	2,554.0	14,367.0	10,366.0
Material Usage Var	8,515.0	1,544.0	45,565.0	22,454.0
Purchase Price Var	(16,445.0)	(12,879.0)	(57,866.0)	(89,255.0)
Rework	15,188.0	8,465.0	122,587.0	72,655.0
Other Variances	6,775.0	2,545.0	119,345.0	35,878.0
	40,176.0	13,583.0	341,787.0	117,874.0
Scrap	12,655.0	8,779.0	190,556.0	89,176.0
Var + Scrap % of Sales			1.4%	0.7%
Budget Sales (Mil $)			36.3	27.8
Curr YTD Sales			26.0	
% Act Sales			2.0%	

114

Jackson quickly reviewed the report, and observed, "I see that your Variances + Scrap have increased from .6% to 1%. Any thoughts?"

"Yes – good question. We expected a few more operational problems with some of our new products. We budgeted a higher ratio of loss as a result."

"OK, but let's look at a few other things. Jason shared some numbers with me, and John gave me the YTD financials. Jason has an annual target of $36.3 million for sales, but John has different numbers. Why the difference?"

"John has the banker's forecast. We're always conservative in our bank estimates – a bit of a safety margin. Jason's sales numbers are our internal budget. Again, as a management principle, we like to keep aggressive targets for the management team."

"Got it. But you're measuring your variance against the budget. Does that make sense?"

"Sure – we measure everything against the budget."

"I understand – but your actual sales are coming in at a run-rate below budget. Said another way, your actual variances are running at 3-4 times the actuals incurred last year. Are you comfortable with that?"

"Again, we always measure against the budget for internal purposes. Remember, we knew that we were going to have some heavier variances with the new products this year, so it seems ok… meets our expectations."

"I'm going to poke at a few other things – kind of naïve questions since I don't know your business. Purchase Price variance is very favorable in both years. Can you help me understand how that works?"

"Sure. When we do our budgets, we really haven't finalized the material prices for the future year. Historically, rather than get caught short with an unfavorable PPV, we automatically build in a 5% material price increase starting at day one of the next year."

"And how does that consider inventories that may be on hand that won't get the cost increase."

"Jackson, you're pretty sharp. That is one of those hidden reserves that I keep in my back pocket."

"I get it. But let's look at the manufacturing variances another way. If you didn't have the favorable PPV, your variances actually total about $600,000 on actual sales of $26 million. Your run-rate is closer to 2.5% of actual sales than it is to the 1.4% calculation you show in the reports. Does that seem to be the run rate that you expected?"

With that quick summary, Bill pulled a calculator from his pocket, punched some numbers, and leaned back in his chair, very concerned. "I… I don't understand how …"

"I'm a bit of a nuisance, Bill, but when I see some of these cushions in your planning, I wonder if you really have tight control over the processes. I'm not opposed to contingency funds, but is there a way to tighten this up a bit?

So for example, rather than just use a blanket inflation factor, could you run a quick Pareto of materials used, and really get a better estimate of price changes expected on the top materials used? You know, the 80/20 rule?"

"I hear you, Jackson, but if I tighten up on my cushions, I could get caught short on some of my other variances. Then we'd be in a real jam."

"Sure, I see that. But without tighter control over all the elements of the business, are we missing major profit opportunity?

OK Bill, let's not spend a lot of time on that. How is your scrap reported?"

Somewhat relieved to change the topic, Bill said, "That's an easy one. When the Work In Process fails inspection, we immediately write off the material value, and clear the stock from the manufacturing floor."

"And what happens to the labor and overhead applied to the product before scrapping."

"Well, because of systems limitations, that disappears into the financials during the final accounting. I'm guessing that it comes through in the book-to-physical adjustment."

"On average, what percent of actual cost does material represent?"

"That's about 20% of total standard cost."

"So when we have a scrap value of $200,000, that represents only 20% of the value added through that manufacturing step. Said another way, on average we are really scrapping up to $1 million of cost."

Now, Bill looked concerned about his losses. Jackson reviewed the concepts with Bill to be sure he understood, being careful not to assign blame.

After they reviewed all the calculations, Jackson summarized, "When I do strategic planning, I like to focus on the risks and opportunities facing a Company on a grand scale. So here we are in a manufacturing & distribution Company with sales in the $25-$30 million range with a 10% return on sales – let's say about $2.5 million.

As I look at the summary we just discussed, I see opportunities that when you aggressively manage – trying to become better than average – of perhaps $1+ million of improved earnings. Again, on the grand scale, that alone could give you folks a 40% increase in earnings. What do you think?"

"OK – I've never looked at things this way before. My overall operating metrics make sense – averages, you know. But it seems like I may have given the managers a bit too much slack when I look at the results. By damn, I've got to kick some butt, and get things back on track- better than average is my goal and it always has been. What are your thoughts Jackson?"

"Have you considered *Lean* business for this operation?"

"I'm opposed to lean because John is a loyal owner. We're not into laying off people just to improve the bottom line."

"Ah, but *lean* doesn't necessarily mean layoffs. Lean is a cultural thing. The overall goal of lean is to eliminate waste. That could be eliminating unnecessary processes and activities, perhaps eliminating unnecessary assets, training personnel so that they do the right thing every time. Maybe implementing routine maintenance or replacing tired equipment. There are many facets to lean business, and I'm not an expert. I've heard of folks improving earnings by 30% just by implementing lean thinking, but it takes time to change culture.

I'll send you a book – 'World Class Manufacturing' by Richard Schonberger - that perfectly describes *lean* thinking so that you can become more familiar with the concepts. After you've read a bit more about the concepts, let's think about how you might consider *lean* in your strategic plan.

One more thing. How have your new product introductions gone during the past few years."

"They've been a bit bumpy. We get through the launch, but it isn't pretty. Glitches – but they happen with every business"

"So, what kinds of things happen during a launch?"

"It seems that we always have some last minute adjustments to the product specs that don't make it the final bills of material (BOM's), the manufacturing routers, and sometimes process instructions are one or more steps behind the final design. It happens when we try to move too quickly."

"So does that add to the overtime, and I think you mentioned that it adds to the scrap, labor variances etc."

"Yes – absolutely. So that's on the manufacturing side, but maybe even more of a dramatic impact is on the customer side. When we promise delivery and they're counting on us, and we miss delivery commitments, they get mad as hell. And they're justified. Adds a lot of angst to the business. Many urgent meetings… sometimes we send our best engineers to their business to fix the product.

It gets to be a mess. Sometimes, we dread new products… but we're dead without them."

"OK, let's be hypothetical. What if we could design a process that gives you on-time product launch, minimal overtime, and keep the engineers in the shop doing their job, rather than chasing their tails around the country – panicked and fixing customer problems. Good or bad?"

"If we could pull that off – well, we'd be happy campers, Jackson"

"Lean!"

"Lean will fix that as well?"

"Read the book, Bill… read the book and you'll be a zealot. Bill, I think that you have a heck of an opportunity here, and I'd like to help you find out how to capture that opportunity in your strategic plan."

Bill seemed more comfortable with the discussion, since they weren't just identifying problems, but possibly identifying solutions that could actually be implemented.

"Jackson, no need to send the book. I'll order the Kindle version, and start reading it tonight.

This is different than I expected. You are more of a solutions guy, than I expected. Let's get to it."

Jackson stacked the papers and notes, and felt very satisfied with the progress during this first meeting.

Meeting with Reg – VP R&D

Jackson adjourned to the conference room, preparing for his meeting with Reginald, the VP of Research & Development. Reg worked with the Company for 15 years, the last 10 years as an employee. John knew many years ago that new product development was a key for his future sales and profitability growth. Initially, Reg worked as a part time consultant, helping Bill to modify some of the existing products.

Ten years ago, John believed that he could support a full-time VP of Research, and he convinced Reg to join the Company. Initially, new product development accelerated so that they launched a new product or enhancement about every 6 months. However, during the past 3-4 years, new product launches slowed as new product complexity increased, and the product launch was plagued by 'glitches'.

A quiet knock on the conference room door announced Reg's arrival.

A tall, bearded man with round metal-framed spectacles entered the room, warm smile and hand extended. "I'm guessing that you would be Jackson. Great to meet you."

Reg's quiet demeanor hinted at his doctoral training. "Glad to meet you Reginald."

"Please call me Reg. I've heard that you've had a few successful meetings with my associates. Seems that your questions are stirring their imagination. How would you like to proceed?"

Reg was accustomed to moving quickly through an agenda.

"Tell me about yourself. I understand that you have a PhD in Metallurgy. What kind of things have you been doing here at the Company during the past few years?"

Reg smiled as if he had been through this many times before. He leaned back in his chair, relaxed and very comfortable, and talked about his life for about 10 minutes. Once he reached the present, he leaned forward and said, "Now that you know about me, tell me about yourself." His search for knowledge continued – he wanted to understand his *interrogator*.

After a 5-minute introduction, Jackson broke from the career history and said, "So tell me how you manage in this Company. Things going well?"

Reg presented 2 folders for discussion. "Would you like a water? It's good to drink about 90 ounces a day…"

"Sure. Thanks."

Reg returned to the table with two Perrier's. During the next few minutes, Reg talked Jackson through the past 8 year's of new product launch history - about 2 new products per year, and then focused on the new product pipeline.

"So does this new product development launch cycle meet your personal objectives?"

"Well, I'd like to have a more active NPD cycle, but things just seem to get in the way."

"What kind of things?"

"Good question. There have been a few that were real knockout factors. For example, the engineers have identified many potential new products based on recent technology breakthroughs, but for some reason the marketing folks don't want the products.

And then, when we get the ideas through marketing concept, the manufacturing folks estimate the cost of the products, and I guess we can't afford to make them at a competitive cost."

"Hmmm. Is it that the marketing folks don't want the products, or is it the customers that don't want the products?"

"Well, I guess in the long run, marketing believes that the customers don't want the products."

"Have you talked to the marketing folks about some of the technology breakthroughs, and asked them to explore the concepts with the customers before the engineers launch into product development?"

"We do that informally, but as I think about the last year, maybe not as diligently as we should."

"How long does it take to develop a new product? You know, the number of engineering hours to launch a new product?"

"While we have technically oriented products, this truly isn't rocket science. Our new products don't require tens-of-thousands of hours of groundbreaking research. We try to use proven technology to improve our success rate and speed to market. As a guess, I'd say engineering time to develop a new product using existing technology might be in the 2,000 hour range."

"And how many engineers do you have in your department?"

"I've got 7 full time engineers, and access to a couple of consulting engineers when I get into very specific technology."

"So, with 7 full-time engineers, let's say you have 14,000 hours of available time for new product development. In a rough calculation, it seems like – worst case – you should have about 7 new products a year."

"Whoa – the simple math doesn't work. The engineers have other responsibilities as well. We support trouble shooting in the manufacturing operations, have personal development time, and quite a few other activities that we need to attend to."

"Got it. How important is new product development to this organization?"

"I think that new product development is essential for our continued success."

"Would you characterize NPD as THE NUMBER ONE priority?"

"I'd say it's a tie for number one. Keeping the factory humming is also number one."

"So how much time do your engineers spend on factory trouble shooting?"

"Well, it's not just factory trouble shooting. The folks also help the customers with some development – maybe some trouble shooting as well."

"And how much of their time do they spend on customer trouble shooting and support?"

"We don't keep track of their time like that. We meet weekly and monthly to establish priorities – focus our energy on the *hot list.*"

"OK. Well let me play some reverse math. If a new product from concept to launch takes – at the outside – 2,000 hours, and you produce on average 2 new products per year, you spend engineering time on other than new product development equal to about 10,000 hours per year. Does that sound about right?"

"Your math is right, given the 2,000 hours for a new product, but that just doesn't make any sense."

"Let me scratch out some timelines – perhaps just exploring some ideas that may help you get additional new products to market."

Jackson grabbed a marker, moved to the whiteboard, and started sketching some numbers and lines.

Engineering Hours

	Q1	Q2	Q3	Q4	Total Year
Total Hours	3,500	3,500	3,500	3,500	14,000
NPD	1,000	1,000	1,000	1,000	4,000
Mfg. Troubleshoot					-
Cust Troubleshoot					-
Development					-
Other					-
Total	1,000	1,000	1,000	1,000	4,000

"So there is the engineering department. Any thoughts?"

"You know, it seems too simple, and yet we're not getting many new products out the door. I think that I need to get a complete timekeeping system in ASAP."

"Well, let's poke at that for a minute. How long will it take to define your system requirements, research the project management systems available, and then install the system?"

"Guessing 4-6 months at a minimum… and I'll have to divert the engineers to the task."

"And can we wait that long?"

"I'd prefer not to wait. I need to understand what's happening now."

"Let me make a suggestion. Rather than immediately put in a full-blown system now, why don't you talk with the engineers – brainstorm what's happening today. Do what I just did – scratch out the concept of hours available, and ask them where the time goes. You might capture enough information initially to redirect the engineers to your main priority – NPD."

They spent the next few minutes outlining an approach to the time-spent analysis. Jackson suggested a one-hour brainstorming session with the team to discover what they believed to be their time commitments. During the brainstorming, it was important that Reg emphasize that, as a team, they were trying to discover why they weren't spending enough time in NPD.

After sipping some water Jackson said, "Now let's focus on two other obstacles to launching a new product. Something about marketing doesn't want the technology that you offer. Talk to me."

"Sure. Our engineers are top shelf. They keep up to date with new developments in our engineering space. For example, last month one of the engineers read about a new composite material that not only conducts electricity, but also can withstand extreme cold down to -100C degrees, and not get brittle. And on the other side, temps can reach as high as 450C degrees, and still maintain its conductivity and shape. This is an extraordinary material.

Al, the engineer, figured out how to mold the material into the shape required for the AB-410 fitting. The only drawback is that the material is a drab green and can't be painted. If it's painted, its conductivity is compromised. Marketing said, 'If it can't be the Company blue, we can't sell it.'

Al was upset about something as simple as color that would kill a potentially major product."

"Sounds to me like it could be a technical wonder. Very impressive. So, do your products need that kind of temperature range to be effective in the market?"

"No. The material would be great on the Mars Rover, but most applications earth-side wouldn't need a quarter of that temperature range."

"Could your existing equipment build such a product?"

"Al talked with the manufacturing folks. I guess that we needed a clean room environment to manufacture these. Virtually any contamination would require scrapping the unit."

"So how did Al get this project?"

"We allocate a certain amount of time to each engineer for their own creative project. I think it's targeted to be about 200 hours a year. We believe that open-ended projects will get us exceptionally innovative products in the long run."

"And how many exceptionally innovative products have you introduced in the past 5 years?"

Furrowed brow, and a concerned look, Reg leaned back in his chair, and thought through the past 5 year's performance. "Damn good question. As I think about the past few years, I can't think of one that's hit the market and been a success."

"And for curiosity, how much does that innovative material cost? I'm guessing that leading edge materials can be very expensive."

"Extremely costly. In fact, Al mentioned last week that we were the only company in Ohio that even ordered a test batch."

"OK. So let me play this back to you. You allow engineers about 10% of their time to work on innovative breakthrough products, and you have 7 engineers with that freedom... a total of about 1,400 hours per year.

The projects are completely at their discretion.

They develop – perhaps as far as a prototype – and present to marketing, which often rejects the innovation because of a potential customer issue.

And there is no advance check with manufacturing to determine if manufacturing of these breakthrough products are feasible."

"Sounds lame doesn't it."

"I'm not opposed to creative thinking, but unless you have an overabundance of new products, would it be worthwhile to realign the resources so that you can make and market new products? And if it's about 2,000 hours for new product development and launch, just by focusing the engineering resource on high probability projects, you'd get an additional new product launched about every 15 months without spending an extra nickel."

Reg was doodling dollar signs contemplating change.

"Reg, let's just spend a few minutes brainstorming and see how the new product development process could change."

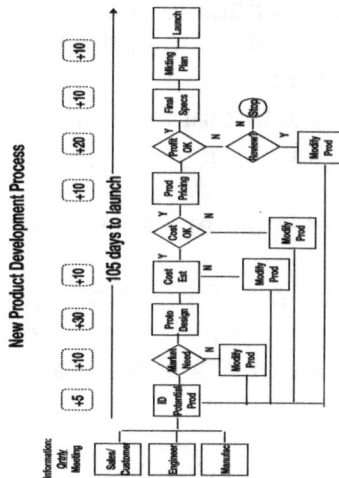

Jackson enthusiastically scratched out a rough diagram on the whiteboard. As he wrote, he explained that on average 2,000 hours were required for a single new product. The Company had engineering resource totaling 14,000 hours a year, so conceivably could produce 7 new products a year. If it were important enough to launch 7 new products a year, Reg should research where the engineering time is invested. If only 60% of the engineer's time were invested in new product development, new product launches would double.

"Jackson, looking at the rough diagram you've sketched… well, I'd really like to double our new product launches. Tell me about the quarterly engineering review."

"Reg, we both know that engineers are driven by innovation. But they have a weakness called 'precision'. They like things to be perfect… and many like intricately designed products. Of course in our brainstorming, I'm exaggerating the stereotypes. By having a quarterly tech-sharing meeting, the engineers get to strut their stuff, and the marketing and manufacturing folks get to understand some of the technology breakthroughs available. The marketing folks are aware of the customer needs. The manufacturing folks would like to produce high quality, and affordable products.

So for example, when the engineers discussed the new material that you mentioned earlier, the marketing and manufacturing folks would have identified obstacles to the successful development, production and launch of new products with the new material.

One other thing I forgot to mention. Collaboration with universities, research organizations and government agencies can be very helpful to identify product improvements that could create major competitive advantage. Just last week I attended a brief seminar coordinated by the Consul General of Canada. In the seminar, they mentioned a non-profit organization called Mitacs. Mitacs is committed to its mission of supporting innovation while working with industry. I think that if you were to establish collaborative relationships with universities, government agencies and non-profits like Mitacs, you may discover some very practical applications that help you achieve your goals.

A disciplined quarterly meeting could also include info sharing by the marketing and sales execs who are more aware of innovations in the field, as well as customer needs. And the manufacturing folks could provide updates about prototype commercialization. Let's say you invest 2-3 hours a quarter dedicated to sharing information and focused on new product launches. Thoughts?"

"Sure doesn't seem like a big time commitment to virtually double new product launches without any additional spending. But I've got to discover where all the engineering time is going. … Just doesn't make sense since they are working overtime and not delivering new products. I've got to get right at that.

What else should we talk about, Jackson?"

"One last thing. How do you folks evaluate new products for development?"

"It's informal. We rough out the production and launch costs, estimate the market potential and if it makes sense, we launch the product."

"And is there any minimum return required? So for example, does a product with a one-year life get the same treatment as one with a five year life?"

"No, we pretty much just determine if the product will make a reasonable gross profit in the first couple of years."

John Davidson Co.
New Product Development Checklist

Product Name: _____

1 Product Description *(Describe both US and International)*

US Operations: *(Include target selling price and target cost.)*

International Operations: *(Include target selling price and target cost.)*

New Product Classification	Enhancement	New Product	New Category

2 Market Conditions/Market Share *(Describe the fit.)*

Key Competitors (Attached List)

3 Product Development - *Description of Process*

5 Timeline Describe *(Development broad timeline - attache GANNT chart)*

6 Description of Launch Process:

4 Financial Summary

	Quarters				Year		
	1	*2*	*3*	*4*	**2**	**3**	**4**
Investment *(Includes Capital & Expense)*							
R&D							
Sales & Marketing							
Manufacturing							
Other							
Total Investment Required							
Sales							
Gross Profit							
Launch & Other Expense *(Describe on attachment)*							
R&D							
Marketing							
Sales Training							
Advertising & Promotion							
Manufacturing							
Total Expense							
Contribution Margin							

5 Financial Ratios:
Internal Rate of Return:
Net Present Value:
Cash Flow Breakeven:

"Let's look at an example template as a way to evaluate a new product. Sometimes when lifetime profitability is considered, products lose their luster. Here's a copy of a template for you to consider before our next meeting. I think that we're wrapped for now."

Reg took a picture of the flowchart on the whiteboard so that he could think about a new approach to product development, and also discover where the engineer resources were used.

Meeting with Bev – VP Human Resources

Thus far, Jackson was pleased with the senior staff discussions. Bev DeSantis, the VP of Human resources, had an unusual background. Surprisingly her undergraduate degree was in pre-med. While John didn't provide much background about Bev, Jackson was intrigued how someone could go from the hard sciences to the less technical side of Human Resources.

John mentioned that she was active in community organizations long before he hired her as VP of Human Resources. Bev was an adrenaline junkie, being an aerobatic stunt pilot. While these two avocations seemed inconsistent, they demonstrated a dedication to purpose not found in the broader population.

When Jackson knocked on her office door, a pleasant voice welcomed him.

"Please, come in Jackson. I've heard a lot about you from the other staff members. I'm quite excited to talk about the business." She guided him to her conference table.

Bev was a 5'8" athletically trim 40+ year-old.

Jackson scanned her office to see the many awards resulting from her interests. Photos of her receiving community service awards and pictures of her flights trailing smoke were scattered around the office walls. Several trophies adorned her credenza.

"Thanks Bev... you have quite a collection of awards... I'm impressed."

"No need to be impressed. The folks that I work for –in the community organizations – those are the ones who are impressive."

After a few minutes of introductions, Bev moved directly into the Human Resources topic.

"How shall we proceed?"

"Well, I'd like to hear about how you run the HR function. You know, what kind of information do you look at... what do you expect of your department... how do you communicate..."

"Sounds simple enough. I've assembled some of the customary information that I review. Let's first discuss how I view the responsibility, and then get into the reporting.

A fact that most executives don't realize is that people costs – compensation, fringe benefits and other people costs - are probably the largest single spending category in their P&L. I would guess that production material cost would be the only other natural spending category that could be as large. I like to challenge the boss with that information, since *people* are more often viewed as permanent fixtures – like the office desk or maybe a laser cutter in the factory.

When I look at the risk of our human resource portfolio, I get nervous – not because we don't treat our people well, but because they can be so mobile. Our most important assets – cliché, I know – leave the building every night. The reality is that the best employees are the most employable and desirable in the market. And believe me, in this competitive world, the competitors know who the great employees are.

In middle market companies, we just don't approach the asset as if it is that valuable.

Just a few weeks ago, I completed an analysis of employee turnover cost. As a line item, the cost is significant – not just for the size of the cost, but also for the business disruption that it could cause.

Let's just review the analysis quickly. I've put this together to get a better idea of what the costs are. At a minimum in a normal year, we spend more than $500,000 on turnover. I put this together as a benchmark for comparison. If we put the $500k into proactive actions, we'd have happier employees and less turnover. Just a thought.

So after my short rant, let's talk about how I manage the Company resource.

In this report, you'll see some of the key statistics.

Sometimes the senior staff doesn't believe the turnover cost, because it isn't a single line in our P&L's, but when I list the costs, the time it takes to recruit, and the number of times that we recruit – well, the costs can be excessive. It is of particular interest when we view these as preventable in many cases.

Employee turnover:	# Months		
(000's $)	1	3	6
VP			
Annual Salary	**250.0**	**250.0**	**250.0**
Search fee cost @33.3%	83.3	83.3	83.3
Relocation			
Temporary Living ($8k/month)	8.0	24.0	48.0
Real Estate Fees, Attorney, Moving	75.0	75.0	75.0
Interim Employee	-	90.0	180.0
All Other	10.0	10.0	10.0
Total	**176.3**	**282.3**	**396.3**
Director			
Annual Salary	**150.0**	**150.0**	**150.0**
Search fee cost @25%	37.5	37.5	37.5
Relocation			
Temporary Living	8.0	24.0	48.0
Real Estate Fees, Attorney, Moving	40.0	40.0	40.0
Interim Employee	-	40.0	80.0
All Other	10.0	10.0	10.0
Total	**95.5**	**151.5**	**215.5**
Manager			
Annual Salary	**100.0**	**100.0**	**100.0**
Search fee cost	25.0	25.0	25.0
Relocation			
Temporary Living	8.0	24.0	-
Real Estate Fees, Attorney, Moving	40.0	40.0	40.0
Interim Employee	-	25.0	-
All Other	5.0	5.0	5.0
Total	**78.0**	**119.0**	**70.0**
Individual Contributor			
Annual Salary	**45.0**	**45.0**	**45.0**
Search fee cost	12.0	12.0	
Relocation			
Temporary Living	-	-	
Real Estate Fees, Attorney, Moving	-	-	
Interim Employee	8.0	24.0	36.0
All Other			
Total	**20.0**	**36.0**	**36.0**

Think about a high turnover year. If I were to lose a VP, a director, half-dozen managers and a dozen line employees, it doesn't sound like a lot, but that could easily add up to $.5 million P&L impact. And that doesn't consider the lost performance impact on the business.

And when we have a pretax income of $3 million, well, that's a very large potentially controllable cost.

Overall, I've tried to manage this portfolio of movable assets with proactive measures.

	# Open	Avg Days to Recruit		Closed This Month
		Actual	*Target*	
Open Headcount:				
VP			90	
Director	2	90	45	1
Manager	4	60	45	2
Supervisor	9	45	30	4
Individual Contributor	22	22	30	11
Total	*n/a*	*n/a*	*n/a*	*n/a*

	Act	Target
Turnover %	8%	5%

Fringe Participation:	%	%
401-k	86%	90%
Health Insurance	90%	90%

Tuition Reimbursement		
Number of Candidates	4	8

ATTABOYS		
# of Sports Tickets	15	20
# Dinners	12	6

Workers Comp Claims	2	0

For the senior execs, we have annual accountabilities –dollars of sales and profitability and department spending. Deep within the organization, we measure costs versus plan."

"Yes, I can see how you focus on some very discreet measurements. By focusing on P&L

items, do you think that you've covered all the essentials to help the Company successfully manage growth?"

"I'm always open to discussion. What are your thoughts?"

"Well, for example, do you have any quantitative measures other than sales, pretax profit and cost measures?"

"Jackson, you're the professor on this. Talk to me."

"When I think of Company performance objectives, I like intermediate goals. So for example, in many companies, careful management of cash flow is critical to their success. Several asset performance measures are easily monitored includes Days Sales Outstanding, and Inventory Turns."

"Are you really trying to turn me into an accountant, Jackson? I'm not capable."

"No, I'll be talking with Mitch about those. But there are other matters. You've mentioned employee turnover values as something that is very important. I'd also guess that the number of new products released, and perhaps the number of new customers engaged might be important measures.

And then, there are process matters that could be measured."

"Help me out Jackson. What would they be?"

"There may also be performance metrics in the manufacturing area such as Scrap as % of sales; perhaps rework as % of sales, variances as % of sales etc. And these are measures that I've talked about with Bill.

Basically, there are many measures that would be ideal to support profitable growth.

And then we get to the personal side of measurement. Do you have periodic performance reviews?"

"Absolutely. We require each manager, director, and VP to evaluate their subordinates annually."

"And what do the reviews look like. Are they going to improve employee performance? Better yet, will they help the employees grow in their careers?"

With that question, she stood and quietly paced the floor. "You know, I make sure that everyone gets an annual review, but when I look at them, the reviews are poor quality. They are no more than *compliance* with the requirement that a review must be done, and not very helpful for the employee. I'm guessing that the execs have never been properly trained to evaluate and coach the employees.

As I think about our management process, our reviews don't seem to link to Company performance other than sales, spending and profit. We don't have any other performance measures, and it seems that some longer-term measures may be very worthwhile."

Bev paused, thinking for a moment. "One other thing that strikes me. We only concentrate on compensation and health care when we talk about the HR function.

Based on some recent reading, there are many ways to compensate folks – well beyond just the paychecks. Just last week I saw that millennials don't necessarily want expensive benefits. They may prefer other amenities like better surroundings, flex schedules and other non-cash features. And you can be sure that I'm not suggesting foosball or billiard tables in the lounges."

"So what do you think that we should do with that information?"

Without hesitation, she responded, "Fix it. You know after our brief discussion, I think I've got some work to do."

Jackson and Bev started to outline some of the items that Bev thought she should be implementing in the Human Resources function.

Compensation
 Exec performance-Strategic   Q1

 Long term incentive comp   Q1
 Profit sharing thru individual cont Q2

 Management performance - Annual Q1
Benefits

 Benefits menu improvement   Q1

 Tactical courses   Q2
 Management courses   Q3
 Tuition reimbursement   Q2
Performance Improvements
 Improved performance reviews
  - Training   Q2
  - Implementation   Q3
Return on Capital
 Improved metrics   Q2
Employee Committee   Q2

After 30 minutes Bev capped the marker, stood back away from the whiteboard and sighed. "That's potentially a lot of money that I'm spending."

"Maybe, but you haven't spent it yet. Earlier you mentioned the cost of turnover. Will some of these items impact employee turnover? And if so, are these HR investments a positive replacement for turnover costs?"

"Yes, but it's still a lot of spending."

"Agreed, but we haven't spent the money, just identified some areas that might improve the management of our most expensive and mobile assets. Think about how much these items might cost, and let's discuss them in a few days. Overall, I like what we've accomplished in the past few hours.

We've concentrated on the most expensive line item in the P&L, and we've identified ways to protect the resource, ways to improve their performance, and increase their career value. Not a bad way to spend a few hours.

Here's what I suggest. Think about this list. Prioritize the list based on your impressions of the value to the Company, and be prepared to discuss the prioritization with the other execs. On my side, I've already discussed some of these topics with the other execs. I've already talked with Bill, Jason and Reg about some of these deliverables. Our goal is to brainstorm these and other topics at the offsite to decide as a Company what are the best actions. It's possible that we can't afford to do any of these things… but I doubt it. There will be a menu of things to be done when we finish the planning.

So for now, v-e-r-y well done Bev.

Just one more thing, Bev. In many companies the Human Resources coordinates many of the community relations activities. What's your involvement in the community?"

"Funny that you mention that. I forgot one area that is a hot button for many of the millennial candidates that we try to recruit. They seem to have a very strong interest in community outreach and support. Historically we've played our part in the community, but when I talk with the millenials it seems that we may fall short of their expectations."

"What kind of activities are you involved with today?"

"United Way gets a lot of attention. Full support of the annual fund drive – nearly 100% participation by our employees. And I've been on the United Way board for about 3 years. We've also participated in the Christmas drive for the homeless. Otherwise, it's been ad hoc within the Company. If an employee is excited about a particular non-profit, we do our best to support the effort."

"How much do we spend on those ad hoc moments?"

"I'd guess a total of about $100,000."

"And it's based on an individual employee's request for support? No formal assessment of the proposal?

"Yes, so far."

"Would your ever consider setting up some kind of employee committee to evaluate and guide the community support activity? Still fund it with the $100k, but let the employees determine how the money is spent."

"Interesting concept. And that would raise the engagement without additional spending. Maybe we could sponsor some charity races... fund some of McDonald house events..."

"Now that sounds like your charitable preferences... do we want to let the employees manage the fund?"

"You're right. I've stepped in to direct, and the concept is to oversee and not manage."

"Now you've got it. So let's add that 'employee committee' to the list of items to consider."

"Will do."

After a few more minutes of discussion, Jackson adjourned their session and relocated to the visitor's office.

Meeting with Andy - VP Logistics

After summarizing his notes about the Human Resources area, Jackson concentrated on the logistics function. Andy Deland, John's stepson, was a recent graduate of Purdue. He has worked with the Company for about 2 years.

John discussed Andy's Company experience as one of exploring project opportunities. During his exploration, he was especially interested in Logistics. While logistics were important for effective customer service, logistics weren't a Company core process.

Jackson encountered similar situations of an owner's inexperienced relatives in senior positions in the Company. In these politically charged situations, he posed questions about Company needs and performance to let the owners form opinions about the best way to manage the organization.

After a few minutes summarizing his thoughts, he entered Andy's office.

"Andy, good afternoon. My name is ..."

Andy interrupted, "Your name is Jackson, and I've anxiously awaited our discussion. Please, come in," as he guided Jackson to the conference table. "Would you like anything to drink? Soda? Water?"

"Sure, let's have a water. Say, you've got quite a view from this office." Jackson scanned the office looking for a topic to start a casual discussion.

"Yes, it sure is. Better than some and worse than others, but I really enjoy the scene."

Jackson spotted Andy's picture grasping the propeller of a Cessna 172. "So, you're a pilot, Andy?"

"Just started lessons within the past few weeks. It's a challenge – you know, edge of the envelope kind of thing. It's a lot of work, but I've never been afraid of challenge."

"So what else do you do for excitement?"

"Nothing for excitement, but recently I've been studying some logistics and operations management books, and I also have the manufacturing book, "World Class Manufacturing…""

"Interesting choice of – can I say hobbies?"

"Yes, for sure. Between the flying and the text books, I'm fully engaged."

"And how did you select the technical fields to study?"

"Look, you know I'm the bosses step-son. If I'm ever going to be successful, I've got to become familiar with all facets of the business. My dad, in his overprotective role, has *allowed* me to work on projects in the logistics area. The other members of the executive team understand that I'm the heir apparent, so they don't challenge me too often. And the logistics area? Well, I guess dad thinks I can't do too much damage to the firm as I earn my stripes."

"And how do you feel about that?"

"It's a placeholder. On the one side, I draw a great salary, but on the other side, I want to feel some pressure. I'd like to operate with greater accountability. Not on a project basis, but I want to be responsible for a function. So for now, I've selected logistics … I can at least add *some* value to the Company, and I'm working with Lean Manufacturing theory, since I believe it is applicable to any function. It's a process thing."

"Ok, I like the way that you think. Tell me what you've been up to for the past year."

Andy talked for a half hour about various projects that he completed. The projects were helpful to improve customer service, but they were low impact. While working on the projects, he always tried to insert himself into more responsible work.

"Andy, how did Bill accept your *Lean* work?"

"Bill is a great guy … long term employee, but quite honestly, he's a bit behind the times. When I've mentioned 'lean manufacturing' to him, he has placated me, but hasn't grasped the potential of lean business. He thinks it requires layoffs – cutbacks. And no, he hasn't read the book on it."

"Would it be worthwhile for you to do a project in manufacturing operations?"

"From a business point of view, absolutely. We've got many opportunities."

"What kind of opportunities do you envision?"

"I've been doing some analysis, and I see too much inventory… scrap losses present an opportunity… rework is a major challenge. As I examine the textbooks, lean could help us improve manufacturing processes, reduce inventory levels, and improve profitability. And I'm a rookie just thinking about the potential. I can't imagine the impact if an expert were to drive change.

Wherever I look, I see opportunity. I've talked with Bill offline – don't want to challenge him in front of his peers – but he's turning out good product overall, generally hitting the customer deadlines, so business as usual is acceptable to all."

"So let's just summarize. You're training in areas that may be helpful to the business, but getting traction within the organization is a bit challenging because you're young, and you're family. You're convinced that Lean Business is critical to the future success of the company. Bill is in mid-to-late 60's, and he likes the old way of doing business. 'Bout right?"

"You've got it."

"Ok, let me play out a scenario. I tend to agree with you that Lean Business is an excellent operating model. I can also understand that Bill likes the historical manufacturing methods. As I think about the organization, it seems that Bill may be retiring sometime in the near future. Does John have any succession planning underway?"

"Not that he has shared… we don't talk much about strategies."

"So let me think out loud for a few minutes. What if the organization decided to create a limited lean manufacturing project? Perhaps using an outside consultant to break through the credibility gap, and with you as the inside project manager. Would that satisfy your desire to deliver on a major project that contributes significantly to profitability, demonstrate credibility and get you into the mainstream of management? And if the project were successful, perhaps you'd be better accepted as a valuable and critical part of the organization.

And let's face it, if a manufacturing project goes well, you could spin the lean concept throughout the organization. Do you think lean applies to – let's say finance, human resources – maybe even R&D new product development?"

"Absolutely – lean is a process orientation and does not necessarily apply only to manufacturing."

"So I'll ask you to think about it and let me know if you have an interest. If so, we'll see how we can get the organization to embrace lean thinking."

Andy's broad smile hinted that he was eager to try this as a way to demonstrate his capabilities. As Jackson left the room, Andy nodded his head and quietly said, "Thank you

Jackson. I appreciate your understanding and your help."

Jackson was very pleased with the potential opportunity for both Andy and the Company. Yes, with this opportunity, Andy would either execute successfully or settle into being a fixture in the Company – yet another relative in a family business.

Meeting with Mitch - VP Finance

Thus far, all the meetings have been beneficial. Jackson was starting to see a path forward to completing the strategic plan. Mitch, the CFO, was next on the list.

Mitch, in his early 40's, joined the Company about 12 years ago as the controller, working for the CFO. About 4 years ago the CFO retired, and Mitch assumed the role. Prior to joining the Company, Mitch worked with several local and regional CPA firms.

Jackson already reviewed the financial statements and identified some potential reporting improvements. Consistent with many mid-market financial statements, the Company focused heavily on basic trial balance reporting – summary revenue, cost of sales and SG&A. There was minimal inventory and accounts receivable reporting.

Mitch's office was smaller than the other executives', and the office had few personal touches. His starkly adorned office had a small conference table; a desk piled with stacks of papers and two LCD computer screens – one larger than the other – almost as a shield to fend off visitors.

Jackson entered the office with his characteristic smile, offering his hand in greeting. "Hello Mitch. I'm Jackson, and I'm here for our 2 PM meeting. Is this still a good time?"

"Hi, Jackson. I know this is the scheduled time, but is there any way that we can postpone this meeting until tomorrow morning. I've had a bit of a blow-up, and if possible, tomorrow would be best."

"No problem. Pick a time, and I'll stop over."

They rescheduled for 8 AM the next morning.

The next morning, Jackson knocked at Mitch's door at 8 AM.

"Jackson, thanks for rescheduling to this morning. I had some rush work to do on an open account receivable... fairly large balance with a Canadian customer. He's a bit challenged... behind his agreed payment schedule, and I like to keep close tabs on him."

"I'm curious. How much is the receivable?"

"In total, it's about $1 million, and about $800,000 is overdue by more than 90 days.

I'm quite sure he's good for it, but he is a very slow payer."

"When was the last time you visited him?"

"Visited him? I'm not sure that I've ever been to his office… just outside of Toronto."

"Well, for a million dollars, I think I'd pay him a personal visit to emphasize the importance of the payment schedule. In fact, I might put him on a prepay for current shipments, and require $100,000 a month on the overdue amount until the old debt is paid up."

"You know, I've never considered a personal visit, but … hey, it is a million dollars…"

As Jackson settled in at the conference table, he said, "Let's talk. I'm sure that you've had a chance to discuss my meetings with the other execs. How would you like to start?"

"I believe that you'd like to hear how I operate."

With that, he described his monthly routine, and shared the financials with Jackson. As they discussed his routines, Jackson asked, "… and how do you work with the future? … Forecast, budgets and maybe strategic plan?"

"Generally, we do the annual budget based on what John wants to accomplish. Usually 3-5% increase over the prior year – straight through the P&L. I develop the master spreadsheet so that his goals are met, and then I pass the numbers to the team.

We've been doing the budget like that for the last few years. As far as forecast is concerned, we just look at the business every month to check our progress. If it looks like we are *seriously* short of the budget, we cut the expenses, or if profits are strong, John will ask for suggestions about how to spend the money. It's a great informal process that gets the team all on the same page."

"Right. I've looked at the financials – great financial summaries, but do you go down another layer through the financials? So, for example, do you develop any analyses covering sales and profits by product line…customer concentration … or maybe manufacturing variance analysis?"

"No, we haven't seen a need for that if the folks are meeting their numbers. If things go astray, the execs will develop an analysis explaining the variances. Our execs are very conscientious and both John and I have 100% confidence in their judgment."

"Ok, let's talk a bit about opportunities."

Jackson then discussed manufacturing operations and variances, lean manufacturing practices, inventory management, accounts receivable management and capital spending analysis.

As he discussed each area, providing examples of analyses and reports that could be helpful to manage the operations, Mitch was silent.

"Well Mitch, this has been a great discussion. What else should we talk about?"

"Sounds to me like you're implying that I don't do a very good job. The kinds of analyses and routine reporting that you've discussed are a lot of work, and I just don't have time to do that kind of work. We've got so many things that seem to crash, I've got to spend my time fixing broken things and I could never have the time to analyze and plan."

"Mitch, don't get upset with our discussion. I'm trying to understand where you are as a Company, so that I can help you improve. Do you think any of the planning and analysis that we've discussed is worthwhile?"

"Sure, analysis and planning would always be worthwhile, but as I said, I just don't have the time."

"Let's find you the time...without increased spending and 80-hour work weeks. Let's make a list of some of the time wasters."

For the next 45 minutes, Mitch and Jackson scratched out notes on the whiteboard. Tasks ranged from IT systems actions to sales and pricing issues, to inventory shortages/location inaccuracies, to accounts receivable errors.

During the discussion, Mitch sometimes became very angry at the work that MUST be done, instead of what he'd like to do.

As the ideas started to slow, Jackson stepped back from the whiteboard. Furrowed brow, he concluded, "Lot's to do, Mitch... what do you think?"

Monthly schedule – possible time wasters		
WHAT	**WHO**	**HOW LONG**
MUST DO		
A/R detail/GL balancing	Joan	4
Spreadsheets...spreadsheets	All	32
inventory/ledger balance	Chuck	8
mfg variances	Chuck	8
collecting old A/R balances	Al	24
reconcile accts-dscts	Al	32
reconcile accts-pricing adj	Al	40
payroll reconciliation	Jennifer	16
commission payments	Jennifer	8
IT breakage	William	20-40
LIKE TO DO		
pricing analysis	Mitch	?
profit by prod line	mitch	?
profit by trade channel	mitch	?
territory sales analysis	mitch	?
planning – near term	mitch	?
planning – longer term	mitch	?
think!!	mitch	?

"I think that we spend far too much time chasing our tails, and too little time thinking about the future. You know, as I look at this list, I just get angry. Damn – I spend far too much time fixing broken stuff. I'm not managing, but I don't know how to get out of this hole. What do you suggest, Jackson?"

"Have you ever heard of Lean Business?"

"Sure, heard about it – not sure how it applies. We're not into cutting personnel. This is more of a family than a business."

"Lean isn't about cutting personnel, it's about eliminating non-value added processes and activities... lean means eliminate waste by identifying things that must be done, then reviewing the entire process to eliminate wasteful actions, documenting the process, select the right personnel, training personnel and then implementing the process improvement. One key to business success is that an organization must continuously improve. I'm no expert at lean, but I've used the concepts to great advantage. The world changes daily. If a company doesn't adapt to change, they're basically going out of business. For now, let's just keep this list as open issues.

Another thing, Mitch, I'm not being critical, but is it possible that the Company could have grown at 10-15% a year instead of – what is the norm 5+- percent?"

""Hold on Jackson. Let's not pick on this Company. We've been successful for about 12 years while some of our competitors have just vanished. We're doing ok."

"OK – now that's a great concept. Is that where we want to be – OK? Or do we want to be great?"

"Of course we'd like to be great, but I've explained some of the reasons for our shortfall. We're definitely not perfect, but we've done all right."

"Is 'all right' similar to 'ok?'"

"You're a pusher, Jackson. Yeah – I get it. So what do you think that we should do?"

"Well, John has taken a major step by opening up his business to strategic planning. I don't have the answers, but you folks do. For the past hour we've talked about the finance operation. In a short time, we've identified many of the time wasters in your department. Now, let's figure out how we can eliminate those wasters and get you in to a more progressive mode. You on board?"

"If I don't have to dedicate 80 hours a week, let's make it happen."

"And what if I just ask you to concentrate on fixing the processes that you've identified as broken so far? Prioritize them based on greatest impact to the business and find the root cause of the problem. Don't try to fix everything at once, or 6 months from now, or you'll be part way through everything and completing nothing. You'll be frustrated. If you want to bounce some ideas around, you've got my number, but I think that your list is a great start on the strategic plan issues."

They briefly discussed the upcoming planning session, and Jackson left for the day, satisfied with all that they had accomplished during the meeting.

Meeting with Vito - VP International

Vito, a true international spirit, spoke Italian, Spanish and French, had more stamps in his passport than a diplomat and thrived on international travel. Being in the same time zone for more than a month was the ultimate torture for him. Vito enjoyed travel to both Europe and Latin America, but seldom visited Asia.

He was seated at his desk scanning emails when Jackson arrived. A brief knock, Vito looked up and immediately displayed a trained salesperson's smile.

"Welcome, Jackson. I've heard so much about you - I anxiously await our discussion. Please sit down," as he motioned Jackson to the head of the conference table.

They shared some small talk about the weather and local sports, and after a few minutes, Jackson redirected the conversation. "So Vito, you know the drill. We'll talk about the International sales operations, and try to understand the best fit with John's financial goals. You comfortable with that?"

"Absolutely. I've actually assembled some of my customary reports so that you can better understand my process. I've been here for about 7 years, so I have a standard routine."

He quickly opened a folder and explained his travel routine, adding some detail as he discussed the periodic tours.

"For sure, I visit my big-5 customers at least once a quarter. It's a straightforward swing starting in the UK, then France, Spain, Germany and Italy. I've been working with the companies in each country for nearly 20 years, and the customers trust me to take care of them. My major customers followed me from my prior company.

Occasionally I make an extra trip to Europe, responding to customer concerns … well, really complaints."

"What kind of complaints?"

"Sometimes it's a product failure that requires either some smooth talking, or maybe some physical tweaking. I may bring along one of the engineers to adjust the product."

"And have you tracked the reason for the product failure."

"Not a whole lot of mystery. It usually happens with new products. In fact, as I think about last year's trips, I think operation's missed a late change order on several occasions."

"So what does an engineer do when travelling?"

"In addition to enjoying the local dining, they just talk about technical topics with the customer to get them to calm down. Most often, the engineer can't fix the problem on site, but engineer-to- engineer they take the emotion out of the failure."

"And then what?"

"After we wine and dine the engineers and the company owners or President, we're friends again, and we re-order the latest product revision."

"So how many customers do you visit on the European swing."

"I usually hit the big customers – about 20 of them – and then I try to visit the smaller customers at least once a year."

"Do you do any prospecting with potential customers?"

"Not much. The international market is very competitive, and new customers are often reluctant to establish a relationship with a US company. ... There are good alternatives in the local market ...guess it could have something to do with some of our historical quality problems.

Heck, if we could just modify our designs a bit to adapt to the European market, I could almost immediately increase my sales – maybe increase by as much as a third."

"And are there major customers who buy our competitors' products that would buy ours if quality were A+ - maybe even more innovative or adaptive to their needs?"

"I would guess. And if they are shipping completed products to the US, buying US components may give them a currency hedge on their costs."

"If we have a trouble-shooting engineer in Europe, could you and the engineers cold-call on prospects and existing customers to discuss their needs?"

"I suppose that we could… just may be worthwhile since we pay to fly them to Europe."

"OK - and how about Latin America?"

"Pretty much the same thing. I call on long-established customers who trust me, and the products that I represent. But it's always a tough sale in Brazil and Argentina. Their economic environment is slightly out of control, and Mitch is very reluctant to give them any open account… always Letter of Credit – FOB Cincinnati."

"Sounds conservative. Do you know if Mitch considers insuring the receivables?"

"You've met Mitch – he's a bit old-school. If it's a big change to business as usual, he's reluctant to change. If it's worked for the past dozen years, why change?"

"Maybe to increase sales… and you didn't mention the Far East. I've heard that Japan and China are booming. Any thoughts?"

"They're not my specialty. If they catch our product line on the web, we'll sell them – letter of credit only. Otherwise I don't spend time with them, since I have no connections."

"Have you done any research with the US Commerce Department? I've heard that they have exceptional resources that exist to promote US business overseas. They have research resources that can help companies identify potential customers… make introductions … help with the required documentation for unusual items. I've even heard of them hosting trade shows for US business. Some of the services are free, and some are fee-for-service, but it's often a great way to break into a new country or region."

"It may be worthwhile researching."

"Out of the – let's say 10 most developed countries in the world – do you think that you could get $2-3 million of sales to new customers? I'd guess that those countries have combined GDP's greater than the US.

And $3 million of new customer sales would increase international by 50%"

"With the right resources, yes, I could – *maybe* – get $3 million of new customers in the mix."

"And then you've got organic growth of existing customers… maybe 5% a year … that is, if nothing drastic happens.

So when we think about the big picture, what does it take to capture that business?"

"You've hit on a couple of things. Improved quality… engineer sales calls … maybe some research with the US Department of Commerce. Maybe have better sales terms. Yes, those are possibilities.

But one of the obstacles is consistent quality – not that we turn out a lot of defects – but if we could get closer to 100% quality that would be great. But I don't have any control over that."

"But our goal is to understand where we want to go and then identify what we need to get there. If quality is a problem, let's focus on the cause and identify what it takes to get to the 100% quality goal."

"So you're saying I can highlight that without Bill blowing a gasket?"

"Look, there are no constraints when we do this brainstorming. It's my job to keep the process moving forward, with minimal angst.

I've already told John that I'll be digging under all the rocks in the Company to identify opportunities."

"In that case, my wish list could get very long."

"And that's what we want to discuss. As a team, if we believe that a viable opportunity exists with reasonable investment, it's our job to identify the opportunity, recognize what it takes to achieve the goal, evaluate the risk and cost, and when we select an opportunity, make a plan and execute it."

"Jackson, you're making this sound too simple."

"No rocket science about the process. The key is not to get bogged down with reasons why something can't be done, and focus on solutions to the obstacles. It's so much easier to grow a company when you brainstorm that way."

"OK, so now I'll be putting my wish list together."

"Can I assume that you think $9-10 million is possible in three years?"

"Fifty percent increase – you're scaring me Jackson … let me put some wish list items together."

"Great Vito. Don't be shy with your list, but understand that you'll be competing with the other VP's for resources. Let me know how I can help.

Janet was a mid-30's woman who has been with the company for 12 years. Her early customer service role and relationship with key customers was the basis for her promotion to VP Marketing.

Her office was pleasantly decorated with a seacoast motif. Janet was very professionally dressed in a navy blue pantsuit, accent scarf and white blouse. Her smile seemed genuine – not an artificial grin. When Jackson appeared in her doorway, she immediately stood to greet him.

"Jackson, I presume?" she questioned.

"Yes Ma'am. It's a pleasure to meet you, Janet."

She guided Jackson to the conference table where a Perrier and glass awaited. Two manila files were neatly arranged adjacent to the refreshments. A bowl of individually wrapped mints was in the center of the round conference table.

"As you might have guessed, I've talked with the other VP's and have a pretty good idea of what you'd like to talk about. Shall we proceed?"

"Before we launch into the business discussion, tell me about yourself. How long you've been here... a bit of your history ... hobbies, vacations. The soft side of business."

The tension of their initial meeting melted.

"Well, ok, but I don't have a very interesting history." She briefly talked about her career with the Company, discussing the exceptional relationships with key customers. She really became animated when she started discussing her hobbies.

"... And I've been working with several non-profits – homeless shelters, food-pantries..." She continued for a few minutes discussing her personal drivers.

"It sounds like you have a very active life. How's the business side of your life?"

"It's quite good. John is an excellent boss. Basically he lets me run the marketing show. I meet with him once a month to describe what's happening, and as long as no one squeaks about problems, I'm on my own."

"So what does your typical month look like?"

"Well, as I said, I meet with John once a month to keep him informed, and then I meet with the VP Sales weekly. He and I generally set the agenda based on what his folks need in the market.

I also meet with the VP-R&D monthly to get updates on the new product development.

And twice a year I get the booth ready for the trade shows.

Other than that, I'm in react mode."

"And react to what?"

"Sales rep's calls for information. Occasionally I need to prepare a quick product summary comparing to a competitive product. And maybe I need to work with the sales reps on a sales proposal, since I'm one of the committee members that needs to approve major price changes."

"Tell me about the price changes."

"Some of our products are in very competitive segments. Reps will call with a price that they need, to get the deal. The rep, VP Finance and I work through the numbers to determine if we can meet the price.

You know, now that you mention it, this happens quite often…maybe 2-3 times a month. And when the reps call, everything stops, since the deals are quick turnaround."

"And how often do you reach the rep's pricing requirements?"

"I'd say more than half the time."

"And what is the basis of the decision?"

"Just the reps input. They're the folks on the front line."

"So, we're in a very competitive business, and a few times a month we get an urgent call for a price adjustment. Have we ever considered doing a competitive analysis for the industry – maybe once or twice a year?"

"That would be great, but we don't have the time to do that."

"So instead, a few times a month, we drop everything, and make a decision based on the reps input – no other source of information."

"Yes, that's pretty much it ... doesn't sound effective does it? "

"And if a product is priced lower than another customer's, and they discover the pricing, will the customers be angry?"

"Yes, that happens, and we've even had retroactive price adjustments for some of our customers."

"Is that good or bad?"

"Probably not the brightest thing we've ever done. But that's the way we work.

"Pricing is one key to profit. Do you think it might be better to develop a strategy that anticipates competitor activity such as new product development and the market itself? Developing a pricing strategy may not define an exact executable plan, but you'd be much better informed if the competitor takes an action. And, let's face it, you really want to be a leader rather than a follower – especially if you want to be better than average."

"Sounds simple enough, but where will we find the time?"

"Well, let's think about your marketing department. It looks like you have two marketing analysts. What's their background?"

"Analyst may be a bit of an overstatement. Neither has any marketing training, but we are exceptionally responsive to customer service needs and sales rep requests. William is analytically inclined, and I suppose with some help he could prepare reasonable analysis."

"What if you and Andy formed a task team with William. I'll make a guess - you could prepare a competitive product analysis in – let's say – 15-20 hours of William's time. If you could help William reprioritize 5 hours a week to prepare the analysis, you could have a viable product analysis within a month. And during that time, William may be doing something that he really enjoys.

That's a 10% commitment to raise the level of the Company's performance. And over 4 weeks, that would hardly be a ripple for you and Andy... would it?"

"On the surface, I absolutely agree. But we've never done such an analysis. What would be included in the analysis?"

"I would probably brainstorm all the benefits of our products and competitors, maybe some web research including complaints about each. We may also include some information about the competitor companies' financial strength, turnover, and also our Company for comparison.

Ideally we'd summarize information that discusses the benefits of our products and Company that are part of the buying decision – time in business, quality, innovation etc. … The basis for a value discussion and not product price."

"Sounds challenging – but the analysis could be very interesting for sales, marketing and the financial analyst."

"Let's talk about some other elements. Tell me about your marketing mix… you know, all the elements that touch the customer and help promote the Company."

"Do you mean actions like deployment of the sales force? The website – new product launches?"

"Yes – but that's just the beginning. I'd like to list all the elements, so let's just scratch them out on the whiteboard."

Jackson pressed to get a complete list of things that had an impact on the market.

	WHO								
	Mkting Dept 1	Mkting Dept 2	Sales	Fun	HR	Mfg	Execs	R&D	IT
Sales reps			x						
Call center			x						
promotional material									
current products	x								
new product intro		x						x	
white papers			x		x			x	
Pricing analysis			x		x				
catalog	x			x					
website			x	x	x	x	x	x	x
trade shows	x			x			x	x	
seasonal themes	x								
periodic mailings	x								
customer co. research	x				x				
keyword analysis	x			x			x	x	
industry trade assoc							x		
board memberships							x		
community service						x	x		
apprenticeships						x	x		

Jackson continued. "OK, now we have a first cut at the shape of things. When I think of marketing, I like to consider every action that affects the business outside the 4 walls. And I like to think of things going out, and things coming in. The list that we just developed is a first pass at how we engage the market."

"Jackson, we've touched virtually every function in the Company. How will the other VP's feel about me stepping on their turf?"

"Their turf is an interesting statement. I like to think of *we* – that is the entire Company trying to win in the marketplace. Once that concept is in place, no one is stepping on anyone else's territory if the activity is properly coordinated. I'm not suggesting that you necessarily direct each of these actions, but rather guide the team to successful use of Company resources.

So let's think about the finance function, working with the marketing department. The finance team is analytical. They can research competitors through D&B reports, and perhaps help the manufacturing folks *reverse engineer* the costs of some of your competitors' products.

HR can be very useful when you develop your website to make the Company more attractive to potential candidates while recruiting.

And to keep going… the R&D folks can contribute to the website by sharing how new products will impact performance at a client company.

There are so many ways that the team can influence the market, it's almost incalculable.

We've done the highlights... can you take this and develop the concepts? Think about the next level down, and how *WE* – the entire Company can become more competitive by working together, proactively rather than reactively – in the marketplace?"

"New experience for me, Jackson... but as I think about how this might be a great way to get the team focused – yes, I'll do it. Can we have another session to review some of the concepts a layer down? And do it before the offsite? I'd like to formalize this and share it with the team at the offsite."

"Deal. Let me know when you'd like to get together."

"Now that I understand the approach, I'd like to get together in the next few days. In the meantime, I'll explore ideas with the other VP's. I'll draft them using the Company against the world theme."

Jackson continued. "So let's summarize. We'd like to get more analytical and proactive in the business. We'd like to analyze where you and your team are spending their time – try to identify the time wasters, and launch process improvements that eliminate the time wasters. We'd like to develop competitive analyses, and pricing strategies that consider the entire marketing mix."

Agreement made, Jackson was thrilled with the overall progress made in marketing. In only a few hours, he helped Janet reorient from a reactive sales/marketing resource to more of a complete marketing function. The concept is one thing, but getting the entire team means breaking down the silos... that could be more difficult. We'll see how John and the executive team adapt to the more thorough marketing concept.

Update meeting with John

Jackson and John met for a casual dinner at Moerlein's Lager House. The craft beers were delicious, and after the first tall ale, Jackson summarized his observations.

"John, you've got an excellent shop – dedicated employees with their eye on the ball. I think that there are a couple of themes for improvement in your operations. Any thoughts what they may be?"

"Let me guess. They think I'm a bit soft with their performance. You know, I don't hold them totally accountable for their actions, as long as we're hitting the numbers."

Jackson responded noncommittally. "Ok. Anything else?"

"I can only guess that they believe that I might be a bit complacent. I don't push them forward hard enough."

Again, Jackson responded, "OK. How do you feel about your management process? Formal enough - too informal?"

"I'll plead guilty to managing an informal organization. And, as a result, maybe I'm leaving some opportunity on the table."

"What kind of opportunities are you letting slip through the cracks?"

"Well, simply put, we run an average operation. Average growth, average profitability, average employee turnover… average… average… average." John seemed resigned to that conclusion.

"I guess that perhaps I don't push hard enough to be the *best*. But, changing now seems like a lot of work, and it might be too disruptive. On the other hand, one reason that I've asked for your help is that I need to change some things to reach meaningful goals.

But when I change the tenor of the business, I want to be sure that I don't abandon any of those folks who have gotten me this far. Do you understand why I'm thinking like that?"

"Something to do with the team being there whenever you needed them?"

"Yes. They've stuck with me in the tough times, and I've tried to take care of them in the good times."

"OK. I've got that. Loyalty is a good thing. Let's talk about a management process change. Something more formal, but not rigid and inflexible. It would be a blend of structured reporting and communications, concentrating on some additional performance metrics – let's call it one layer down from the top financials. The metrics might also be non-financial metrics."

"Like?"

"How about something that measures new product development progress on specific projects? Or maybe starting a "Lean Business" initiative? And I'll confess right up front, I'm a *Lean Business* fanatic."

By this time, dinner had arrived, and they ordered another craft beer.

Jackson directed the conversation to more casual topics while dining, knowing that he would concentrate on the tougher topics as they finished the meal – perhaps with a single malt.

After the scotch arrived, Jackson migrated to tonight's core discussion.

"John, I see great opportunity for your business. You are correct in the self-assessment that your operation marches to the leader's charge, 'Let's be average!'"

John leaned forward trying to capture every word, since his future may be built around Jackson's observations.

"Now for sure, this is not a criticism. It's an observation from the viewpoint of someone who's seen many businesses. My suggestion overall – improve your reporting – examine another layer of information and challenge your team to not only explain the results, but to describe the corrective action taken so that you become a continuous improvement business."

"And what do you think the reaction to that will be?"

John said, "Keep going."

"First of all, it will initially be more work. It will put pressure on the team, but you can manage the impact by selecting priority projects. For example, your new product development is wandering, and as a result new product launches are – well, you've said it – average. I know that the team is working long hours, and they are diligent in their efforts, but they seem to be spread across several priorities. Find out what they're spending time on, and you'll be able to determine if that's where you want the investment."

Jackson knew that their NPD time wasters were due to manufacturing failures, and a failure to coordinate activities among the critical resources – manufacturing, sales/marketing and engineering. The simple fix was to summarize where the time was spent, and decide if that's the best way to operate the Company.

"The next area of opportunity might be in the manufacturing area – concentrating on quality, new product launch, logistics, and training."

"Ah, yes. You've had a chance to work with Andy in logistics. Did I tell you he is my stepson? He's a good kid… smart as hell and works hard. Gotta get him some *chops* so that the executive team respects him."

"How do you plan to 'get him his chops?"

"Hire you." John smiled. "You're the guy who sees things differently than I do, and I need your insight to get this business to above average."

"I understand, and I'll help you develop a program that will increase Andy's responsibility and accountability. Then you'll be able to understand his potential. And what are your thoughts about Bill?"

"Bill's one of those guys that I can always depend on. He's been with me through some challenging times. I admit that he's not the most progressive exec in the business, but he keeps the manufacturing operations under control. No major surprises." As he said that, he leaned back in his chair, smiled and sipped his scotch. "But while he hasn't killed me with major surprises, he doesn't seem to run out of smaller surprises. But overall, I like the guy."

"So Bill is – what is it, mid-60's? How long will he be around? One year? Five years?"

"That is a good question. I've avoided the topic altogether. I'm nervous, because I don't have a second in command in manufacturing."

"Good or bad?"

"If I said *average* for a business like this, are you going to make me buy this dinner?" John laughed about the cost of dinner.

"I agree with your assessment of average – for this kind of business. Is your goal to be average?"

"Point taken. Are you suggesting that I bring in new talent? Bill won't be comfortable with that kind of change, and it will be expensive."

"Let's not try to solve that now… we can handle that kind of question during the strategy sessions with the team. Talk to me about logistics?"

"You mean let's talk about Andy? Andy is smart as hell. His age is somewhat of a barrier - no major experience - but he's done some worthwhile projects that have improved customer satisfaction and reduced some costs."

"But is he in the management mainstream – serious performance accountability – or operating on the fringes?"

John looked down at the table, lowered his voice as if guilty of a charge, "Fringes. I've got to get him in mainstream so that the team respects him for his performance and capabilities, and not just because he's the boss's son."

"Agreed. Bright kid... energetic... anxious to learn. Did you know that he's been studying manufacturing to broaden his background?"

"Didn't know that. Is that one of his main interests?"

"It is for now, but I think the over-riding interest is to get experience that will help you grow the business profitably. And logistics and manufacturing may be a great place to start. So let's spend a minute on lean thinking – the Toyota manufacturing method.

I've talked about manufacturing operations and business process improvement with Andy. He seems very excited about the topic and we discussed the book – 'World Class Manufacturing'. He's been reading the book and trying to apply the principles.

So when I blend all these things together, a thought occurred to me. What if we got Andy involved in a serious project based on Lean Thinking? A project that involves him with the

operation's team, and if he does a great job –
average is unacceptable - will that get him
some chops with Bill and the team?"

"Could be. Is he capable of this new kind of
thinking?"

"You said it – young smart and energetic. And
if done properly, an outside consultant –not me
– could help him develop and execute a
program that could bring your business to
above average performance. Interested?"

"Yes – and would that also help bring Bill
along?"

"Possibly, but let's not build expectations too
high yet.

One last thing. When I get into the offsite
meeting, I turn over a lot of rocks. I've
encouraged the team to be open with their
comments. I like to challenge the organization,
and if I do my job right, we may get into areas
that are uncomfortable for you. I always keep
an eye on the boss to make sure we don't get
too deep into the delicate tissue, but I do want
to warn you.

When we get into open discussions, I'll press
for the good and bad. I'll dig into competitive
strengths and weaknesses, and you might hear
some things that are *news* for you.

For example, a few years ago, I was going
through the offsite preplanning with a client

who provided me with a *complete* list of a half-dozen strengths and weaknesses. I mentioned that if we didn't identify 30-40 items, he shouldn't pay me. The client smiled thinking he just made the deal of the century – a no cost strategic plan.

During the offsite, we filled flipchart pages covering three walls of the conference room – I think there were 47 items identified before the brainstorming was complete.

To his credit, the owner was not the least bit defensive throughout the process. In fact, after the meeting, he elbowed me gently in the ribs, smiled and said, '...you've earned your fee, bub... had no idea what was below the surface...'

Any comments, John?"

"So I should be prepared to hear some things that might bother me?"

"Only if I do my job, and your team is forthright."

"And I'll assume that starts us on the journey to excellence... let's get on with this. I'll put on a Kevlar vest and deal with it real-time."

"Ok. We've covered the main topics tonight. This is going to be a very successful planning process, John. Shall we get together tomorrow to establish the macro goals you'd like to accomplish during the next few years?"

They scheduled a 9 AM meeting for the next day to outline John's goals.

Jackson was very pleased with the progress during the dinner. John was on board with the major opportunities identified. Jackson also knew that he could guide the executive team to a successful strategic plan, but the final solutions had to be theirs – not the outside consultants. Without their enthusiastic support, the plan would fail.

Jackson Planning Meeting with John

"John, that was a great dinner last night. We covered many broad topics, and today, I'd like to zero in on some things that might surface in the offsite. Shall we begin?"

Jackson walked to the whiteboard.

"So let's start with the destination. For the past few years, you've grown at – what, about 5%?"

"Yes, somewhere around that. We haven't set the world on fire, but I've been reluctant to push the team too far. They've been great working with me for years, and, well, I just want them to enjoy the success we've had without giving too much stress."

"Got it. But now we're thinking of accelerating growth. What were we thinking, about $50 million of sales with a 10% return?"

John's grin was unbeatable. "Well, yes, that would be nice."

"OK, then let's rock. What do you think will be the keys to that growth? Shout them out."

John had the napkin with some notes from last night. "I'd like more new products… I'd like the international business to really add some value to the company… it would be nice if the inventories were lower – you know to improve cash flow. Something occurred to me this morning – is it possible that employee turnover is too high? Do I dare say worse than average?"

"Could be, so we'll just list it on the board. What else?" Jackson liked to keep the pace of brainstorming at a high rate. "C'mon John, this can't be everything."

"OK, now I haven't given this a lot of thought, but could we just crank up the sales performance?"

"Specifically, what are you looking for?"

"Well, it seems that we have a very stable – good, but stable – group of customers. If we want to grow quickly, I think that we might want some new customers."

"Got it. While we're talking about outside the four walls, tell me about your vendor management."

"Bill does a good job with that."

"Good or great?"

"OK, let's put that on the list. Let's increase vendor performance requirements. They could use a little heat."

"And do you just want them to supply raw materials? Are there other benefits when working with the vendors?"

"Like what?"

"Do the vendors have any special capabilities that might be more efficient than what you can do in-house?"

"Now hold on. I told you I didn't want to reduce any heads. Are you taking me to outsourcing?"

"Don't think of it as outsourcing. Think of it as freeing up what might be expensive internal resources for more value added work for the Company. We're just brainstorming. We can scratch it later. What else would you like to do?"

"You know, when we have our monthly meetings, the meetings don't have any life… no energy. We do the same thing every month. … Look at the numbers, and compare them to the budget. I don't know what I want, but it would be nice to have something different."

"So do the meetings drone on about 'we missed sales by x. Expenses are down by x. We added a headcount in engineering… blah blah blah. And it doesn't seem like there is a strong force driving the business."

"Yes, you've got it. I'd like it to be different – not sure how."

"Do you report against development objectives?"

"Not really. We just get a status – more or less, on time or delayed. Pretty simple stuff."

"Does your delegation of responsibility require performance, or is the reporting more of a narration of what went wrong or right?"

"I guess it's more of a reporting function… a narration."

"Well, how do you prepare a budget?"

"I like to keep that simple. I'll develop a goal – oh, maybe 5%+- growth - and task Mitch to put a spreadsheet together."

"Does the team feel like they own the budget?"

"Not sure, but they know we've got to meet it."

"Do you have one set of numbers?"

"No, we do one for ourselves, and a high level one for the bank. Gives me a bit of a cushion so that we don't get into trouble."

"And how do you fold in business improvements?"

"They are handled more informally."

"OK – got it. So here's our list of 'wishes.' Happy with the list?"

"Seems a bit long, but, sure, I like the list of thing that I'd like to do."

"Let's kick this around a bit. You've identified some tactical things that you'd like to see. I've added another column to your wish list. These might be process improvements that will get you where you want to be. Any thoughts?"

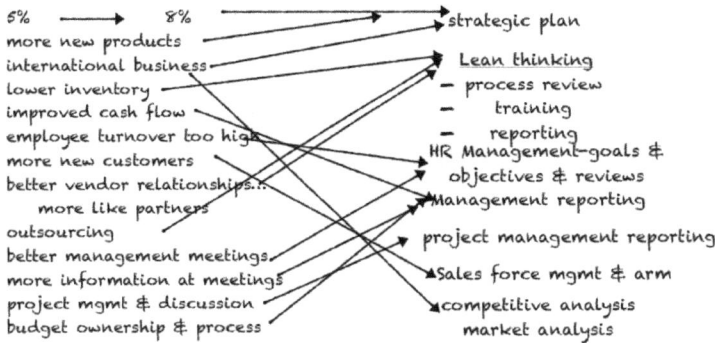

5% ──→ 8%	strategic plan
more new products	
international business	Lean thinking
lower inventory	— process review
improved cash flow	— training
employee turnover too high	— reporting
more new customers	HR Management-goals &
better vendor relationships.	objectives & reviews
more like partners	Management reporting
outsourcing	project management reporting
better management meetings.	
more information at meetings	Sales force mgmt & arm
project mgmt & discussion	competitive analysis
budget ownership & process	market analysis

"Sure. You've got a helluva lot of arrows. We've taken a dozen things and condensed them into the program of the month. Is that about right?"

"Sometimes you might think that, but these factors will help you accomplish your profitable growth objectives. The beauty of getting your key execs in the room is that they become part of the solution.

We'll set up the agenda so that each one gets the chance to talk about their function, and discuss how it might relate to the financial goals.

I'll lead with the financial goals, and then let them provide input into how these numbers can be achieved. My commitment to you is to identify the factors that will allow us to reach the $50 million, and then decide if you want to invest time and money to reach the goals. It's always a trade-off of risk and opportunity."

Jackson Planning Meeting with Patricia

Patricia awaited Jackson's arrival in the conference room.

When Jackson arrived, Patricia welcomed him at the conference room door. "I'm so glad that you were able to fit us in your schedule, Jackson. I'm excited about this initial planning stage – a broad brush of the future. How would you like to proceed?"

"Well, you've taken the first step. Sounds like you are quite excited about this, so let's begin."

Jackson started the discussion about her long-range goals, and how she thought she could accomplish them. Did she want to keep the Company for another 20 years? … Sell the Company within 3-5 years? What kind of growth was she expecting? …Products and product lines? …Distribution: US; Global?

As they explored the various topics, Jackson went to the whiteboard and started listing concepts and ideas… product lines, sourcing, distribution, employees, roles and responsibilities.

After an hour, he and Patricia created a rough P&L using averages based on Patricia's knowledge of the business.

	2017	2018	2019	2020	2021	2022
Millions US $						
Inflation		2.0%	2.0%	2.0%	2.0%	2.0%
Price Increases		2.0%	2.0%	2.0%	2.0%	2.0%
Baseline	6.0					
Pricing Impact		6.1	6.2	6.4	6.5	6.6
New products						
Soft Goods		0.6	1.2	1.2	1.8	2.2
New product lines						
Sport			0.3	0.6	1.0	1.5
Hard Goods				0.2	0.2	0.2
	6.0	6.7	7.7	8.4	9.5	10.5
Market channels						
Baseline	6.0	4.5	4.5	4.4	4.3	4.5
Mass Market		1.5	1.0	1.3	1.7	2.0
Web (US)		0.5	1.3	1.9	2.4	2.5
International		0.2	0.5	0.8	1.1	1.5
Total	6.0	6.7	7.7	8.4	9.5	10.5
Geography						
National	6.0	6.5	6.8	7.6	8.4	9.0
International		0.2	0.5	0.8	1.1	1.5
Total	6.0	6.7	7.3	8.4	9.5	10.5
Gross Margin		4.0	4.4	5.0	5.7	6.3
SG&A		3.0	3.3	3.5	3.8	4.2
Pretax		1.0	1.1	1.5	1.9	2.1
Pretax % Sales		15%	15%	18%	20%	20%
GM %		60%	60%	60%	60%	60%
SG&A % Sales		45%	45%	42%	40%	40%

The rough P&L showed potential growth to $10.5 million of sales, with profits increasing to about $2 million.

"OK Jackson, I'd be crazy to say I don't like this future projection… but is it really possible, or is it a feel-good wish list?"

"That's something we'll have to sort out as we meet with the team. But for now, let's think about the concepts that we've discussed.

First of all, the estimates are only as good as the assumptions behind the financials. So before we're done, we need to validate the assumptions.

Let's talk about them for a few minutes. We've assumed that if you keep the same products, your business will be flat – that is, if it doesn't go under first."

"C'mon Jackson. That sounds a bit rough."

"Yes, it is, but I want to be sure that you recognize that in business, you either move forward or backward – there is no standing still. Think about it. In our connected world, you could now sit at your computer, dial up a UK Company, and have a product shipped to your home within the next 10 days. The wonder of the Internet.

So, for planning purposes, we'll assume that your baseline is flat. … Might be ultra conservative, but it's an assumption.

So that means you need new product development. Earlier we prepared a possible NPD process. Any thoughts?"

"Jackson, I've reviewed our earlier work – thinking about Natalie and Dave – critical skills and workloads. I've got to concentrate Natalie on NPD – no question. And I need to reevaluate the entire management team."

"I agree. But let's not do that now. Let's just know that we must complete an organization review, and think about the whole organization in the context of NPD, and getting the daily routine shifted to others.

And if we load up Natalie with a key NPD task, will she make the same salary – considering she will be a key to growth?"

"I'll have to change her compensation. In our last session, you convinced me that she is critical. I'm thinking about bonus, maybe some ownership interest."

"We've reviewed two essential areas – new products and key personnel. When I look at the P&L, I see two other growth concentrations – international sales and web sales. Let's talk about your resources to deal with those."

They discussed the Company's limitations for E-Business, the Company's website, and the concept of a small US business selling internationally.

It was clear that the Company lacked e-business talent, and she couldn't afford fulltime employees to develop and manage the web.

Several of the areas where the web would be instrumental in the Company's growth included product research and marketing intelligence; communications with essential contacts outside the Company; and finally the web can be used to process transactions – buying and selling.

Patricia decided to:
- Expand product design research … maybe using contract designers, considering the number of free-lance professionals around the world.
- Expand US and international sourcing. This becomes even more important if the Company decides to do pilot runs before full-scale launch.
- Research branding and marketing resources.

Transaction processing – selling over the web – may be a key growth area, since the bricks & mortar sales limit her distribution today.

No matter where they looked, the web skills were critical for growth, and Patricia did not have a current resource.

She needed to identify and acquire skilled resources to manage these opportunities.

"As we talk about all these 'new' responsibilities, you've just doubled my time in the business. You can't be serious."

"Great point, Patricia. Use the web for recruiting."

Also, you'll need to delegate, Patricia. Let's load up the staff schedules, and keep pushing responsibility down through the organization.

One other factor to consider. You're a fledgling business… small by many standards … and you need some great people to make the plan happen. You are competing for talent – against other companies your size, and mid-to-large sized companies. How will you recruit that kind of talent? Bigger salaries? Bonuses? Working conditions? Can employees bring their dog to work? What are your thoughts?"

"My goal is to have a business where associates enjoy coming to work. I don't think I can make them rich, but I can make their work life more rewarding. I'm just not sure what the right mix will be."

"So let's add that to the list of action items. Let's call it corporate culture."

After they completed the discussion, Jackson summarized with bullet points on the whiteboard:

Organization Review
  Corporate culture
Update Job Descriptions
Compensation Review
Resource Requirements
  Web expertise
  Branding Expertise
NPD – Basic & Pilot Products

"Thus far we've outlined our mission, broad financial goals and we've identified some of the major activities to complete. Next, we'll have, your staff give a short presentation about how they can contribute to the success of the Company. I'll coach them so that it will be successful.

I'd guess that we want about 15 minutes from each attendee.

I'll show the draft financials with your growth objectives. This will be a short discussion to help them orient to the bigger business. Then we'll talk about the competitive environment. Company strengths and weaknesses, and how the functions work together to achieve our goals.

I'll caution you now that when I get to strengths and weaknesses, you may be in for some surprises. When I get to the really delicate areas that are too sensitive, give me a signal and I'll back off, but our goal is to make the team part of the solution. We don't want this plan to be forced on them. Sound good so far?"

"When they get into the weaknesses, how tough does it get?"

"I won't let it get personal, but I will ensure that their voices are heard – up to a point. Again, if we listen, we may discover many very simple things that will help this Company grow and prosper. Comfortable?"

"I can tell you I'm a bit nervous about opening up to criticism, but I guess I'll have to trust you."

"It shouldn't be a problem. I've spent enough time with the folks that there won't be any bombshells in the discussion.

So for next steps, I'll update the financials, send them to you for a final review – and don't be shy about your comments. I'll develop an agenda. Once you approve the agenda, you can send it to the team."

"Jackson – this is new turf, but I like the approach. Let's get this bus rolling."

Jackson assembled his papers took a picture of the whiteboard, and moved to the conference room.

Jackson meeting with Patricia's staff - Natalie

This was a very busy time for Jackson, since he was managing two strategic plans – one for Patricia, and one for John.

John's planning was going very well. Today Jackson would spend the entire day in individual meetings with Patricia and her staff.

Jackson would meet with David, Tom and Natalie the operation's managers, and Tonya the Controller.

Each of them had important roles in the Company, not only due to their specific skills, but their ability and versatility to work in other functional areas in a small organization.

Patricia and Jackson decided that it would be best to work with the ops managers first to get a better understanding of the business, before meeting with the controller.

Natalie, day shift operations' manager, was an essential employee. She was Patricia's first employee, and was instrumental to meet customer demands. She worked well with the hourly employees, and managed customers extremely well. Her personality was open and friendly, yet she was a driven taskmaster.

Patricia arranged for Jackson to meet with Natalie in the small conference room, allowing total candor and a confidential workspace.

Natalie, seated in the conference room when Jackson arrived, was comfortably dressed in designer jeans and sweatshirt. She didn't notice Jackson's arrival, as she was reviewing documents.

Jackson knocked quietly on the conference room door to avoid startling Natalie.

Natalie's stern face broke into a broad smile - she stood and greeted Jackson. "Welcome, Jackson. I'm glad that we could arrange to meet during the day. It's been quite busy around here. Sorry about these docs, but I wanted to get through some of the paperwork while waiting.

Patricia mentioned that when we met I should be straightforward with my answers."

"Yes, Ma'am. I think it's great that we could meet during a workday. That will give us a chance to stroll around the operation while it's working. You can tell me what's happening. Shall we take a stroll?"

Natalie stood and guided Jackson out the door and to the left. "Absolutely. Do you want the nickel tour? Or the full Monty?"

"I'll let you be the judge, Natalie. Say, how long have you worked with Patricia? Tell me about yourself."

Natalie worked with Patricia for 5 years starting about 2 years after completing high school. She was very young to be responsible for daily production, and the design work but she was enthusiastic about her role and her contribution to the business.

"Let's start with what we call the receiving/warehouse area. Shipments arrive from – well, really all over the world. We like to clear receiving and restock the warehouse as quickly as possible, but we're a bit behind now… maybe as much as a week, until we get the stock on the shelves.

One of our biggest challenges is hiring and scheduling people for consistent work flow. Employee availability is lumpy, and some weeks we've got incoming product stacked to the ceiling. But we always manage to get through it." With a grimace, she added, "…eventually."

"Once the receiving is cleared to the warehouse location, we can work the incoming orders. The next room has the assembly worktables. Things are informal in the assembly area. Most times we process orders on first-in-first-out basis. Things really get crazy when we have backorders. The clipboards on that wall are color coded to reflect our backorder processing. Red boards are priority… orange and yellow are next."

Jackson observed, "That Red board seems a bit overstuffed. What's up with that?"

"That is a monster. The new Vietnam supplier isn't well organized and they've fallen behind in processing. It's really a shame, since they have great product and design… they actually produce our hottest product right now. Fashion is quirky and sometimes it's a flash of demand, sometimes it's sustained demand over 4-6 months, and sometimes it's a complete bust. They are hot right now."

"And what are we doing about it?"

"Daily Skype calls to Chien, the owner and entrepreneur. He is such a pleasure to deal with, but he just doesn't have the processes to support such a great product."

They spent the next few minutes discussing Chien's product. Natalie continued. "It is a combination of superior quality print silks, clever design and packaging. There are two primary components – the printed scarf itself, and the packaging that's a printed silk pouch suitable for sunglasses, makeup or other necessities.

The closures used to secure the pouch are backordered. I guess a bigger Vietnamese company has cornered the supply and Chien's supply is carefully rationed.

I've talked with Patricia about having the closures made here in the states so that we can satisfy customers' orders. She's been reluctant to move on it. While Chien's products seem to have a sustained demand, if we can't ship the product, it could have a short life."

She continued to discuss the operation. Incoming materials were stored alphabetically by source, since products were fashion driven, and therefore unique by supplier.

"Can I guess that fashion accessories might be seasonal, and in some cases Chien's products might be "A" – or best seller's this month - and "C" seller's in two months?"

"Sure, that happens."

"And would it be worthwhile changing stock locations to reflect seasonal trends rather than alpha based?"

"Never thought of it. This is the way we've managed since day one, and it's worked."

They continued the tour. The assembly area was a large room with long tables used to select merchandise, wrap, package, and prepare a label for shipping.

"One reason that we've done so well is that every item is gift wrapped. We like everyone to open a package – even if they ordered it – to feel like it's a very special gift. Some of our competitors save a few cents, and just brown box and ship the product. We love to make the gift connection."

"That's a clever marketing touch. Talk to me about the packaging and shipping process. It seems that people are doing a lot of moving around. Label printers at each end. Stocking areas with what looks like the gift packaging in bins, with small piles of material near each worker. Anything special about that layout?"

"Just that it works, and we've kept the informality so that folks are comfortable. It's a quick tour, but there really isn't a lot to see. Back to the conference room?"

"Yes. Patricia tells me you spend some time researching designs and materials. Something that you enjoy?"

"Yes, for sure. I'm a bit of a romantic… I came up with the idea of everything is a gift-wrap. I also spend a lot of time *on the web* researching trends, materials, and designs. I try to spot what's hot before it becomes in high demand here in the US."

"And your training?"

"Finished high school and didn't have enough money to go to college. Started with Patricia and never left. She takes good care of me… we get along well … and she appreciates my work."

"How so? The appreciation, I mean."

Her eyes flashed with excitement. "Well, just at random, she might give me a gift certificate for Macy's…maybe a Jack Ruby's restaurant… or a weekend for two at a spa. She does it with a smile and a hug. I think it's just a great relationship."

"How many of the new products and designs do you personally identify and source? Is it 5% or 50%?"

"I identify maybe 150% of the products, and then the team decides which ones would be best to launch. Mostly, we think about market response. And when the designs look great, we try to find a reliable source. Sometimes our suppliers send prototypes for us to evaluate, but not too often."

"So out of all the products launched, would you say you've discovered half of them? …More?"

"Truthfully, I've found probably 90% of the products launched. It's really the team that narrows the selection for launch, but other team members don't really scour the market for new products."

As they returned to the conference room, Jackson asked, "Can you describe your workday?"

As she discussed the workday, Jackson asked questions to better understand her contribution. She normally works from about 7:30AM-6:30PM. Her first hour is getting the day's schedule organized, and her last hour is completing all the administrative tasks like time sheets, emails and other correspondence. Whenever possible, she scans the social media for information that might be helpful to the business – customer observations and ratings, competitor observations etc. Fridays include weekly duties such as summarizing production, completing payroll summaries, and responding to customer correspondence. Her evenings and weekends include new product research that ranges from fashion trends to unique materials, and identifying new suppliers.

She likes to do that kind of research evenings and weekends, since it is her quiet, creative time. No hard deadlines or schedules to meet.

"Any thoughts about things that we should do differently, Natalie?"

"There are always things to do differently, but we just never seem to have the time to change."

"Can you give me a *for instance?*"

"I'm not complaining, but I've been doing the – I'll call it the production work – for 5 years. It can get to be routine, and I really enjoy the new product development … and I seem to be pretty good at it.

Also it would be great if we could take some time out of the hectic day-to-day schedule to reorganize a few things. For example, our inventory methods don't seem to be very efficient… not sure how to change it, but I'm guessing with a little thought we could cut out a lot of wasted time.

And speaking of wasted time, we have to train folks far too often. Turnover on the packaging line seems high because we only hire full-time employees. I can guess that there may be folks out there who would enjoy working a few hours a week, without a full-time commitment.

And just between us, I wish I could get some formal design training. I'd like to get out of the production ops and focus more on new products."

"Natalie, I like the ideas we've discussed. Talk to me about the design training. What are you thinking?"

"UC has a creative arts program – I think it's called DAP – would be nice to take a course there – even if it was Saturday's. I think I could improve the pace of new product introductions if I knew more about creative fashion. Now it's just trial and error."

"This has been a great discussion, Natalie. Thanks for your time." Jackson concluded that she was a dedicated, and talented employee. It would be wise to protect her from the competition.

Jackson meeting with Patricia's staff - David

Jackson asked Natalie to introduce him to David, the other Operations' Manager.

David was a thin, high energy, fast-talking and somewhat skittish individual. His deep voice was noticeable over the din of activity.

"David, great to meet you. Is this a good time to talk?"

"Yes sir. What would you like to discuss?"

"Well, I'm sure that you've heard I just want to talk about what your role is in the Company. You know, your everyday activity."

"Yes sir. Please come over to my workspace."

His worktable was unusual in the Company. There were two stacks of various colored folders on the right side of the table. His "In" and "Out" boxes were also on the right side of the table at the front, to provide easiest access for anyone dropping or retrieving messages.

The left side of his table – an area about 10 inches wide – held a small collection of multi-colored sharpies, a stapler, two pads of Post-its (a yellow and a blue), a calendar with notes at various hours of the day, and a yellow pad.

"Sir, please be seated. Would you like any refreshments? I have water and coffee."

"No thanks. I'm glad that you could fit me in your day. It seems quite busy around here."

"Yes sir. It has been busy. Shall I start?"

Jackson nodded.

"My day begins at 7:30 AM. I check my calendar for any upcoming commitments. I make sure that I've prepared for the meetings and clear up any last minute issues from the day before. I also review the production schedule for the day so that I can give the team the right production goals.

At 8:00, we have a team meeting with the production associates. It's our organizing *huddle*. We discuss hot issues – for example, any major orders that must get out that day, and any expected production problems. I also encourage the team to speak up about anything that's on their mind.

The *huddle* takes no more than 15 minutes, and then we launch production ops. Throughout the day, I circulate among the associates to make sure that they are hitting production targets. Sir, if you look over to that wall, you'll see our production performance. We assign a new scribe each day on a rotating basis to record production on the chart, and also list any problems.

My job is to keep the production on schedule. When major problems are identified, we may call another huddle. At times, I may have to do some assembly, or scout components to make sure we hit our numbers.

We seldom miss our daily numbers. The only time that happens is with a rush order."

"And how often do you get rush orders?"

"We probably average about once a week. Unexpected, but a pleasure to serve the customers."

"What are your current run rates?"

"Normal production for an 8-hour shift is about 600 shipments. On a great day when everything goes well, we can ship as many as 1,000 shipments... but that doesn't happen too often."

"So what do you think it would take to hit that 1,000 level every day?"

David's eyes rolled and then he winced. "I think a miracle. Day-in and day-out... wow, that would be a staggering increase. And let me think about that. If you're saying averaging 1,000 a day, that might mean that some days, I'll have to hit – what, maybe 1,500 a day? Guaranteed, we can't do that the way we operate today."

"So, if we want to increase our business by 50% during the next 3 years, what should we be thinking about?"

"Sir, that's a surprise question that I'm not prepared to answer."

"So without deep thinking, do we need to double the work space? Add some equipment? Change our processes? Bigger warehouse? Any initial thoughts?"

"Training... more people ... more space ... and that's if we only continue to do the same things we're doing today. If we get creative and add any new products or additional processing, we'd have to rethink everything. On the plus side, it would be great if we could grow by 50%, but I'd like to think very carefully about how to do that."

"Anything special that you'd consider?"

"It sounds crazy, but at the gym we sometimes talk about our business challenges. Lately, many of my classmates have been talking about *lean thinking*. They are very excited about it, and on the fringes, it sounds almost magical. So maybe we should explore *lean* – whatever that is."

David discussed his normal routine for the next few minutes. There weren't any major activities that hadn't been discussed before.

"David, this has been a great discussion. I especially like the way you keep a tight rein on the operation… daily monitoring with goals… work huddles…"

Jackson moved to an empty conference room to summarize his discussion. He was very pleased at David's tactical capabilities. Once an activity has been properly defined, he would definitely be able to execute. His high school education was supplemented by his military experience. Patricia may need to invest in supervisory training to get him to the next level. Overall, this was a very successful meeting.

Jackson meeting with Patricia's staff – Tom

Tom was the most reserved of all employees. While friendly, he was focused and task oriented. He would do as instructed, but he was not a creative thinker – he was a good soldier.

Tom was an operations manager who had reached his highest level of effectiveness. He assumed the Operations Manager role when the business got so large that Patricia needed another supervisory person who could do more than just assemble orders. Unfortunately, Tom was unable to perform advanced operation's manager duties.

Jackson meeting with Patricia's staff - Tonya

Tonya was a quiet 20-something who learned basic accounting skills at the local community college. Her role was straightforward – prepare the accounting records. Patricia approved every invoice, regardless of size, and she also manually signed every check and cash transfer request.

Tonya was proficient using "Quick Books" for record keeping. She performed no analysis and viewed the job as processing accounting data.

Tonya's skills were limited by her education and her desire to grow in the accounting field.

As the Company continued to expand, Tonya may constrain growth. Jackson would need to discuss Tonya's limitations with Patricia.

Jackson & Patricia: Set the Agenda

Jackson was seated at the conference table making some last minute agenda notes.

"Thanks for joining me Patricia. This shouldn't take too long – let's call it a final agenda-setting meeting. I've had the chance to meet with Natalie, Tom, David and Tonya and wanted to review where I think the 'offsite' will take us.

First, let me confirm that you've got some dedicated employees. Natalie and David have a strong interest to make this Company very successful. They were a bit surprised when I shared your financial vision of the next few years, and they were both enthusiastic and concerned."

"Concerned?"

"Maybe I should say apprehensive about the growth. They are very busy today, and they were not sure how to grow by 60% in the next few years. For sure, it's a big number, but when you break it down, I believe that it's achievable.

I have the notes from our earlier discussion – today I'd like to make a few additions."

Jackson pulled the notes from his earlier discussion with Patricia.

Organization Review
  Corporate culture
Update Job Descriptions
Compensation Review
Resource Requirements
  Web expertise
  Branding Expertise

"This was our starting point. Natalie is a very bright employee. Highly motivated, and inquisitive. I guess that's been proven through her design work.

I think she is still underutilized. To get the best results you may have to restructure her role, and dedicate her to design. While I didn't suggest that to her, we did discuss her normal routine. As you think about her day-to-day workload, have you thought more about reorganizing?"

"OK, Jackson. Sure I'd like to have Natalie spend more time on the fashion side, but I'm not sure I can afford it."

"Well, the real question is can you afford not to? And while we're on personnel, what are your thoughts about David?"

Patricia hesitated, becoming somewhat thoughtful, as if she were now reviewing David's performance.

"David is a real trooper… and I mean that literally. He is former Army supply. He does an excellent job – very organized, and works well with the team. I like his style."

"Well let me play the devil. Natalie is a creative talent, and David is a tactical talent. Once the goals have been defined, he organizes the work, assigns the employees, and gets the job done."

Patricia corrected Jackson. "Associates, Jackson… associates."

"Yes, the associates. What if you just increased his span of control? Let him manage the incoming receipts, and warehousing, and let him push some of his current responsibility down through the organization."

"And hire more people?"

"Could be. I'll break your business down into a few categories. First and most important - new products that must be launched on time. You and Natalie make that happen. Second, I'll call it the direct activity of handling the merchandise – receiving, warehousing, assembly and shipping. This is comparatively a lesser skill requirement. There will be more available personnel to do these kinds of tasks. Would you agree?"

"I'm not sure in today's world that they are more available. But I would agree that there is less training involved."

"And as a result, can we say less business risk?"

"Agreed – especially when compared to the creative side, and engaging production sources."

"And lastly there is an administrative and executive side of the business. Working with suppliers … negotiating contracts … organizing logistics … business strategy … customer relations etc."

"I understand. Three major responsibilities. OK, I'm on board."

"Now, when we think of these three primary responsibilities, how do we best staff the functions?"

"OK, Jackson. I see where you are going. I'm not sure how I can sort all that out in the next few days."

"Well, let's not. Let's talk through the challenges during the offsite."

"And let the team work through it? They… you're making me nervous again, Jackson."

"I'll facilitate the discussion, but if we get them to help us solve the resource problem, they'll have some skin in the game, and be more likely to implement the solution. Game?"

"Ok… I'm going to trust you on this, Jackson. But I'm concerned."

"Understood. If we get into areas that you are very uncomfortable with, wave me off.

Here's the way I expect the offsite to go. We'll need to get an awareness of the financial goals by sharing the broad-brush P&L with the team. Once the impact of the high growth is accepted, we'll discuss what the Company's Vision and Mission will be. We'll let the team work through that, and not just show them the one we developed a few days ago. I'll make sure that, if nothing major arises, we get to where you will be comfortable,

From there, we'll discuss the various functional areas. We both know that the team will be looking for more investment – in people and process, based on my earlier discussions with the team.

From there, we'll discuss strengths & weaknesses, competition, and then we'll wrap up. The whole offsite will take about a half-day. I don't think we'll get much input from Tom and Tonya, but we'll have them participate to reinforce your management structure.

You comfortable with that agenda?"

"As we've discussed it, yes, but will the team surprise us with any unknowns?"

"It's definitely possible, and if we're not prepared to deal with the items, we'll place the item in the Parking Lot. Ready to launch?"

Patricia nervously agreed. "Let's go. I'm excited, but apprehensive."

Three Amigos #3

Doug suggested that the group meet after the first few consulting meetings so that John and Patricia could share their learning. Tuesday night at Jeff Ruby's would be a relatively quiet place to meet. Doug reserved a table at the back of the restaurant near the windows.

Doug – dressed more formally than the others in a blue blazer and striped tie - was already seated when John and Patricia arrived.

"Welcome folks – glad that we could get together. It's been a few weeks, and I was wondering how the *strategic planning* was going." As he spoke, he smirked when he said *strategic plan*.

He continued, "Guys, since you're spending the big bucks on Jackson, I'll pick up tonight's dinner, so let's just enjoy the evening."

Teased by his sarcasm, John and Patricia's broad smile boasted of success – perhaps by capturing an expensive dinner, or maybe because they were pleased with their planning thus far.

Patricia responded first. "Doug, that's wonderful. I haven't had a Ruby steak in a few months, and my mouth's already watering. You pick the wine – red if I can influence your decision."

John chimed, "Ditto, Doug. And since you're buying make it a v-e-r-y nice red." The three had been meeting monthly for the past 2 years, and this banter was customary.

After the first 10 minutes of gossip about the Bengals and Reds, a touch of Cincinnati government, Doug mentioned strategic planning.

"So, you've been working with Jackson for a few weeks. You've spent a few thousand bucks. Any thoughts?"

Patricia responded, "Jackson is a very interesting character. For a Company my size, I was concerned that he was serious overkill. But the ground rule that he offers is, 'If you don't see value, I won't send you a bill.' That basically removed my risk.

So far, he's spent a few hours with me talking about my goals – personal and business. We developed financials that will help me reach my goals, and from there he's talked with key employees."

Doug leaned forward. "Patricia, you only have – what 15-20 employees? Whom did he talk with, since most of your folks are hourly factory workers?"

Patricia bristled. "Doug, you've got a fairly large Company, but that doesn't mean that my folks are unskilled employees. They've created some miracles during the past few years, and I'm very proud of their work ethic and performance. Back off a bit."

Somewhat startled, Doug's eyes cast downward for a moment and he apologized.

"Sorry, Patricia. So what's been accomplished during the few hours?"

"Jackson's met with the key employees, toured the operation, and talked about the future. One of the unique talents he seems to have is the ability to relate to the team. He's also explored their creative side by talking about – for example, 50% growth in the next 3 years."

Doug's eyes widened, and he stuttered, "50% growth? How could you possibly…" and his voice trailed off.

"When I think about my current product line, trade channels, logistics supply chain, new product design and a standard introduction process… well, as crazy as 50% sounds, I truly believe that it's possible. Can you imagine?"

Doug thoughtfully swirled his wine, "Discussing changes to trade channels, supply chain and new products. Sounds very risky to me."

"When he first talked about them, I was very nervous… my reaction was the same as yours. He talked me off the ledge, and step-by-step, we discussed high-level obstacles to change.

On the surface, solutions seemed possible without just plain stupid risk. But there is risk."

John was silent until now. "Did he hit you with a contingency plan discussion?"

"Yes - briefly. And even the contingency plans seemed reasonable. And this is before we have our offsite meeting."

Doug chuckled. "You're beginning to sound like corporate America with an offsite. Big bucks to get conference rooms, amenities and travel."

"Not so, Doug. He uses the term offsite to designate a time and place of unavailability to the production team. We're doing it in our conference room – Panera for the food. Out of pocket, maybe $100."

"So if he's working with your operation – what are you $7 million with 15-20 employees – maybe he's not going to do so well with your Company, John?"

The food arrived when Doug asked John that question. "Let's skip business for a few minutes and enjoy the beef."

For the next 30 minutes, they discussed family vacations, politics and sports. As the table cleared, preparing for deserts, Doug turned to John. "So if Jackson does small companies, how could he adapt to the mid-market? - A Company of your size"

"Pretty much the same way. He's talked with me to understand where I want to be in 3-4 years, and we've shaped out how it's possible?"

"So what growth do you expect?"

Self-satisfied, John leaned back in his seat, "We're targeting 50% growth as well." Leaning toward Patricia he added, "But it will take us 4 years – not three."

Doug appeared agitated. "C'mon John. Do you really believe that you can grow by 50%?" He paused briefly, "But then again, if you buy the market by ravaging your earnings, I suppose it's possible."

"You don't give me much credit, Doug. Unprofitable growth is a waste of time. I'm now earning about 10% on sales, and we're planning 10% on sales. Not only that, I'm planning to improve my ROI."

"Now that's just BS, John. Can't be done. I've been in business for nearly 28 years, and I've tried all the hocus-pocus management theories that the consultants conjure, and those are mutually exclusive goals."

"Doug, I've read the same books that you have – mainly because you've recommended them. Now I'm not going to say I have a magic bullet, but Jackson and I have talked about the business. We've discussed the market, competitors, new product development, the impact of technology, performance improvement programs for the employees, lean business – so many topics.

By looking at a high level, we've talked through sales growth, logistics and supply chain, and lean business concepts. At a high level, it seems that I have inefficient assets – inventory and receivables – ineffective new product development – and worst of all, while I've thought I take care of the employees, I haven't managed them as a prized investment.

It's not that I've been negligent, I just haven't been as progressive as I should have been."

Doug was now becoming defensive. "So you're going to launch into the program of the month?"

"No, not the program of the month, but a strategically planned upgrade to my entire business process. There are things that I can do immediately in new product development, manufacturing ops, and finance that don't cost a nickel, but will improve the value of my Company."

Feeling cornered, Doug summarized, "Well, it sounds like you folks have sipped the Kool-Aid. I'm sticking with my strategic planning process and will let you folks drive on. Hey, this has gotten far too serious. Let's have a single malt and wrap up."

Small talk completed the evening. Doug parked with the valet – John and Patricia walked to the parking garage.

"So Patricia, what do you think?"

"If you mean about Doug's commitment to continue without a detailed strategic plan, I think it's a mistake – but he's entitled to his opinion. Personally, the more I think about Jackson's questions and approach, the more convinced I am that we should proceed. You?"

"I'm at a different stage of growth, and I'm 100% convinced it's the right thing to do. And it's not just the questions he asks, but the topical areas that he covers. I think about running the business, and he thinks about thin slices of the business… how to improve the new product development cycle time… our sourcing channels… sales channels. I'm aware of all these items, but he's been asking the tough questions about today and the future. Yes, I'm all in on the process, and we'll see where it will lead. In general, I'm learning about how to think strategically."

"I'm glad you feel that way, John. I'm a little out of my depth, and hearing your commitment makes me even more determined. Be talking with you."

Offsite With John

While many offsite meetings for larger companies are held in a resort setting, John decided that the country club was a good choice – no travel expense and still close to the business in case of emergency. The club boardroom had a large whiteboard and several flip charts.

An array of pastries, hot coffee and water, and a bin filled with a selection of juices and spring water awaited their arrival.

The team's scattered arrival – generally 10-15 minutes ahead of the start – was consistent with the theme of 'on time means 15 minutes early'. Dressed business casual, they spoke in quiet tones with an occasional nervous laugh, not knowing for sure what to expect from this meeting.

Jackson was at the head of the conference table, closest to the white board. He greeted each executive personally – smiling and hoping to allay the tension.

At 8:00AM, John started the meeting with a warm greeting. "Folks, today we're launching a new phase in our business. While historically we've talked about the future, and general strategies to improve the business, today we're going to take the first step at a more formal strategic planning session. You've all had the chance to speak with Jackson. Your candor was critical for him to understand our business.

Jackson and I have talked about the future and my personal and business goals. My objective – simply stated – is to make this a more valuable business while adding career value for each of you. We've had those discussions before, and today, we'll define the actions necessary to reach those goals.

Jackson has developed some financials – don't be alarmed when you see them. He and I have discussed the concepts, and they seem to be within our grasp. Today, with your insight, we'll better understand what is possible and not just the boss's dream. Please, continue to be candid with your discussion. There are no right or wrong answers. And now, Jackson, it's your show."

Jackson displayed the first slide with the agenda.

Meeting Agenda

1.0	Introduction	John	8:00-8:15
2.0	Financial goals	Jackson	8:15-8:45
3.0	Functional Discussions		
3.1	Sales	Jason B	8:45-9:15
3.2	International	Vito A	9:15-9:45
3.3	Marketing	Janice V	9:45-10:15
3.5	BREAK		10:15-10:30
3.6	R&D	Reg T	10:30-11:00
3.7	Manufacturing	Bill K	11:00-11:30
3.8	Logistics	Andy	11:30-12:00
3.9	Finance	Mitch D	12:00-12:30
	LUNCH		12:30-1:00
3.10	HR	Bev D	1:00-1:30
4.0	Competitor Discussion	Jackson	1:00-2:15
5.0	Strengths & Weaknesses	Jackson	2:15-3:15
	BREAK		3:15-3:30
6.0	Summary of Meeting	Jackson	3:30-4:30

"During the past few days, we've all had a chance to discuss how we would develop the plan. The process is straightforward. I've prepared a draft financial statement as a straw man. It's not correct… not accurate, but just a quick and dirty summary of where we think we can be in a few years.

When you see the numbers, don't be shocked, because we're going to be thinking differently, starting today. Something that I say that always alarms the owners: WE HAVE UNLIMITED RESOURCES… DON'T BE AFRAID TO SPEND JOHN'S MONEY."

John smiled and clutched his chest as if he were having a heart attack.

Jackson continued, "I say that for one simple reason. You folks are all conscientious. For years, you've stayed within spending constraints as dictated by the budget. As we launch this strategic plan process, if you continue to think with those constraints, we'll miss opportunities. Historically if you had a breakthrough idea, and then thought about the Company, you might say, 'John would never purchase that new machine… or John would never add another salesman…etc.'

If we think like that, let's not do a strategy, and just prepare an excel spreadsheet using the same paradigm as always."

At this point, Jackson made eye contact with each participant. "So let's get creative, and rather than have a rallying cry of 'let's be average,' let's say 'Let's be great?"

Jackson always used that phrase at every kick-off meeting to break the barrier of complacency.

"So let's take a look at a strategic P&L. First let's look at sales."

Strategic Sales Plan

	2017	2018	2019	2020	2021	2022
New Products			1.0	3.0	7.1	13.3
Share growth			1.0	2.0	4.0	6.0
Market Growth			0.9	0.9	0.9	0.9
Baseline	27.8	30.0	30.0	30.0	30.0	30.0

As the slide flashed across the screen, eyes opened wide.

Mitch, the CFO, was first to speak. "So we're going to increase by 60% if we do a great job today?"

"Worried?"

"Not worried since we're only scratching numbers. But that's a helluva jump."

Reg observed, "Excuse me, but that shows $13 million of new products. That's a bit concerning, since we've never added more than a million in any single year."

"Excellent observation, Reg. Has John ever given you an unlimited budget before? Spend whatever it takes? Let me show you the next slide."

Reg squirmed in his seat.

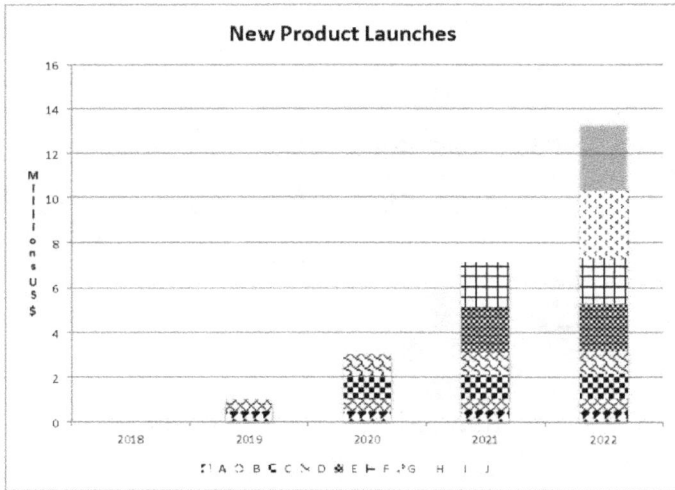

New Product Launches

Jackson continued. "You folks are the experts, but when we look at the potential new products forecast – most of the new products are at $1 million or less in the launch year. Sounds familiar, Reg?"

Without responding, Reg nodded.

"And we really don't start getting the big additions until 2021…3 years from now. Now let's step back for a moment. No spending constraints… so you've got the engineers and assets you need for development. Perhaps we have some development agreements with UC… perhaps we outsource some of the development. And maybe – just maybe – we purchase a new product or license a product. Are you still worried, Reg?"

"I suppose when you open the spending gates – I guess it's up to our prioritization and execution. But we talked about our capability to execute to a schedule. We haven't done so in the past."

"With resource constraints, Reg. And perhaps a development process that isn't the smoothest… maybe with some distractions…"

Bill rapped his knuckles on the table. "Yes, we have distractions. Get rid of those and NPD might go more smoothly."

Jackson quickly responded. "Exactly, Bill. So now we're saying that we have unlimited money, and as far as distractions are concerned, isn't that under our control?"

"Under our control as long as customers don't need their product on time…" Bill mused.

"I like the engagement. Bill, Reg, it almost sounds like you're in the game. Just to confirm, we're going to assemble a plan that I believe can be 100% implemented, with the right discipline. That's why we're together here today. YOU FOLKS are in charge. You are the disciplinarians.

Now let's look at the full P&L."

The next slide displayed profitability that, once again, seemed unattainable.

000's US $	2017		2018		2019	2020	2021
	Amt	%	Amt	%	Amt	Amt	Amt
Sales:							
Metal Fab	11,750.0	42.3%	11,550.0	38.6%	13,500.0	16,000.0	20,800.0
Casting	8,055.0	29.0%	8,350.0	27.9%	9,000.0	10,500.0	12,000.0
Resale	4,555.0	16.4%	3,500.0	11.7%	4,500.0	5,500.0	6,000.0
International	2,955.0	10.6%	5,915.0	19.7%	6,800.0	8,100.0	9,720.0
Other	455.0	1.6%	635.0	2.1%	1,000.0	1,200.0	1,500.0
Total	27,770.0	100.0%	29,950.0	100.0%	34,800.0	41,300.0	50,020.0
Gross Margin							
Metal Fab	4,700.0	40.0%	5,197.5	45.0%	6,075.0	7,520.0	9,776.0
Casting	3,222.0	40.0%	3,340.0	40.0%	3,600.0	4,725.0	5,400.0
Resale	1,138.8	25.0%	875.0	25.0%	1,125.0	1,430.0	1,560.0
International	1,625.3	55.0%	3,549.0	60.0%	4,080.0	4,860.0	5,832.0
Other	113.8	25.0%	127.0	20.0%	200.0	300.0	375.0
Total	10,799.8	38.9%	13,088.5	43.7%	15,080.0	18,835.0	22,943.0
SG&A							
Selling	3,332.4	12.0%	4,492.5	15.0%	5,046.0	5,782.0	6,502.6
Marketing	1,666.2	6.0%	1,797.0	6.0%	2,088.0	2,478.0	2,751.1
R&D	1,388.5	5.0%	1,497.5	5.0%	1,983.6	3,304.0	5,002.0
Financa	694.3	2.5%	748.8	2.5%	835.2	991.2	1,300.5
IT	555.4	2.0%	599.0	2.0%	696.0	826.0	900.4
Legal	555.4	2.0%	599.0	2.0%	600.0	600.0	600.0
HR	416.6	1.5%	449.3	1.5%	522.0	619.5	750.3
Other	-	0.0%	-	0.0%			
Total	8,608.7	31.0%	10,183.0	34.0%	11,770.8	14,600.7	17,806.9
PBT	2,191.05	7.9%	2,905.50	9.7%	3,309.20	4,234.30	5,136.12
					9.5%	10.3%	10.3%
Employees							
Operations	55		48		58	59	66
Sales/Mkting	18		20		22	25	26
Admin	6		7		7	8	8
Total	79		75		87	92	100
Sales/Emp	350		400		400	450	500

Mitch tapped his pen on the table. "Excuse me, Jackson, but those earning numbers look a bit aggressive. Is that after we spend all of John's money to get the sales?"

"Excellent question, Mitch. A few highlights for you to think about.

First of all, think about those new products that Reg and Bill will develop and successfully launch. Do innovative new products have average or above average margins?"

"If we do our job right, better than average margins."

"So, a profit lift compared to average. And let's talk about operating leverage. Right now, if I increased sales by 20%, would you need to add 20% to the fixed assets? Add 20% to the HR, Finance, QA departments?"

"Probably not... but the profits still look steep."

"I understand your concern, Mitch. Humor me – think about these values with an open mind, and let's drive through the agenda. When we're done, if we – that's the entire team – does not believe that the numbers can be delivered, we'll change them. Agreed?"

John leaned forward. "You better believe that I'll change the numbers. Jackson, I'm trusting you to keep us under control."

Vision/Mission

Jackson continued. "So now you've seen what the future can be. Let's think about the business, and not even consider the numbers.

Who are we?"

Jackson gazed around the room and repeated the question. "So who are we?"

Reg responded, "What are you looking for, Jackson?"

"What defines us as a company? Are we a non-profit organization?"

John raised his hand and cleared his throat. "We better not be," and the team laughed. "But I will say we have a core idea that it's ok to have happy employees, satisfied customers, and we can make money."

"So we're a profit oriented organization, that produces *stuff*. Anything in particular?"

Bill offered, "Metal fabricated and precision cast components."

Keeping a quick pace, Jackson said, "Ah yes, based on our manufacturing capabilities. So we'll do precision cast parts for ..." leaving the sentence unfinished.

"Precision requirements... aircraft, automotive, medical devices," Jason offered.

"OK. Commodity products? Or are we top of the heap?"

Janice leaned forward, "I think we target the premium segment..."

Jackson continued the brainstorming session challenging each comment by the team. While there was no apparent direction in his challenges, the team seemed to guide him to the mission statement that he scratched on the whiteboard.

MISSION STATEMENT

Profit oriented
Metal fabrication
cast parts   precision
commodity
complex   → highly
engineered
premium market
high quality   employee
development

midwest values ethical
US based
Global ————→ M&A?
progressive
willing to invest

JV
distributor
licensing
Acquire??

exotic mat'l?

treat employees,
suppliers &
customers with respect

Jackson summarized, "OK. I'll put together a more formal mission statement, but it seems that:

John Davidson Co. is a highly ethical, industrial products Company that develops, manufactures and distributes complex, highly engineered and premium value, metal fabricated parts and castings serving the global markets. The Company will treat employees, suppliers and customers with respect. Our business will grow organically, and through acquisition, licensing, and joint ventures.

This, of course, isn't final, but it helps us frame our strategy to accomplish our mission. The idea of a mission statement is guidance for the organization. The mission can change, but if we've done our job right, it shouldn't change frequently unless something monumental occurs.

So the mission describes what we believe we can do, but it also gives us boundaries for what we can't do. For example, if we had a great opportunity to invest in a chemical processing plant, which would not be within our mission, so we wouldn't do it. However, if we discovered a great opportunity to JV with a company that developed a processing technique for an exotic metal, that would initially be within our mission statement. Any questions, knowing that this isn't final?"

Bill's question was straightforward. "So if I had an opportunity to pick up a contract for, let's say, a simple stamping that just about anyone can do... low margins, but great overhead absorption, we wouldn't do it, although my total profits would increase?"

"Now I'll give you a waffling answer. There may be circumstances where we would venture outside the mission statement, but it would be an exception. In your example, if we had an unusual amount of excess capacity, and the operation was simple turnkey without a lot of engineering support, we might just accept the order if we were financially stressed. But generally, we wouldn't dilute our focus from the main mission. It's really a judgment call. But remember, the mission is a guide, not an inflexible rule."

"Ok, I understand when you say guideline. Circumstances may push us outside the lines."

"For sure, and John's the guy that makes those ultimate decisions."

"So, for now, let's discuss the functional areas. Our objective in this segment is to get a better understanding about how the functions work. It will help each of us understand the complexity of the operation, and also help us coordinate the activities among the functions so that the best Company decisions are made.

Let me illustrate. Mitch may believe that a new data system is critical – sorry to pick on you Mitch. The system would cost in round numbers - $1 million. Bill has a proposal for a $1 million multi-axis mill that will allow the Company to enter a new segment of precision metal fabricated products. In the example, the Company only has $1 million of available capital. What should we do?"

Jackson looked at each individual and continued. "If the accounting system is ready to crash – say we will no longer be able to bill customers – we'll probably invest in the data system, and Bill may have to outsource to a high-tech vendor. Agreed?"

Jackson awaited a response and then offered. "There's usually more than one answer to a business problem, but when we all know the circumstances, it's much easier to make a proper decision.

OK, now that we have some life in this party, let's move on to the individual functions. We do this because every day, each of us work diligently in our function and may not appreciate the other functions as thoroughly as we should. This gives each of us the opportunity to strut our stuff.

Of course, I've worked with each of you so that we stay on track... so let's roll."

Bill, talk to us about the manufacturing area."

VP Manufacturing discussion

"Thanks, Jackson." Scanning the executives around the table, he launched a slide. "Jackson and I spent a few hours together during the past week. It was disconcerting ... uncomfortable." With those words, he looked directly at Jackson, a small nod, and he continued.

"While he never said we weren't functioning at 100%, his questions pushed me to read a few books, and think differently about our business. Between "World Class Manufacturing," Henry Ford's book "Today and Tomorrow" and "All I Need to Know about Manufacturing I learned in Joe's Garage," I decided it was time to think differently. Check out this first slide." With that, he moved through the progressive slide.

TODAY'S THINKING

$$A = PY + i$$

$$A_{verage} = P_{rior}Y_{ear} + i_{nflation}$$

TOMORROW'S THINKING

$$A = (PY + i) + (C+E) - (W+LO)$$

$$A_{verage} = (P_{rior}\ Y_{ear} + i_{nflation}) + (C_{reativity} + E_{xcellence})$$
$$- (W_{aste} + L_{ost}\ O_{pportunity})$$

"So what does this really mean? Folks, historically we've run the business as 'x%' over the prior year, and we were happy. It really got to me when Jackson asked, 'So your message when leading the manufacturing group is 'Let's Be Average!' bothered me.

I've never considered ourselves average, but when I thought about the manufacturing operations, I really couldn't be comfortable to say that we were anything other than average.

After I read the books, I decided that we – and I – needed to change. That's when I developed the equations. Sure, it's a bit schmaltzy, but I kind of liked the idea of an equation – especially since it focuses on specific actions.

Let's think about average performance. If we in the manufacturing operations perform our day-to-day work excellently – is that a word – or operationally perfect, that's not average… and it's under our control. If we become extremely creative, well, that's not average – and it's under our control.

And waste and lost opportunity – they speak for themselves.

So I looked at some of the manufacturing metrics, and I want to change some things. While I'm not exactly sure how to do some of these things, I know that they can be done. And given the unlimited pile of money that John will dedicate to the effort, let me share my thoughts."

John squirmed in his seat a bit, but smiled and cheered Bill onward. "Spend some bucks, Bill. I'm with you on this, so let's roll."

Bill's next few slides focused on several manufacturing metrics from the past two years. As he reviewed the information, he related the data to his initial equations.

(000's $)	Current Year	YTD Prior Year	2016
		Cost (Income)	
Manufacturing Var:			
Labor Usage Var	97,789.0	65,776.0	60,155.0
Labot Rate Var	14,367.0	10,366.0	12,657.0
Material Usage Var	45,565.0	22,454.0	5,677.0
Purchase Price Var	(57,866.0)	(89,255.0)	(66,757.0)
Rework	122,587.0	72,655.0	66,998.0
Other Variances	119,345.0	35,878.0	38,767.0
	341,787.0	**117,874.0**	**117,497.0**
Scrap	**190,556.0**	**89,176.0**	**77,989.0**
Var + Scrap % of Sales	1.0%	0.6%	0.6%
Budge/Actt Sales (Mil $	36.3	27.8	26.9
Curr YTD Sales	26.0		
% Act Sales	2.0%		

"While I haven't done extensive analysis, I want to share some information with you. The details of the manufacturing variances are included in the total cost of sales. Historically we haven't published the details of the variances. We've never thought it worthwhile to bury you with the manufacturing details. Now, when you're looking at the summary, remember that variances are the difference of what things actually cost by unit, compared to budgeted standard costs. When we look at this summary, a *positive* number is unfavorable. It's an unplanned cost. It's a bad thing.

Thus far in the current year, we've spent about $400,000 more than we expected to produce the product. That is the summary of all the variances except purchase price variance. And favorable Purchase Price Variance, or

PPV offset these excess operational costs. PPV is the difference between the raw material costs budgeted and that actually incurred. Said another way, historically we've conservatively budgeted material costs – that is we've overestimated the costs in the budget – since we know that unplanned bad things happen.

If we were operationally excellent, conceivably that could give us another $400,000 of earnings.

Then I skip down to the scrap line, with scrap of $190,000. Historically, we've been at .6% of sales, and that is the industry average. Yes, you heard me right – AVERAGE – which historically meant that we were OK. Now, when I look at the number – Jackson actually spotted this – the scrap has been measured as a percent of budgeted sales, not actual sales. So, while we thought that we were ok, our ratios are actually worse than average.

Again, let's think about this differently. If the scrap were saleable, does this represent potential sales of about $300,000, and additional gross profit of about $100,000, given our historical averages?

When I look at our pretax earnings, the operational excellence of just those items could increase our profits by nearly 15%."

At this point, Mitch was feverishly jotting notes, as he leaned into the discussion. "Bill, this is great insight. I'm not sure that you can capture all that opportunity, but I really like how you're thinking about the operations."

Bill continued. "And so far we haven't even touched the creativity part of the business. As I've thought about our new product introductions – well, once again, we haven't been the most effective. I'd like to work more closely with Reg to figure out how we can improve our new product launches. And when the engineers aren't working on new products I'd like to focus on manufacturing improvements.

I've heard that in the automotive industry, cost improvements should *at least* offset inflation each year. In our case, that would mean a cost reduction of 3% a year. We've never done that. I think strategically I'd like to plan that we could offset inflation with process improvement.

And when I think about all of our processes, I'll guess that we aren't the most efficient in some areas. For example, in the stamping area, we don't have the most modern equipment."

Bill paused briefly to allow the team to absorb the discussion. Bill then turned to John.

"John, I've held off capital spending requests for the past few years just to preserve cash flow. As part of my strategic planning, I'd like to review the fixed assets in manufacturing operations, and do some make versus buy analysis. The older equipment often isn't world class, and some of our vendors – those that have the modern equipment – may be able to give us a better cost than production in-house."

John interrupted. "Bill, that might bump into my goal of no layoffs. If we outsource some of the work, what impact will that have on the workforce?"

"I share your concern, John. A couple of things. First, we now spend about $400,000 in overtime costs. Eliminating overtime is not a layoff. As part of any analysis, I'm going to take the approach of, 'What is the best economic decision?' We may find that obsolete equipment is costing us quality – think of the scrap, rework, and overtime – and excessive overtime to meet schedules. And maybe lost sales.

I'll work with Mitch and his analysts to get a sharp pencil on the task, and we'll do the math and, working with you, figure out the best way to proceed. I don't want to hide behind our principle of no layoffs without understanding the financial impact. And it may turn out that the labor impact may be offset by reduced overtime – and that cost is at time-and-a-half."

"I surrender, Bill. Let's get the financial information, and then we'll have the data to make a decision. I've got to tell you, I'm blown away at how rethinking beyond averages opens so many opportunities. Amazing."

"One last thing, John. I've been walking the plant floor with the new equation in mind, and the reference point of the books I've read. Our inventory turns average 2 – 2.5 a year – within the industry averages. Well, the equation suggests that there is waste and opportunity in the inventory. When I look at our inventory investment, I think that we are a long way from *Just-In-Time* – JIT - inventory. We're more like *Just-In-Case* - J-I-C. If we could just get a half-turn more through the process, that would add about a million dollars to cash flow."

As the team looked on, they busily took notes. John jotted a few notes and said, "Bill, I hope that you shared your equations with the others. I'm somewhat speechless when I think about how I've tethered us to average, rather than push us to excel. That's on me... and thankfully, you've accepted the strategic concept and run with it."

Bill continued, "Now to do all these things, I'll need some investment. I've read the books, and can see the opportunities, but I haven't executed in any of these areas. I could tell you that this may take a few million dollars to implement, and that might be the right number overall, but instead, I'd like to ask for this to be self-funding on a project-by-project basis.

I've put together some time-lines and investment requirements for the items that I've discussed. I've also identified deliverables so that I'm accountable. These are best guess, since this is new turf for me, but I want to get started.

And typically, I'd be talking about headcount, but since I don't have a clear understanding about the impact, I'm going to leave the headcount as is for now, with the understanding that things could change.

So for a quick summary of what I envision during the next three years, let's review my objectives:

Description	2019				2020	2021	Cost (000's)	Purpose
	Q1	Q2	Q3	Q4				
Engage Lean-Business consultant							100	Annual coaching cost to improve operations.
High-low Manufacturing standards review (top 50% of production)								Operational excellence
Review & change Purchase Price methodology								Operational excellence
Root cause scrap analysis								Waste & lost opportunity
Engineering focus-cost reduction								Operational excellence
Production assessment: make vs. buy (high-low processing areas)								Operational excellence; waste; lost opportunity
NPD process assessment								Creativity
Inventory & logistics review								Operational excellence; lost opportunity

I've categorized the tasks into the actionable elements of the equation – Excellence, Creativity, Waste and Lost Opportunity. These will be our marching orders rather than just manage the manufacturing operations.

Note that deliverables pretty much stop in 2020, because I don't know what I don't know. In fact, even these deliverables may vary when we get some outside support. But rather than just say we're going to get better, I wanted to put some accountability in the plan.

And John, it isn't critical that I get the outside consultant in house ASAP. I think that in every case we can make progress, but with a pro in the mix, I think that progress will be quicker, and the consultant will more than pay for themself.

And that's manufacturing operations. Questions?"

Reg immediately slowly applauded – clapping sounds piercing the air every second or two. "Bill, for an old guy you have flipped this place upside down. I really like the way you've changed priority from managing the business to specific actions that will help us be a better Company. Bravo."

Mitch chimed in, "Sounds to me like you just added some action items to my strategic planning. I've struggled with how to make the finance more essential, and closing the books faster just doesn't seem to have an impact. But the kinds of analysis that you're looking for... well, it seems that finance has become more of an essential part of the executive team. More work for sure, but I think I like the approach."

Jackson stood – broad smile of congratulations – and said, "Bill, you've done some great work. You've read the books and drunk the Kool-Aid. Well done.

And now, let's move to Jason for the sales operations. Jason – it's your show.

"Bill, first – WOW. You're a tough act to follow, but I'll give it my best. I really like the equation that you developed. By breaking down the management responsibility into actionable tasks, you can easily develop improvement goals.

After talking with Jackson about resources, and how we sell, I've done a similar analysis.

Historically we've focused on selling to the market. We've had informal input about the competition… we've had some input into the new product development… we've worked a bit with Janice in Marketing. Launch a new product… maybe have a goal of getting new customers. And it's worked out reasonably well. Sales goals – you know the +3% a year – well, we've met them.

During the past week, we've done some analysis – quantifying things like we've never done before.

We've looked at our current base of actual customers and potential customers… we've done some ranking." Looking directly at Jackson, "Thank you Jackson…excellent insight into resource allocation… and we've built a matrix of our sales operations.

Jackson, you'll be familiar with this. And Mitch, we couldn't have done the background analysis without your help and your analysts.

My gosh, I'm amazed at the information available in the data system. While it might be difficult to get to, it's a wealth of information.

Customers								
	A		B		C		Total	
Territory	$	#	$	#	$	#	$	#
East								
ACTUAL-2018	8,966	36	1,755	155	1,554	344	12,275	535
Target 2019	9,800	40	2,000	170	1,700	350	13,500	560
potential - new customers	2,500	12	6,000	50				
South								
ACTUAL-2018	10,144	47	1,988	245	1,386	299	13,518	591
Target 2019	11,000	50	2,400	250	1,600	300	15,000	600
potential - new customers	2,500	12	4,000	30				
West								
ACTUAL-2018	6,998	32	2,655	324	1,063	410	10,716	766
Target 2019	8,000	35	2,900	330	1,100	400	12,000	765
potential - new customers	2,500	10	6,500	50				
Total								
ACTUAL-2018	26,108	115	6,398	724	4,002	1,053	36,508	1,892
Target 2019	28,800	125	7,300	750	4,400	1,050	40,500	1,925
potential - new customers	7,500	34	16,500	130	-	-	24,000	164

So in our plan, we're looking at our sales opportunities in a much more strategic way. After Jackson's guidance, we sorted the current customers into three buckets – A-B-C.

"A's" are accounts with more than $500,000 annual sales, "B's" have between $50k and $250k, and "C's" have annual sales of less than $50k. We identified these strata by looking at existing customers … there is a natural break at each of those levels.

This helps us to invest our sales and marketing resources wisely. So for example, we want to invest more in those accounts with the greatest potential.

This is the first time we've done this kind of analysis, so components may change as we proceed, but the concept is to understand the actual sales, identify potential customers and develop a sales plan that addresses the opportunity. We have several layers below this summary - customer by customer etc.

When we analyzed our sales goals of – for example 3% growth rate – it just didn't seem to be enough growth, given the *potential* "A and B" customers, existing customer growth and new product introductions.

Jason paused – looked at Reg and nodded. "Right Reg?"

"You betcha! They'll be on time this year."

"While I haven't buried you with all the details behind our assessment, it seems that we have tremendous opportunity in "A" accounts in the East and West. And different reasons for each.

In the East, there have been numerous acquisitions by European companies. That opens up completely new opportunities to reallocate my resources.

In the West – well, that is just too much geography to cover with the existing reps.

We also analyzed our selling process, trying to get a handle on the sales cycle time. As you might expect, "A" potential accounts take quite a while to close. Our best guess at this time is anywhere from 9-15 months from initial contact.

"B" potentials close in about 9 months.

We've also analyzed our closing ratios. To be honest, we haven't tracked close rates in the past, but we've guessed that we have a 30% close rate. We'll start tracking these stats in the future.

In addition to new customers, we need to keep existing customers happy.

I'm sharing all this with you because it's an entirely new process - in addition to our basic selling.

When you look at the numbers, you'll see a great opportunity in the Western Region. We hope to complete an analysis of the best selling approach in the region. We're now thinking of breaking the West into two territories, complete with additional sales reps and a regional manager. An alternative that we're considering is manufacturer's reps – little to no fixed cost, and it might get us in the remote markets more quickly and efficiently."

Jason looked at John to see his reaction to the proposed additional spending. John nodded. "Please continue. I like the analytical thinking, Jason."

"We'll have the analysis completed in Q1 next year, just to warn you. And Mitch, depending on the outcome of the analysis, we might have some pretty large expenses during Q2-4."

"Got it."

"So we've discussed the sales force, and potential new customers… call cycles, and closing rates. Do you remember that I mentioned that we don't have any easy way to monitor these factors?

Well, that leads to the next investment. We need a CRM system to manage this resource. There are some rudimentary standalone systems, and then there are the full-blown Salesforce.com applications. We don't have any recommendation yet, but we also expect to complete the analysis in Q2… hopefully you can help us with the financial analysis, Mitch."

Mitch agreed.

"And then we want to look at the allocation of all our resources by customer classification.

Historically we've been fortunate to have a great sales force, which has great relationships with the customers. Let me say, the "A" customers. We've tried to understand why our customers stay with us, and also how we manage our sales resources.

When you look at the projected 2019 sales, you'll see an overall 10% increase. Anybody nervous about that."

John leaned forward, elbows resting on the conference table. "…Two emotions … nervous and excited. I'm anxious to hear how you'll grow at more than double the market rate."

"There are four main components to that growth:
- New customers, with a planned close rate... closer management of the sales force.
- Keeping existing customers... making them extremely happy with our service and products. For that we need the entire team to hit on all cylinders.
- Timely new product introductions.
- A small price increase – average of 2% - based on competitive analysis. And yes, we need your help with that Janice.

When we focus on each of those components, and think about our marketing mix, we want to target each element of spending to achieve those overall goals. We won't just have a rep do all the selling. We'll have other touch points with our customers, so let's look at the mix."

Mitch was making notes as Jason discussed each element of the proposed spending.

Jason continued. "We've identified about 160 "A" and "B" accounts with a potential of nearly $25 million of sales. We're going to allocate about one-third of our sales resource to those potential accounts. I know it sounds like a lot, but this is an investment in our future.

Description	A		B		C		Total Spend		
	Act	Pot	Act	Pot	Act	Pot	Total	Act	Pot
Reps									
Base	500	300	200	150	25	25	1,200	725	475
SPIFS	50	100		50			200	50	150
Inside Sales	50	25	100		75		250	225	25
Travel	50	50	75	25			200	125	75
Advertising	350		100		50		500	500	-
Collateral Mat'l	100	100	50	100	50		400	200	200
Trade Shows	75	25	50	50			200	125	75
Website		25	25	25	25		100	50	50
Promotions	150		100		50		300	300	-
Other	50		50		50		150	150	-
Total	1,375	625	750	400	325	25	3,500	2,450	1,050

Think about lifetime customer value. If we can secure a new "A" account, that's at least $500k of annual sales… about $150k of gross margin from an account that should last indefinitely if we do our jobs right. Every 10 years, that's $1.5 million of gross margin per new account.

Comments about dedicating one-third of the resource to potentials?"

John raised his hand, "And are you comfortable that two-thirds of the resources dedicated to holding $14 million of margin annually is the right mix? I'd hate to lose customers…"

"That's why we're reviewing the concepts today, John. I need everyone to work with me – I need your insight - because we are talking about some significant changes in how we run the business.

So let's continue. We lean heavily on the personal approach to the "A" and "B" actual and potential customers that account for about 75% of our sales. You'll see reps with a heavy concentration on those larger accounts. We're shifting salesmen from calling on "C" to "B" accounts, and some "B" accounts to potential "A". We're going to manage the "C" accounts with an inside sales function. And yes, that may mean some additional spending – guessing an incremental $50k/year. We'll also manage the "C" accounts with improvements to the website – yes, it's an additional cost.

If you step back, we're taking a sales person that costs $150k a year from "C" accounts to selling to "A" and "B" actual and potential.

We'll need to evaluate our sales force, because it requires a different kind of rep for prospecting versus what I'll call account management. We've scheduled that sales force evaluation for the 2nd quarter.

Did you notice the line *Website*? I've gotten together with the sales team, and we're not comfortable that the site gives us what we need. As we shift resources among the 6 classes of customers, we need the website to help us manage the "C" relationships, and also entice the potential A's and B's. We think that we need to redesign the website… and that will cost money and time. An updated website is scheduled for 3rd quarter launch."

Mitch winced. "So in the ideal world, you want a new CRM system AND you want an updated Website?"

"I'm following John's ground rules of *'Let's spend some money.'* I know that will strain the organization, but I'm thinking that I'll ask for what I need, but understand that spending is based on what's best for the corporation. I'm guessing that we all have a wish-list, and some things will be reprioritized."

Jackson responded. "That would be a correct assumption. We're dealing with somewhat of a simultaneous equation that we all need to solve. OK, Jason. This is a very analytical approach to the sales resource, and I think this is great stuff. You've done your job thinking outside the box."

Smiling broadly, he said, "And I'm not done yet. This last part is more of a theoretical discussion, but our sales team visits with customers every day. We hear what's happening with our competitors – personnel, new product development etc. We'd like to somehow get involved with the new product development process so that we can share our observations. Is that possible?"

Reg sat up in his chair and said, "You just did! Have you been looking at my presentation?" Jason scoffed.

Reg responded, "No, really. I've got that as one of my objectives. We want to hear what's going on in the market."

And Janice added, "And I have you on the hook in my presentation. We want to hear what's happening in the market. You folks are on the front line and a key to competitive information."

"So there you have it. Let me put the quick summary of my line items.

Description	2019				2020	2021	Cost (000's)	Purpose
	Q1	Q2	Q3	Q4				
Implement new sales call and management plan	→							Efficiency
New Product Introduction		→	→					Creativity
Western Territory Analysis	→							Opportunity
Sales Force Evaluation		→						Effectiveness
CRM Selection & Installation			→		→		50	Effectiveness
Website upgrade					→		100	Opportunity
New Product Committee					→			Opportunity
Marketing Intelligence Committee					→			Opportunity

Any questions?"

This time John led the applause with a rhythmic slap about every second.

"Ok folks. This approach is so scary good, I'm speechless. I remember last year's *budget* discussion. Wasn't it something like, 'I'd like to increase sales and earnings by about 3%. Can we discuss?'

And from there we explained how it would be nearly impossible to get that kind of growth. This year we focused on the actions that will help us run the business better. Things that will change the course of our business. Well, for sure you've identified things that will cost me, but I think that the concepts are well thought out, and it's merely a case of available resources.

Guys, you've set a high bar for the rest of the team, but I'm guessing that they won't disappoint. Well done, and let's keep this going."

VP International discussion

Jackson stood and motioned everyone to stand and stretch. "Everyone, let's just take two minutes to stand and stretch – reach for the stars…just like we're doing in the discussions.

After a brief pause, Jackson continued. "Vito, we need a bit of International flair. You're up. Drive on."

"Buenos Dias…Guten Tag … Buona sera.

I'm going to have some fun with my discussion. I guess that we all know that there are about 320 million people in the US, and the rest of the world has about *6 Billion* people. Well, that's my market."

Jason quickly interjected, "So that means your sales will be about 20 times that of the US?"

The team enjoyed the jibing, and Vito continued.

"Thanks for hitting that softball pitch, Jason. In fact, there is a tremendous opportunity in the international segment. Especially when we focus on the industrialized nations that are key producers in our market segment.

My analysis is a bit different than the others. I focus not on countries with large populations, but rather on major companies that can use our expertise. We have barriers as a US company, but we have some unique advantages as well.

There are about 40 major companies that use our products or our competitors'. That is my target. But I don't think of just those companies, I think of the locations that use our products, so rather than just 40 potential companies, I have nearly 500 separate locations that we could sell to.

Historically, I've worked through distributors that sell products to my target customers in some countries. Distributors cover about 4 countries in Europe, 4 in Latin America, and 3 in Asia. After speaking with Jackson, and thinking about the kind of sale's efforts that we need, I'd like to add an employee – I'll call the person a business development person.

Their role is not just selling to target customers, but rather expand a business relationship with existing customers and build relationships with new customers. I'd like to get deeper penetration to large multi-national companies.

I've recently met with a US Commercial Services Department executive, and we will be using several of their resources to expand and build the international business.

Specifically, I'll be using them for market research, personal introductions to key potential customers, and when there seems to be a prime market with numerous potential customers, we may even have a mini-trade show. That is where the new individual will be instrumental.

The Commerce Department research costs are minimal – perhaps less than $50/hour – their local contacts are superb, and their purpose is to help US companies expand export sales. Given their contacts, I expect to provide developmental seminars with local governments and organizations to expand our brand awareness. We have an exceptional brand that is virtually unknown in several fast growing Eastern European countries that are rapidly expanding their production and sales capabilities.

Specifically, I'll be adding *countries* to our customer list using more distributors, and the business development person.

I'll also need some language flexibility on our website so that these new customers can access our resources. While on-line ordering may be difficult due to the language requirements, we may want *local* language for some of the greatest potential sales countries.

And of course our most important technical and sales material should be translated to the local language. While I expect the leaders in the target customers will speak and read English, it's the engineers and the product designers that will ultimately make the recommendation, and I can't rely on them to have bi-lingual capabilities. I'm expecting language translation eventually to include Spanish, French, Italian, Portuguese, Russian and Japanese. There are so many dialects in China; I think that English will economically solve the sales requirement.

You'll see how I've prioritized these languages based on my expected sales volume. Over the next three years, we will be sold into at least 4 new companies, with multiple locations – as many as 25 new direct customers, when you consider the locations.

I expect my sales to increase from about $6 million to $9+ million by 2021. This, of course, includes new products that will be adapted to the local market." Looking at Reg, he continued, "Right Reg?"

Vito continued, "We'll also be expanding our participation in the International trade shows – going from 3/year to 6/year. The increased number of shows is due to the number of countries where we will sell. We are adding shows in countries where we have customers, but haven't done shows in the past.

Description	2019				2020	2021	Cost (000's)	Purpose
	Q1	Q2	Q3	Q4				
Market Research	→						20	Creative
New Product Introduction		→	→				35	Creative
Trade shows (8)		→	→	→	→	→	100	Opportunity
Website upgrade				→			?	Efficiency
Collateral material translation			→		→		25	Opportunity
Business Development Addition			→				100	Opportunity

Questions?"

"Vito, that is one heck-of-a rapid fire summary of how you're going to re-launch the international operations. I'm also very interested in your spending. What is that – an incremental $300k/year?"

"Yes John. But if we want to increase sales by 50%, we need to make some kind of commitment."

"Ok – you're definitely thinking outside the box, and we all know that there could be enormous demand for the product. Can we meet offline to discuss some of the background information on your plan? I like the thought of an expanded base of countries… the value of a relationship in the international market is critical, when you consider the distances and social differences. Overall, I like how you think. Now it's our job to fit the spending and risk profile into the entire Company package. Well done, Vito.

Is it about time for a break, Jackson?"

"It's not only ABOUT time, it IS time for the break. Back in 15 minutes folks."

The team immediately scattered for the rest rooms. John and Jackson huddled near the windows.

"Well, Jackson, you told me you were going to change the way they think, but I never expected this much progress. I'm embarrassed that for the past few years I haven't tapped into their creative energy."

"Not a problem, John. We're under way as of today. You've got a good team and they'll respond to the right kind of challenges – if you listen to their input.

For now, let's get back at this."

VP Human Resources discussion

When the team reassembled, Jackson introduced Bev. "Bev, it's your show."

"Thanks for the opportunity to discuss the Company Human Resources. Little known fact. Did you know that other than materials purchases, the people costs represent more than any other category in the Company's spending? People spending includes salary & wages, fringe benefits, bonus, commission etc.

As a Company, we talk about HR more as a commodity product than a critical resource that drives the organization.

Let's do a brief comparison to something that Bill mentioned earlier. We have accounting information about materials – the purchase price and the usage of materials. We also develop performance standards for every SKU in the building. That is, engineer's study, calculate, define norms of performance – and then we report against all those well-defined standards.

We also heard Bill talk about the efforts that will be used for process improvement. Perhaps even employing outside consultants that will introduce new methods and processes to make us more competitive.

And then we get to Human Resources.

Historically, the big thing with HR is, 'what is the annual pay increase? How much will benefits cost us this year?'

But what can we measure that will help us better manage the Human Resource – the 2nd largest single spending category in the Company?

When was the last time we had an employee survey that asked this resource what they think about the Company? And to the executives in this room – how have you managed this very expensive resource? And I'm not talking about getting the day-to-day tasks done. I am talking about how we manage a scarce resource critical to the business.

I've looked at a sampling of annual reviews that we have completed. The reviews typically focus on how the employee performed tasks, but I saw very little about how we can help them develop their future… coaching… how they can become more valuable to the Company. The reviews are a few paragraphs – quite often warm and fuzzy – softball comments of what a great job they've done.

When have we actually coached them… improved their skill set so they become more valuable to the Company … discuss how they can improve our operations?

And what have we done to educate them – and I'm not just talking about task education like running a press. I've checked with the regional chamber of commerce, and the national human resources organizations about training offered provided in progressive companies. We don't measure up."

The silence in the room was austere – the execs didn't even shuffle papers in their self-conscious embarrassment. Bill and Mitch simply stared at the pages on the table.

Jackson felt the tension build throughout Bev's dissertation, and could resist no longer.

"Wow, Bev. When we said that we were looking for breakthroughs, you certainly didn't disappoint. I like the information that you've presented – but what should we do about this?

Do you want us to ... well, what do you want us to do?"

She folded her hands, somewhat uncomfortable with her assessment of the organization's HR performance. She cleared her throat.

"I apologize for my rant. This isn't about your performance. It's a self-assessment of *my* performance. I've been responsible for the Company HR for several years, and I've let you down. I've failed in my responsibility to help you manage this most important – and expensive - component of our Company.

I haven't worked with you to help you develop competitive training programs, to help you implement meaningful goal-setting and personnel reviews, to help you identify relationships with trade schools, universities and organizations that provide the resources that we need to be competitive.

I'm responsible for HR. I'm the one that should understand how to protect the resource, and help develop policies with your insight to nourish these critical associates."

John interrupted. "Ok Bev. It seems that we've all been a bit behind the curve on capturing opportunity, and this meeting is our renaissance. You know, under your guidance we've grown successfully for the past few years. Maybe we could have done things differently – maybe better, or could be worse - but none of us has done more than average.

We've survived one of the worst recessions in the last 75 years, and we've come out smiling. We've adapted to prevailing conditions and done a good job.

This meeting – and working with Jackson – gives us an opportunity to reignite our enthusiasm, and become a better organization.

So, after the past few minutes of self-flagellation, I'm guessing that you have some proposals to get us to the front of the competitive world. Let's get to the solutions. Agreed?"

"Sure thing, John. I – well, when I looked at what could have been, I've been very embarrassed."

"Ok- so what will we do about this?"

"Folks, I need your help. There are so many things to consider that I think as a group we need to decide what's best for the Company. I've made a list of things to consider, but the last thing we should do is let me proceed without your input.

Our turnover rate has been a bit high in the lesser skilled areas. I think that we need to assess our compensation package for entry level workers."

Bill, who employs most of those blue-collar workers, spoke up. "I'll agree with that. What's the best method to do that?"

"I think the local chamber of commerce is a great place to start. Is anyone a member of the local chamber?"

Silence.

Jackson interrupted. "Well maybe that's a good organization for the Company to be involved with regardless of the HR focus. Any thoughts?"

John nodded agreement, and waved for Bev to continue.

Bev continued. "Bill, you've got the greatest immediate exposure to turnover – especially in the machinist and fabrication area. I'd like to start reaching out to the local high-schools, trade schools etc. – maybe to set up apprentice programs, or part-time student internships."

"Sounds like a plan…"

"Also, when we looked at the turnover numbers, it seems that the younger engineers stay for a few years and move on. I think some kind of survey with the millennial engineers – as well as the others – would be worthwhile. Ideally we'd initially – and maybe annually - engage an outside survey firm to manage the survey to ensure confidentiality.

In the literature, it seems that millennials have different work/life objectives. I'm not talking about having billiard tables in the cafeteria, but they have different drivers. We'd pick some of that up in the surveys, but one outstanding item seems to dominate. That is community involvement... you know, participating in charity events, maybe have the Company sponsor some events... mentoring students. I really don't know what's best, but again, let's research and get a plan together."

Reg smiled when he heard 'community involvement'. "Funny you mention that. A couple of the younger engineers were in my office last week asking for some sponsorship money for a walk for kids, or something like that. I offered $1,000 and they were extremely happy."

Jason nodded agreement. "I had a similar request from some of my folks – I gave a $1,000 as well."

John leaned in. "Anybody else contributing?"

Each executive nodded that they had also donated to various charities during the year.

"Ok, so our heart's in the right place. Seems like we should be thinking about this as a Company, and make strategic donations. Bev, did you mention that millennials want to get involved with that kind of charitable activity? Seems like we should form a committee including the millennials to help us make better decisions."

"Got it. And to continue, let's talk about our annual review process. Anybody think that they do a great job in the review and coaching process?"

"I have the largest organization in manufacturing and warehouse, and I can tell you that we haven't done a great job. We've only focused on Company deliverables- on time shipments, inventory shortages, errors on the floor. It's a complete miss on my part – the coaching aspect. When you first raised the topic I knew it was a miss. Can we develop some kind of standard performance review?"

"It's on my list, Bill. And I'd also like to investigate some kind of formal training or education process where the Company reimburses outside training."

"Sounds expensive."

"Mitch, you're right that it may cost money, but when Jackson and I talked, we focused on the cost of turnover. It's a hidden cost, but you can't imagine how big it is. Think about the recruiting fees, potential relocations, temporary help, lost productivity, delayed shipments. There are so many costs that could be avoided by more effectively managing our human resources. I'll go through the numbers with you offline.

And remember, I'm just presenting alternatives. I know that we can't solve all the issues in 30 days… and that everything is a trade-off.

And for those at this table …" She briefly looked at John. "For those at the table, I think that we need to look at the overall compensation plan. John and I talked about the growth plans – up what is it, 40-50% in the next few years. Well, we need to be hitting on all cylinders, and an incentive compensation plan with solid metrics might help us get there."

John responded. "Thanks for touching that hot potato, Bev. Yes, Bev, Jackson and I have been discussing executive compensation. I'm open to the discussion – no promises, other than I'll keep an open mind to anything that helps us manage the Company better."

"So let me summarize. We have s-o-o-o many open questions, and opportunities. Here's my list of action items.

Description	2019				2020	2021	Cost	Purpose
	Q1	Q2	Q3	Q4			(000's)	
Workforce Comp & Benefits Review	→						20	Opportunity
Executive Comp Review		→					35	Creative
Upgrade Performance Review Process			→				100	Opportunity
Employee Survey	→						?	Creative
Training & Apprentice Programs		→					25	Efficiency
Community Services Committee			→				100	Creative

And you'll notice that I don't have any tasks in 2020 or 2021. I think we heard this earlier. I don't know what I don't know. If we establish and continue the listed programs, I think that we'll figure out what comes next. Any comments?"

Jackson stood and walked to the white board. "This morning has been a real knockout so far. While we've had a few bumps in the road, let's look at what we've accomplished by thinking differently. Instead of debating whether, and how we will increase sales and earning by – shall we say 5% - we've focused on the actions that will actually create the opportunity to increase the business well beyond 5%.

When we get to the competitive strengths and weaknesses, I think that you'll see how the functional self-assessments have pre-empted the competitive discussion. We've identified *HOW* we will manage the business better.

I think that you've taken the TNC mantle…" He selected the red marker and scratched on the board while saying, "…that is *THINK - NO CONSTRAINTS* – and run with it." This is truly outstanding. Let's keep up the good work.

Next up – Janice, you're on.

VP Marketing discussion

Janice moved quickly to the whiteboard, holding the black marker. "I'm going to be far less formal in this discussion. I'll scratch some things on the board, but want you to solve my problem.

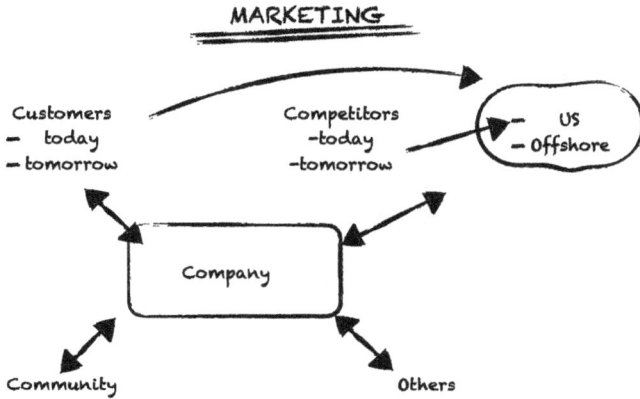

MARKETING

Customers
– today
– tomorrow

Competitors
–today
–tomorrow

US
– Offshore

Company

Community

Others

We know that our products are first class...
better than most of our competitors once our
products are formally launched and debugged.
During the past few years, we've had some
launch challenges, so we've done a soft launch
initially. Not a lot of promotion until we get the
initial response from the users. While on one
side that's great – since we are actually in the
market and can boast about it - but does our
reputation suffer as a result?

And did I mention that we're often the close
second product introduced into the
marketplace? Can you imagine if we were first
in the market, and had the best product when
first launched – soft or not?

So, a question – how can we get first class
products in the market before anyone else?"

Bill cleared his throat. "I think part of it is what I mentioned earlier. We've got to fix our manufacturing processes so that we don't have so much breakage."

Jason jumped on the opportunity to speak. "I'd like to get my reps involved in the new product discussion. We have insight as the front line people. We also hear the wish list from our customers."

Reg spoke out. "And you haven't heard from me yet, but I've got to get the market insight – from the customers – tied in with my developers, and then we've got to work things through with Bill's teams. In the past, we've designed some exceptional products that were either too difficult or expensive to produce, or the market doesn't want them. It's a crazy way to run the business."

"Ok – so we need to have some kind of new product development committee with input from sales, engineering, and manufacturing."

"And don't forget the finance function," Mitch added."

"Great – committee formed. We'll sort out the details offline."

She scrawled NEW PRODUCT COMMITTEE on the board.

"So now I've got some insight into the products that we will develop. And how should we price the product. Cost plus?"

Jason shouted, "I'd like to be price competitive."

"Do you mean lowest price? Would that erode our quality image? Do we want to take the chance?"

The executives were silent.

She continued. "I'll suggest that we want to have a gross margin that allows us to invest in the business, while maintaining the quality image in the marketplace. I'll call it a pricing strategy. And once we define the pricing strategy, we'll back into the manufacturing cost. Reg, I won't call it reverse engineering, but won't it help if we know the margin required and the price that the market will tolerate? Then we can design the product that manufacturing can produce for us to make a profit."

"Agreed."

She wrote PRICING STRATEGY on the board.

"Now, I'll make an assumption that we can get to market first. Will that help?"

Mitch leaned forward. "Just guessing, but a quality product first to market gives bigger margins. I'm all for flawless early introductions..."

Reg and Bill exchanged looks. "Reg and I have been talking about some kind of defined new product development process that will give us timely, first quality products without a pile of scrap, rework, overtime, expedited shipping costs and discounts because we've missed target dates."

Mitch contributed. "Absolutely."

"We need some kind of new product development process. Who should develop the process?"

John interrupted, "I'm just thinking out loud, but it seems that sales, R&D, manufacturing, marketing and finance should be involved - same as the committee."

Heads bobbing endorsed the team identified.

Janice scratched across the white board, NEW PRODUCT DEVELOPMENT PROCESS.

"So now we have a first quality product, launched on time, with excellent margins since we're first in the market. Great.

Now we get to my world. I like to think of the universe of customers, competitors, the community and others – maybe government agencies, municipals – who knows. My job is managing product and Company information flow in and out of the Company, and supporting the sales, product development, Company image and branding. I'll just call this the soft side of marketing.

A few minutes ago we heard Vito discuss the need for translations to – what was it, about 4 different languages? What's the market in the target countries? For our products, is it $1 million or $1 billion? And who are the competitors, and do they make any money?

Vito, I like the preliminary research that you've done with the US Commercial Services department, and I especially like that you want to get some on-the-ground research done. I'd like to work with you on the competitive analysis, and perhaps think about the marketing strategy of launching in numerous countries. You ok with that?"

Vito's head bobbed agreement.

Janice scrawled FOREIGN MARKET ASSESSMENT/MARKET STRATEGY across the whiteboard.

"Vito and Jason, you mentioned that you wanted to attend 6 trade shows. I clearly understand that you want market visibility, but will that be the most effective use of our investment? Said another way, you've done a great first pass at the marketing mix that we have. I'd like to help you when you do alternative analysis – you know, trade-offs among customer facing touch points."

Jason's body language hinted reluctance. "Um, sure, if you think that you need to be involved."

"Do you know what I'd really like to do is share what we know about the competitors, and the overall market information. After talking with Jackson, I started to root around for public information about competitors, the economy, expected market conditions. I'd like to share that with you – it may affect how you approach some of our customers.

One other thing I'd like to do, if you agree. We'd like to set up some Internet searches for information about your key customers and competitors. Whenever any information hits the market, we can get you the information ASAP so that you can react to it. Maybe adjust a presentation... drop a note to the customer when you see they did great things. That kind of market intelligence."

"So you're telling me that you'll set this up and keep me informed about current events that might affect my customers?"

"And your competitors."

"Let's do it."

She wrote COMPETITIVE INTELLIGENCE on the board.

"And then we get to what I'll call the public relations portion of the marketing function. Would anyone like to write white papers? Perhaps give seminars? Participate in panel discussions?"

Reg looked up from his notes. "I've got some engineers that really light up at those kind of opportunities."

Bev volunteered. "Is that also the kind of thing that keeps employees challenged and gives them a bit of personal development?"

"OK – let me just add that to the list," as Janice wrote on the board – PUBLIC RELATIONS.

"John, that no doubt means you'll be speaking to groups touting our great Company."

"I guess it's only fair that I take a few assignments in this strategy. So tell me, Janice, where did all this information come from?"

"Closet MBA in Marketing, John. Just never felt the Company was ready for an intrusive set of new ideas. When Jackson and I talked, I just decided it was now or never. And then, when I looked at our current set of activities… let me just say that the marketing team will be excited to crack open some new responsibilities. They'll still get the day-to-day *stuff* done, but through prioritization and planning, we'll make it happen.

I have just one other major topic to explore... I think that we need an overall market strategy. Right now we seem to be in many product areas. Is that what we want to do in the future, or do we want to be exceptional in a few?

I haven't done a detailed analysis, but it seems that we have expertise in electronics, hydraulics, some chemistry, metal fabrication and castings. Do we want to be in all those areas, or should we focus? Focus based on market potential, growth rates, profitability, and competition? And when we think about our product lines and distribution channels, are we distracted by too many options?

Folks, with your permission, can I write DEVELOP MARKETING STRATEGY?

The question hung in the air, since this was directly challenging John's philosophy of 'let's get sales."

John was motionless, staring out the window. After a minute of silence, he scanned the attendees, making eye contact with Reg, Jason and Bill.

"I think that's a darned good idea."

Janice scrawled across the board DEVELOP MARKET STRATEGY.

She smiled broadly and said, "That completes my discussion. I'll put some timelines together and look for your input. Thanks all for removing the handcuffs."

She then presented a slide with topics and timelines listed.

Description	2019				2020	2021	Cost (000's)	Purpose
	Q1	Q2	Q3	Q4				
New Product Committee	→							NPD
Pricing Strategy		→						Profit
New Product Development Process	→							NPD
Foreign Market Assessment		→					20	Growth
Competitive Intelligence Process			→					Growth
Develop Product/Market strategy		→						Growth

Everyone laughed, since she had already defined her goals and timelines. Bill broke the silence, "You sandbagged us!"

Janice smiled, "Maybe just a bit."

"Jackson rapped the table twice. Let's take 15 minutes to absorb what we've covered this morning. We're a bit behind schedule, but the time has been well worth it. See you in 15 minutes."

Jackson and John immediately huddled. "Jackson, that was one helluva session, and we aren't done yet. It's is startling what we've talked about this morning. It almost seems like we have been treading water and not moving forward. Can this really work?"

"For sure John, but we're talking about culture change. We can list the projects and get all excited about the possibilities, but it's a lot of work. Every day, every week, every month we need to accomplish elements of every one of these tasks. If we don't, you'll miss major opportunities. That doesn't mean you'll crash and burn, but you'll have an opportunity cost.

John, your job, once the planning is complete, is to guide and coach these execs to success. That means that you'll need to change priorities as things happen, and you'll have to focus on the progress made rather than misses that will occur.

I don't think I've ever seen a plan that was executed flawlessly. But a plan that is relentlessly pursued will take you closer to your goals. This has been quite an exceptional session. Your troops are doing a v-e-r-y good job at breaking down the barriers."

After a few more minutes, Jackson restarted the meeting.

VP Finance discussion

"Well, I know that you've all been anxiously waiting for a spectacular presentation from the most dynamic finance exec in the room. And rather than disappoint, let's get going.

First of all a confession. After Jackson slapped me 'upside the head', I decided to do some self-assessment. Bev beat me with the self-immolation, but I will confess.

During the past few years, I've gotten a bit entrenched – some might even say stale."

"Nah… not a chance mister tightwad," spoken in unison by several execs.

"OK – hold the hostility. After talking with Jackson and Bill, I discovered manufacturing accounting and financial analysis. And as Jackson and I talked about finance, I discovered what I would kindly refer to as *breakage* – in my department. Jackson and I analyzed how much rework the finance and IT departments perform. Bill you were like a rusty knife when you discussed manufacturing accounting, and it was painful.

When I looked at my department's work routine, I was shocked. So that I don't completely beat this to death, I'm making a promise today to fix the train wreck I've referred to as finance.

When I'm through with the list of stuff, I'll ask for your insight… I want you to wear yourself out with things for me to do. I want the entire wish list on the table so that I can prioritize actions to make my department the most productive finance department you've ever worked with. Agreed?"

The team was somewhat shocked at the confession. "Fasten your seatbelt, Bean-counter!" Bill couldn't resist the opportunity to have some fun with Mitch.

Mitch's first slide was very straightforward.

		2018				2019	2020
		Q1	Q2	Q3	Q4		
Improve Procedures							
A/R detail/GL balancing	Joan	$$					
Spreadsheets...spreadsheets	ALL						
inventory/ledger balance	Chuck	$$					
mfg variances	Chuck		$$	$$			
collecting old A/R balances	AL		$$				
reconcile accts-dscts	AL		$$				
reconcile accts-pricing adj	AL		$$				
payroll reconciliation	Jennifer		$$				
commission payments	Jennifer		$$				
IT breakage	William		$$				
strategic imperatives							
pricing analysis	Mitch		$$				
profit by prod line	mitch			$$			
profit by trade channel	mitch			$$			
territory sales analysis	mitch			$$			
planning – near term	mitch				$$		
planning – longer term	mitch				$$		
IT sysetms Review	mitch					$$	

"Now let's be clear, I've used dollar signs to confirm that each of these tasks will add to the Company's profitability. You'll see finance staff members with many tasks to complete. These early tasks are fixing the broken processes that we've tolerated for years.

And then I move from accounting to risk management. When I think about risk, I also include the positive side called opportunity. And to me that means using some of the analytical talent in-house for profit analysis and planning. That will be on a tactical basis for specific product lines, territories, and new product development assessment, as well as business planning. The first installment of business planning is what we are doing today.

We're also going to change how we budget, if John agrees.

Those are all the finance items, and as I look at our goal of $50 million annual revenue, I've got to be sure that our data systems environment can meet the needs of this high growth business. Said another way, I don't want finance and IT to be a constraint to our growth.

Let me take just a few more minutes to show you an example of improved analysis and reporting. Bill and I have spent a few minutes discussing the reporting that he needs to better manage the manufacturing operation. Without getting into too much detail, in finance we have a responsibility to provide information to you folks so that you can manage better. That means we need to give you accurate, timely consistently prepared information that helps you.

Bill and I scratched out an example of a report that we'll start preparing in Q1 next year. Here's a quick snapshot:

Manufacturing Cost

Month: _____

	Month		Description		YTD	
Act	F(U) Plan			Act	F(U) Plan	
	Amount	%			Amount	%
			Headcount			
			(Amount in 000's US$)			
			Capital Spending			
			Production Cost at Standard			
			Materials Variances			
			Material's Usage Variance			
			Purchase Price Variance			
			Total Materials Variance			
			Labor Variance			
			Labor Usage Variance			
			Labor Rate Variance			
			Total Labor Variance			
			Overhead Variance			
			Overhead Spending Variance			
			(Over) Under Absorbed Overhead			
			Total Overhead Variance			
			Scrap/Reject			
			Rework			
			Total Variances			
			Overhead Spending			
			Compensation			
			Benefits			
			Maintenance			
			Insurance			
			Supplies			
			Travel			
			Depreciation & Amortization			
			Telephone			
			Freight			
			All Other			
			Total			

While it gets technical and is geared to Bill's responsibility, we'll compare actuals to plan. How'd we do compared to what we expected to do? We're going to start thinking differently for each functional area, and I need your help to get you the right information.

Any questions?"

Reg asked the first question. "So will you be developing some kind of analytical approach to new product development? Something that I can apply quickly, because we're ramping up the NPD work soon. And also, I'm going to need some help understanding where my engineer's time is going. A specific task in my commitments, but I'm going to need your help with that."

Jason saw the Q3 timing for sales analysis in the earlier summary and said, "You know, I've gotten some religion and need the sales analysis sooner if I'm supposed to get my job done. The projected sales growth that we're looking for needs to start immediately."

"Thanks for your comment Jason. Jackson mentioned that once I opened the door to analysis, the demand might be too much. Folks, while the finance and IT departments are my responsibility, we're really a service organization, and you are my customers. I have some corporate things to do – the timing is non-negotiable – the rest of my time is yours. As far as timing of other tasks, may I suggest that we leave the timing as is for now, until I get a better idea about the resources available. If I can fix some of the broken processes, I'll have a much better idea about available resources. Once I get a handle on resources, I promise that WE – that's everybody in this room - will work out the priorities together. Agreed?"

John nodded, "Seems reasonable that we schedule after we understand the resources available. Great job Mitch. Seems like you've taken this strat planning to heart. Anything else to discuss?"

After a few moments awaiting a response, John continued, "Reg, I think that you're next on the agenda. Let's roll."

"Thanks John. It seems that much of my thunder has been taken. Now, we all know that I'll be working with Janice, Bill, Mitch and Jason to improve the new product development launch timetable.

Thank you for your attention." Smiling, Reg began to move toward his seat, as if the discussion were complete.

With large applause, the chant "Encore" arose from the executives at the table.

"OK, so you want more detail? Well if you insist.

As we've all done during the past week, I've done a preliminary review of my department. Strange thing. I've got 14 engineers, all capable of designing new products for this high-powered production machine. I've also estimated that it requires about 2,000 hours to develop and successfully launch a new product.

Seems like we should have 7 new products each year. … But we don't.

I've also discovered that our engineers have developed some of the most sophisticated new products that our customers could ever want, and they don't buy them. Hmmm...

And these sophisticated new products developed by these extremely talented engineers somehow can't be produced at any reasonable cost. Hmmm...

When I look at the grand scheme of things..." He looked at Jackson, smiled and nodded. "... In engineering, it seems that we haven't been thinking about our customers. And when I say customers, I mean that R&D has not been responsive to Bill, Jason, Mitch, and Janice... and did I mention those organizations that actually buy our products – Jason, are those the folks we call customers?

From this point forward, Jason, I'm counting on you to provide insight into today's customer needs. Now that doesn't mean just what they want today, but thinking ahead about trends that the sales force sees.

And Janice, given your marketing expertise, I'd like your insight into market trends – whether it is particular products or competitive actions.

Mitch and Bill, help me to understand what things cost so that we don't charge mindlessly down a rabbit hole of failed new products.

Overall, I'll summarize my goals as follows:

Description	2019				2020	2021
	Q1	Q2	Q3	Q4		
Engineers Time Study	X					
NPD Process Template	X					
NPD Fin Eval Template		X				
NPD - Prod #1			X			
NPD - Prod #2				X		
NPD - Prod #3					X	
NPD - Prod #4					X	
NPD - Prod #5					X	
NPD - Prod #6					X	
NPD - Prod #7-10						X

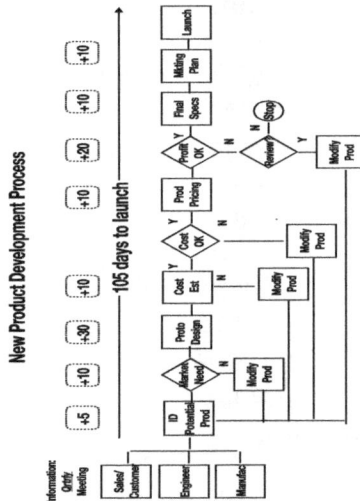

New Product Development Process

105 days to launch

+10, +10, +20, +10, +10, +30, +10, +5

Information: Qrtly Meeting — Sales/Customer, Engineer, Manufac

ID Potential Prod → Matls Avail? (Y/N, Modify Prod) → Proto Design → Cost Est → Cost OK? (Y/N, Modify Prod) → Prod Pricing → Profit OK? (Y/N, Modify Prod) → Review? (N/Y, Stop) → Final Specs → Mktng Plan → Launch

This first flowchart is a quick summary of how long our new product development should take. When you look at the summary, you'll notice that in a normal process without any major problems, we should be able to develop and launch a new product in about 105 days."

John and Bill were surprised at the chart. Bill said, "So why does it take us 2-3 times that amount to develop and launch?"

"Distractions, Bill. One of my projects is to discover what those distractions are, and eliminate them." Reg then spent a few minutes reviewing the detailed chart, responding to questions as they arose.

After a few minutes of discussion, Reg projected a new chart. "As I mentioned a few minutes ago, our engineers have been allowed to spend time on pet projects. Historically we haven't done much to guide the selection of their projects, considering their creative imagination to be a great source of ideas. We've looked at the results of their projects, and while we've had some limited success in product development from these creative projects, we're going to redirect them to higher probability launch products. Mitch and I have huddled to create a template that we'd like to use to evaluate NPD projects." Reg launched the next slide and reviewed the elements of NPD projects.

"This template will allow us to evaluate the NPD proposal. We've already agreed upon a New Products Committee, and now we'd like to evaluate new products using this template. The driver is long-term profitability.

And I'd also like to share my thoughts about what may be important to evaluate new products. Mitch and I spent a few minutes discussing critical points of information, but this is the *Cliff Notes* version. There is a lot more development to do, but I wanted to share this with you today.

When you think about finding the lost engineer time – we're not sure exactly where yet – the standard development template and timeline, and the required financial analysis, we expect to have leading products launched on a predictable schedule, with higher margins. Comments?"

John Davidson Co.
New Product Development Checklist

Product Name: _____

1 **Product Description** *(Describe both US and International)*

US Operations: *(Include target selling price and target cost.)*

International Operations: *(Include target selling price and target cost.)*

New Product Classification	Enhancement	New Product	New Category

2 **Market Conditions/Market Share** *(Describe the fit.)*

Key Competitors (Attached List)

3 **Product Development -** *Description of Process*

5 **Timeline Describe** *(Development broad timeline - attache GANNT chart)*

6 **Description of Launch Process:**

4 **Financial Summary**

	Quarters				Year	
	1	*2*	*3*	*4*	**2**	**3**
Investment *(Includes Capital & Expense)*						
R&D						
Sales & Marketing						
Manufacturing						
Other						
Total Investment Required						
Sales						
Gross Profit						
Launch & Other Expense *(Describe on attachment)*						
R&D						
Marketing						
Sales Training						
Advertising & Promotion						
Manufacturing						
Total Expense						
Contribution Margin						

5 **Financial Ratios:**
Internal Rate of Return: _____
Net Present Value: _____
Cash Flow Breakeven: _____

John stood, walked up to the screen to examine the NPD template. "You and Mitch developed this?"

"Yes, John – with some great insight from Jackson. We had some side discussions with Jason, Janet and Vito, but they haven't seen the finished product yet. And I say finished, knowing that we are always looking for improvements. Suggestions?"

"After just a quick scan, I like this. Considers all the cost buckets, and probable sales and margins. Better yet, you've included a section for launch expenses. This is a great start. Thanks."

"Looks like a lot of work, Reg." Bill was visibly concerned about the amount of work to be done.

"First of all, don't be frightened off by the topics – 'launch expenses, capital and other developmental expenses.' This is a broad checklist and not accounting precise. Mitch and I would like to get an idea about the costs and returns to the Company. In some cases, a simple answer such as 'less than $10,000...or maybe min/max estimates...' helps us understand whether we should move forward... small, medium, or large investment.

We also thought about the risks of an entirely new product versus a modification to an existing product. I'm sharing this with you now so that you can start thinking about the business checklist. I'd like to finalize the template during the first quarter. OK?"

After a few moments of silence, Jackson thanked Reg, and introduced Andy.

VP Logistics discussion

"Thanks Jackson. As you know, I've spent a lot of time on special projects during the past two years. The projects have been valuable to me and quite often to the Company. Recently, I've been working with the Lean Business concepts based on the Toyota Manufacturing method.

I've learned a lot, and for my Strategic Plan discussion, I'd just like to challenge us to think differently. 'What if' is the question that I challenge myself with every day, and today, I'd like to share the challenge with you."

As he launched his first slide, the music from Star Wars played in the background, and the following scrolled upward from the bottom of the screen.

A long time ago, in a different galaxy…
It is a time of fierce competition where small and large corporations have attacked our market share, stolen our customers and kidnapped our best engineers using advanced management techniques to win the competitive war…

During that battle for customers, they have launched new products at a rate unseen in our history.

Andy continued, "OK, I've had a bit of fun with this. Just as in Star Wars, I think of competition as waging a war on our Company. And I don't like losing wars. So I've studied some management techniques.

So here's my challenge for you.

Let's think about a Company – not necessarily ours, but, let's just call it "X" Company. Now in this Company, with sales of 100, and pretax earnings of 10, I'd like to challenge how we think. As a young radical, I want to change that Company's pretax earnings to 15. Whattayathink troops?"

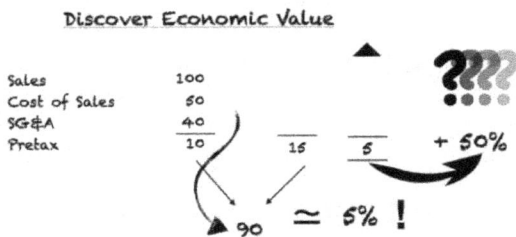

Discover Economic Value

Sales	100	
Cost of Sales	50	
SG&A	40	
Pretax	10	

15   5   + 50%

▲ 90 ≃ 5% !

"I think that you've found a stock of legalized marijuana."

"Or you've taken one too many tours on the bourbon trail." The team enjoyed the challenge, and responded exactly how Andy wanted.

"Well, as we all know, I'm one of those theoretical college boys, and…" as he finished the sentence, the bottom of the slide appeared, "I'd like to think of the increase of $5 to Pretax Earnings as only a 5% change, not a 50% change."

Mitch perked up immediately, "What kind of funny math are you using? It's a 50% improvement and it's just not possible to increase earnings by 50%. I think we need to talk, Andy."

"I hear exactly what you're saying, Mitch. And your math is correct, but I look at this in a completely different way. See, I think of the change of $5, as only a change of 5%, based on $90 of input. Cost of sales and SG&A costs to this Company total $90 of input, so, all I'm really asking for is a change of 5%."

Bill next objected. "Andy, it's a 50% change in profitability."

"I agree that it's a change to profitability, but when we look at the resources applied, it's 5% of resources applied. Simple math."

Janice stood and walked to the screen, carefully examining the math. "Andy's right. The math is simple when you change the thinking. Clever, Andy. So now what do we do with that information?"

"Glad you asked, Janice. We've heard of the Lean Business concept – and no, it doesn't necessarily mean layoffs. While I'm a rookie at the thinking, I like to think of it as squeezing the waste out of a business.

So in these slides, I'm going to challenge each of us to 'Gimme-5.' That's right, I'm looking for 5% of our resources to be applied to value added activity.

Discover Economic Value

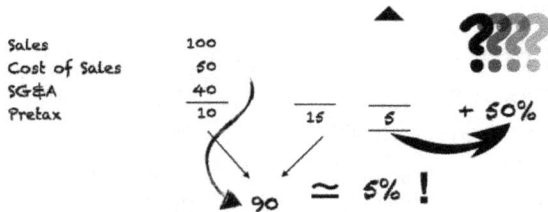

Sales	100			
Cost of Sales	50			
SG&A	40			
Pretax	10	15	5	+ 50%

90 $\simeq$ 5% !

What if you could:
- ... increase R&D spending
- ... add sales force coverage
- ... license new products
- ... improve competitive analysis
- ... increase advertising
- ... increase technical training
- ... implement lean business process
- ... reduce working cap requirements
- ... reduce cap-ex requirements

without spending more money.

So, in this next slide, let's change how we think once again. A company has functional needs.

Logistics, operations, marketing, sales. These are primary functions – things that add value to product or service as we deal with the customers.

But there are other needs. Sometimes we call it overhead – functions that a company needs to stay running. Can you imagine operating a company without finance?"

Bill spoke up laughing, "One can only dream, Andy!"

The entire team laughed. "Well functions like Finance, HR, IT, legal – they are secondary functions.

And within the functions, people do stuff – I'll call them activities. There are direct activities – my definition of course – that directly add value to the product or service delivered to the customer. And there are indirect activities – activities that don't necessarily add value to the customer. Things like internal reporting."

Jason chimed in, "I'm all for getting rid of all internal reporting."

Again, the entire team laughed.

"OK, so we're all on board with eliminating indirect activity – so we no longer need time reporting to prepare payroll."

"I'd like to keep payroll in the indirect activities," Bill offered.

"OK, so we agree that certain indirect activities are necessary to run the business. Well, now that we understand some of the elements of the company, I'd like us to challenge everything that we do, and try to save 5%. And when we find that 5%, let's shift as much as possible, from indirect to direct activities, and from support to primary functions. Agreed?"

"So you want to make the accountants sales reps when we find easier ways for them to do their job?"

"That's a thought, but that's not where I'm going. What if we can eliminate wasted activity – fixing broken accounting processes that Mitch mentioned earlier - and have the accountants spend more time in manufacturing analysis. We could possibly help Bill find the reason for scrap.

Or maybe we could help Janice perform competitive analysis – using the analytical and math skills that the finance people love doing.

And when we find that 5% - well, who knows what we could do with the time.

Now, using a lean thinking process, and thinking of economic value, it would be great if we could shift that 5% of economic value to more value-added use.

Without getting into too much theory, we all perform activities to improve the value of the

Company. So for example, Jason sells to the customer. That's a primary function – a function that directly contributes value to the customer. And Mitch is in finance. The reference books describe that as a support function. A Company can't do without finance, and still function, but often, the finance function doesn't directly add value for the customer.

And within the function, we perform direct and indirect activities. So for example, when Jason is in front of the customer, he's performing a direct activity. When he is spending weeks preparing budgets, that's an indirect activity. … Doesn't really add value to the customer activity. So if we hunt for that 5% - let's take Jason's time as an example – and reduce his efforts budgeting, he has more time for direct selling. And how would we do that?"

Mitch picked up his head, "Talk to those financial analysts, Jason. We can do a pretty good job budgeting."

"That's right, Mitch. So ideally when we undertake this review, we would like to shift our activities from indirect, to direct, and from support functions to primary functions.

Let me give you some examples. Jason, the finance folks can do competitor analysis for you and your team. They can also help you folks do pricing analysis.

And for you, Bill, the finance folks can start digging into the manufacturing accounting to help you identify where we have profit opportunities."

Mitch added, "I think that would be the variance analyses that I mentioned earlier. It will help you identify where expectations differ from actuals, Bill."

"Right on. It's somewhat of a theoretical approach to value, but I think that you can see the overall benefit if we take a *lean look* at the business.

Here's the slide that pictures the theory.

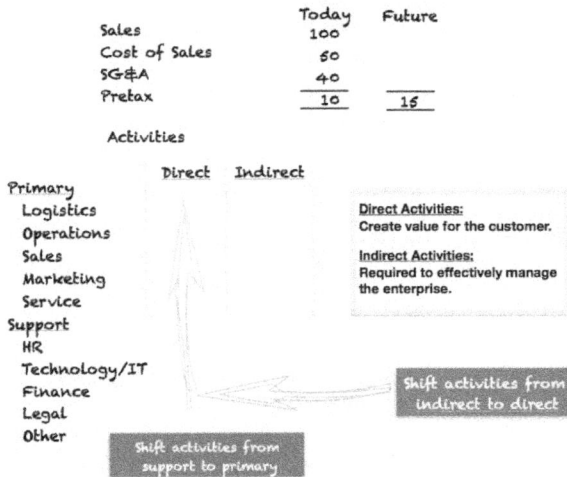

	Today	Future
Sales	100	
Cost of Sales	50	
SG&A	40	
Pretax	10	15

Activities

Primary	Direct	Indirect
Logistics		
Operations		
Sales		
Marketing		
Service		
Support		
HR		
Technology/IT		
Finance		
Legal		
Other		

Direct Activities:
Create value for the customer.

Indirect Activities:
Required to effectively manage the enterprise.

Shift activities from indirect to direct

Shift activities from support to primary

"So there you have it. I'd still like to work on some of our logistics challenges, but I'd like to suggest that we start a Lean Thinking project. I think that the best way to proceed is to hire a consultant for a specific project. Based on my research, most of the Lean experts expect that the investment will be self-funding. And if you look at the 5% value, it sure seems reasonable.

Any thoughts?"

Bill walked to the screen and reviewed the concepts. "Jackson mentioned lean as well, and I've read the books. And let's face it, a 5% improvement in our business process is chump change. I'd like to propose that we do lean in the manufacturing area, and since Andy is so enthused, I'd like him to be the internal exec responsible for the project.

Andy, do you have any objection?"

"I'm all in, Bill. In fact, without knowing how a project is managed, I'd like to sign up for a project a quarter, until we discover more about the process."

John was quietly seated at the back of the room. "So, if we discover opportunity – you know, competitive analysis, eliminate broken *stuff,* will this give us the financial resources to grow even more quickly? I'm thinking more profitability analysis will help us focus on valuable actions… no extra cost, and we'll then have resources to invest in the Company. So, for example, if we can make the sales force more productive, we may be able to make more sales calls. And if we make more sales calls, given our average 30% closing rate, we may get more customers, and that will give us more sales… more gross profit to invest in the Company.

And if we eliminate waste in our R&D process by working as a team in new product development – well, wouldn't it be nice to have a flawless new product launch. And in fact, would we have even more new products to launch?"

Jackson walked to the front of the room, "So it sounds like that's a go. Agreed?"

After unanimous agreement, Jackson called for a 15-minute break.

Jackson and John huddled at the back of the room.

John looked at Jackson and asked, "What just happened?"

"I think it's called teamwork… focused teamwork. I'm excited about how this is turning out. Not scripted per se, but it certainly went in a positive direction.

Strengths & Weaknesses Discussion

"Folks, let's fill our coffee cups and get back to work. We've had a very successful start. The background and candor you've shown has been instrumental in gaining a thorough understanding of our business. Now, let's talk about competition.

The first thing we're going to do is list the competitors. They could be direct competitors – here in the region – or international competitors who are on the fringes. There are no rules for this other than start shouting out the names of the competitors."

Marker in hand, Jackson stood ready to list competitors on the flipcharts.

As the group of executives shouted the competitors' names, Jackson scratched out the phonetic spelling of each.

Competitors

Name	Size	What makes them great	What makes them vulnerable
Haloren Enterprises	<100	Engineering skills	slow response
Act Now Castings	<20	Sales terms	Owner's age
		Flexibility	Informality
Jansen Controls	<100	Relationships	Sales force
Entourage Industries	<20	21st century Equip	Location
Selnick Co.	<100	Reputation	lack personal touch
Butters & Flyn	<20	Sales force	
Begley & Assoc.	<100	Video & website	
Bonje' Ltd.	<100	Location	
Tippe Inc.	<20	Pricing	
Jemme Ltd.	<10		
Harbrecht &Schism	<100		
Jacksonville Ltd.	<100		
Masters & Brellan	<100		
Markers Precision	<100		

As the pace of the competitor listing slowed, he quickly focused on competitors with more than $500 million of sales. "So, let's talk about what makes them great." Jackson continued to press for quick responses. He knew the rapid pace would not allow them to edit their responses, and he would receive unbiased answers to his challenge.

Once the 'great' traits were exhausted, he focused on competitor vulnerability. He peppered the session with questions, hoping to spur additional strengths and weaknesses. "Can you give me an example?" Throughout the brainstorming, the team was fully engaged, interacting among themselves as well as providing material for Jackson to record.

Once the comments for the greater than $500 million segment slowed, he shifted to $100 million or less.

"Let's spend a few minutes on the smaller competitors."

"Hey, Jackson, why did you separate the big boys from the small guys?"

"No deep science. It just seemed that they might be two different competitive groups. So let's spend some time on the less than $100 million... more of our size competition. Now I'd like you to individually rank the top 5 competitors. Think about these strengths and weaknesses, and what we see in the marketplace. Who causes us the most grief?

Who do we go up against more frequently?
Who is the most difficult to compete against?

Once we have those ranked, we'll go through
our strengths and weaknesses and do a plot.
Questions? OK, let's have at it."

Competitors

Name	Size	What makes them great	What makes them vulnerable
Haloren Enterprises	<100	Engineering skills	slow response
Act Now Castings	<20	Sales terms	Owner's age
		Flexibility	Informality
Jansen Controls	<100	Relationships	Sales force
Entourage Industries	<20	21st century Equip	Location
Selnick Co.	<100	Reputation	lack personal touch
Butters & Flyn	<20	Sales force	
Begley & Assoc.	<100	Video & website	
Bonje' Ltd.	<100	Location	
Tippe Inc.	<20	Pricing	
Jemme Ltd.	<10		
Harbrecht &Schism	<100		
Jacksonville Ltd.	<100		
Masters & Brellan	<100		
Markers Precision	<100		

Jackson continued. "OK, now let's spend
some time talking about these lists. Strengths
& weaknesses for our size competitor. Talk to
me about the Sales Force – both a strength
and a weakness."

Jason immediately responded. "Depends on
the company. For example, Jemme Ltd, and
Butters are both owned by old timers. Their
sales force is weak in both places, but the
owner – the chief sales person – has great

relationships with several of his most important customers.

And when we look at sales terms and flexibility, we go nose-to-nose with the owners, and they pretty much do as they please. It's the relationship that is the key."

"OK – so now we have a list of strengths and weaknesses for all our major competitors – small and large. Let's make a list of our strengths and weaknesses.

So let's begin – it can be strength or a weakness. Bill shouted "Responsive…" Someone else called out, "John."

Jackson kept the pace lively and continued to press for business attributes. Several times members questioned a trait, and Jackson reinforced that there should be no critique of the words, but just a continuous flow of information. We would discuss each trait once the list was complete.

After about 15 minutes, the pace slowed.

Strengths	Weaknesses
Responsive	Sales terms
Flexible	Asia sales
Key relationships	Few new customers
Sales Reps	Unfocused R&D
John	Linkage with universities
Mfg engineering support	Late Product intro's
Dedicated employees	Quality problems
Solid customer base	Pricing
Vendor relationships	New engineer turnover
Midwest location	Compensation
Health insurance	Career opportunity
Community involvement	Data systems
	Financial analysis
	Tech equipment
	Community involvement
	Management training

"Ok – now that's a list. Let's see. We've covered People, Product, Plant, Processes and Market. Seems like we've done a fairly good job with the list. Before we rank the items, do we need to explain any of them?"

Reg spoke, "What do we mean 'unfocused' New Product Development?"

Jason responded. "Maybe that's the wrong comment, but what I was getting at is that our new products seem to be late – we're followers – and when they're introduced, they're not always ready for introduction – glitches."

Reg was uncomfortable with the response, but knew it was not the right forum to defend the situation.

Jackson continued. "Other comments?" After a brief pause, he continued, "Now, I'd like you to take a Post-It, and rank the top 5 attributes. Number from 1-5, with 1 being the most important in our business. Once the ranking is complete, we'll plot the results against the top 8 competitors, and see what we see."

Jackson walked to the refreshments to pour an orange juice while the team completed the ranking.

Once the ranking was completed, Jackson plotted the information on a series of graphs. He suggested that the participants take a 15-minute break while he plotted the results.

As the team reconvened, Jackson flipped to his first chart. "So here's what we've done this morning. We've discussed the competitive environment – that is 'who are the most important competitors?' Once we had the overall list, we mined your experience to identify those considered to be the most formidable competitors. We then identified their strengths and weaknesses.

With that as a background, we self-examined our Company… strengths and weaknesses … and ranked the most significant variables. Whenever possible, we grouped the traits into meaningful and actionable items… for example, Human Resource factors.

And finally we plotted competitors and their strengths and weaknesses based on priorities. The size of the bubble is relative to the size of the companies.

So in this first plot, what do we see?"

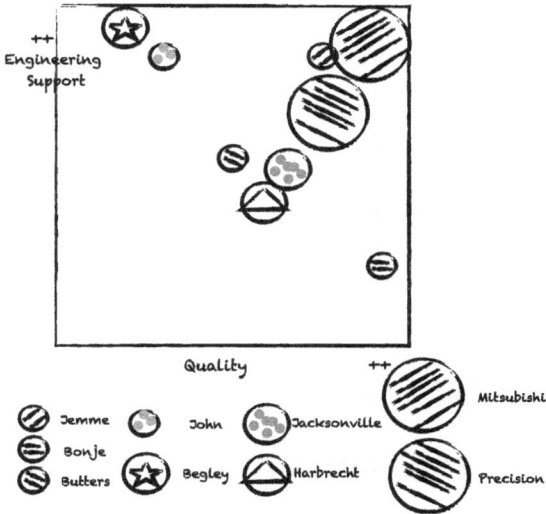

Reg observed, "It looks like we believe that most of our competitors have better quality than we do. That almost seems inconsistent with the high marks for engineering support."

Bill suggested, "Reg, I think the high grades for engineering support relate to – once we discover a manufacturing problem, your folks fully engage and resolve the issue."

"And from the sales side, when my customers have a problem, you get your engineers on the job as quickly as possible to resolve the issue."

Jackson let the discussion play out for a few minutes, and then questioned, "So is it a good thing that we are responsive to problems identified? Or is there a better way to manage this?"

"Jackson, when you and I discussed the R&D function, we puzzled over why we didn't have more new product development. Well, the answer is that we're fixing things and not developing things. I think that we need to fix the new product development and manufacturing interface so we don't send out problems."

"Any thoughts, team?"

All at the table agreed with the assessment.

"Ok – what else do we see?"

Janice leaned forward and said, "If we fix the new product development and management interface problem, will that also solve the quality problem?"

"Possibly. Thoughts Bill?"

"I think that we'll discover other issues. Late change orders, and some outdated manufacturing equipment might impact the quality assessment."

Jackson created a side list of open issues, and continued.

"Observations about this next slide?"

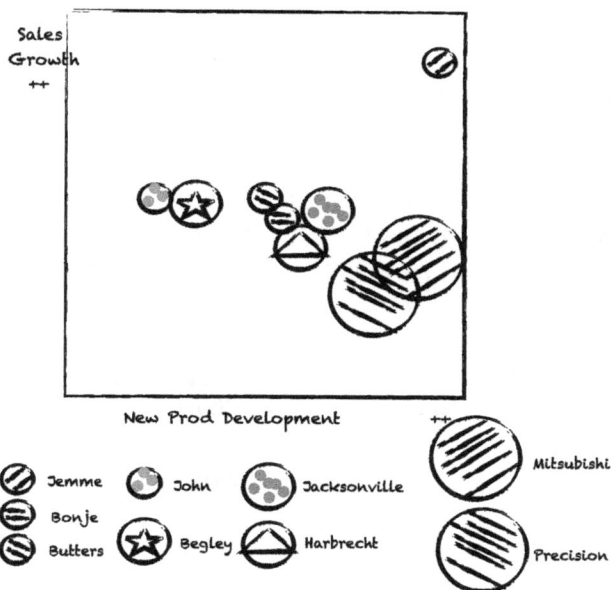

Sales Growth ++

New Prod Development ++

Jemme
Bonje
Butters
John
Begley
Jacksonville
Harbrecht
Mitsubishi
Precision

"It seems like the global companies do a much better job at new product development.
…Likely the global resources. But their sales growth is not stellar. Maybe the product line is below their radar."

"I'd agree with the radar. And they sure do have deep pockets. I'm more concerned about the little guys that seem to beat us to market. What the heck?"

Reg offered, "I'm going to guess that it's because our engineers are fixing problems rather than developing new products."

"And our sales growth is average, while Jemme seems to be great at new product development, and sales growth."

"That's an easy one. Roger, the elder statesmen in the industry, runs his company at his pace. He's an old school engineer, and he believes that new products are the lifeline to business. As an older guy, he tinkers and grows the business through new product development... new products equal sales growth."

"So you say older guy. Did we say that they have sales of less than $10 million?"

"Yes – that's a best guess. And I think he's in his early 70's?"

"Do you think he'd be interested in some kind of JV – or maybe, would he sell out to us? That could be an answer to our being an industry follower... using his creative genius could be very helpful. And – an additional $10 million might get us to the ultimate goal much faster. And the larger companies have excellent NPD, but aren't as good at selling. Would they be willing to sell their orphan products?"

Jackson listed possible acquisition on the flipchart.

"OK – let's get on with the next chart."

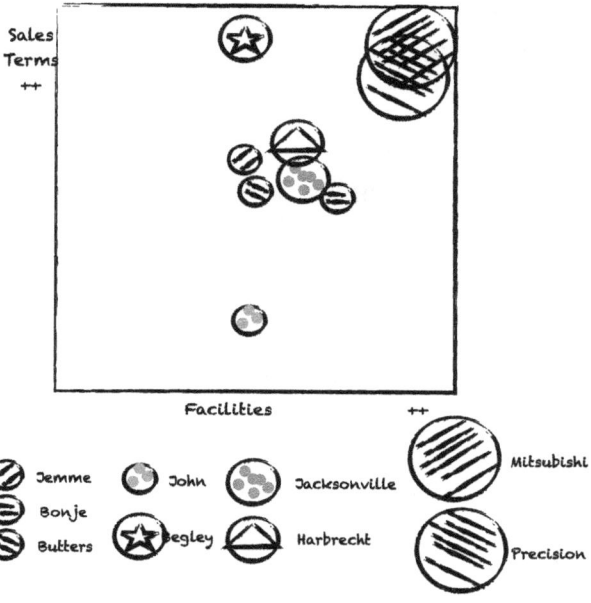

"What's happening in this slide, folks?"

Mitch's head popped up. "Bet there are issues with the Letter of Credit and tight credit terms. Right?"

Jason nodded affirmative.

Bill added, " And some of manufacturing equipment is tired. But I've intentionally kept capital spending low."

John interrupted. "Understood, Bill. And I appreciate your frugal behavior, but my goal is to grow this business at accelerated rates during the next few years, and if we need more advanced equipment, let's get that on the table. If I know what we need, and have a

321

reasonable estimate of the likely return on investment, I can make an informed judgment. For now, I'd just like to have the opportunity of your insight."

Jackson followed John's comment. "Folks, I am extremely pleased with your insight today. Let's keep up the good work."

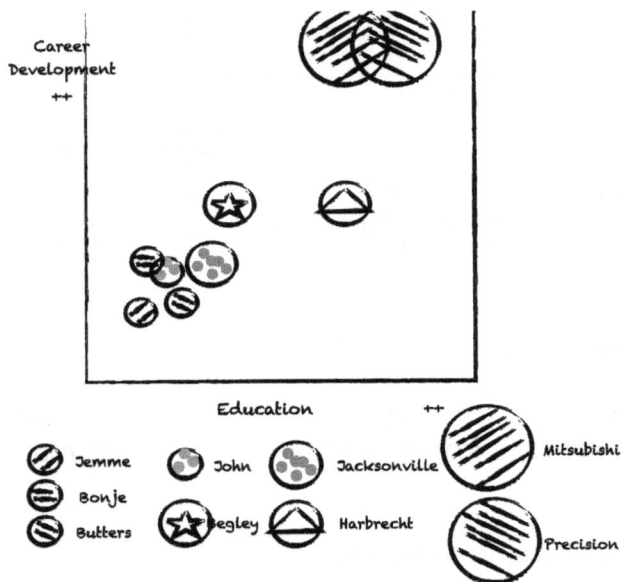

"So now let's look at what I'll call the soft side of the business. I've plotted the 'career development' and 'education' on this chart. Anything strike you?"

Bev was first with an observation. "Sure, the billion dollar companies have great career development opportunities, and they have the money to invest in education."

John observed, "We've been bouncing along the bottom of both career development and education opportunities."

Jackson asked, "Is that good or bad?"

"I'll speak for the R&D shop. Engineers are interested in careers. If I don't have a growth shop for them, it's difficult to get some of the best – even if they are entrepreneurial and want to be in a small company. And as far as education is concerned, if we only have outdated equipment – or to be less negative – not the most current equipment, they train on state of the art equipment in the universities, and move backwards to come here."

"So when we listed education as a weakness, what kind of education were we looking for?"

"In some cases, it's technical – something as basic as Excel or PowerPoint, or maybe the engineers CAD/CAM - but we also need management training so they feel like they are preparing for the future career."

"So let's talk about specific training that would be helpful. Our goal is to brainstorm the list of things, and we can prioritize the list later."

```
9 Excel
10 PowerPoint
8 Presentation skills
7 Sales training
5 Negotiation skills
6 Supervisor skills
1 CAD/CAM
2 Management skills
5 Delegation skills
5.1 How to run a meeting
4 Finance for non-finance
4.1 budgeting 101
3 Sensitivity & politically correctness
```

"That list doesn't seem to be overpowering. Any thoughts?"

Bev suggested, "There doesn't seem to be anything extraordinarily expensive. For example, it's not getting an MBA. I'll do some initial research – but can we rank them right now from most to least important."

Jackson opened the meeting to the ranking, and summarized for Bev. "Here you go, Bev."

"I think that we're pretty well wrapped for the day… and a very successful day it was. Do you want to close the meeting?"

"Yes, I'll do that …"

John concluded the meeting with a brief summary. "Team, this was one helluva day.

I'm amazed at the creativity, the forward vision, and the self-assessments that examined each functional area. I couldn't be happier about the results of the day. Jackson will summarize the meeting and review the commitments with each of you personally, and then we'll get together once more to finalize the plan

Once we've done that, it's up to us to deliver.

Thank you all for your creative approach … your candid assessments … and your feedback about the process and the proposed changes that we are going to make.

Congratulations on a very successful meeting."

With that closing, John moved to a cabinet and removed a box containing small, gift-wrapped packages – each containing a Mont Blanc pen. "Thanks for your help today – a small gift to recognize your creativity and candid assessments of this business. Well done."

Offsite with Patricia

The conference room was set for the team to be comfortable in this first strategic planning meeting. Patricia welcomed Natalie, David Tom and Tonya who arrived about 15 minutes before the scheduled start, not knowing what to expect. The conference table was set with coffee, orange juice and a selection of pastries.

A flipchart and multiple markers were ready for the session.

Jackson was distracted as he linked the computer to the projector.

Once everyone was settled Jackson greeted each person individually.

At 8:00 AM, Patricia moved to the front of the room, opened her arms, smiled and said, "Welcome to our first strategy meeting. I know that you've all had the chance to meet with Jackson, and you may have some notes about things that you'd like to change.

I'm very excited about this opportunity to focus on the future. Jackson told me that he's had an excellent discussion with each of you – so for now, let's go to Jackson."

"Thanks Patricia. These meetings are the highlight of my month. We get the chance to explore ideas and concepts that we may never have considered before. Patricia has assured me that nothing is off the table in this meeting. So let's go. And did I mention that Patricia said that money is no object – she has access to unlimited funds." After a moment's pause, he continued.

"Our agenda will cover about 4-5 hours, depending on how deeply we get into the topics."

He showed the agenda slide.

Introduction	8>00	8:15
Vison/ Mission	8:15	8:45
Framework: People, Process, Plant/ Assets, Product, Market	8:45	9:00
Competition	9:00	
Strengths & Weaknesses		10:00
Break	10:00	10:15
Brainstorming	10:15	12:00

After a brief discussion, he showed a chart. "How does this sales chart look to everyone?"

Sales

	2017	2018	2019	2020	2021	2022
Sales	6.0	6.7	7.3	8.4	9.5	10.5

He left the chart up for a few minutes, and said. "A goal that we've considered reasonable is that sales can increase – and I mean profitably increase – from about $6 million to nearly $10 million during the next few years."

Natalie raised her hand and said, " But that means if we're now pushing through 600 orders a day, we'll need to go to 1,000 a day on average. I don't mean to be negative, but we're struggling to reach the 600 a day average. How will we do that?"

"Great question Natalie. And Patricia and I challenged each other with the same question. Increasing from 600 to 1,000 has several basic assumptions. One assumption is that we will have the same average sale per order. So let's say that today's average is $50/order. What if we were to have $100/order? Would that require nearly doubling the number of orders processed?"

"Absolutely not. But why would people buy in larger quantities?"

"What if we were to have more premium products – e.g. higher priced products - for sale? Would that be reasonable?"

"Yes, but we'd have to find those products and source them. Who would do that?"

"And that's why we're sitting here today.

I wanted to shock you folks with what could look like a very aggressive – maybe even unachievable – goal. But to get to this higher level, we've got to think differently. So as Patricia has said, everything's on the table.

Our current vendor pool could change… our current product line could be upgraded… we could use other methods of distribution. Anyone heard of the internet?"

"But Jackson, we don't have any Internet experts. How can we possibly sell more over the Internet?"

"Get the resource… hire a consultant… train someone inside. You folks are hitting this right on the target. There are many obstacles to this kind of growth. Today, we're going to identify them, and figure out how we can afford to hire resources, or train today's employees to get the job done.

I'm not so negative to say it can't be done. So let's spend some time thinking about how it can be done."

The room fell silent as people tried to understand what Jackson was saying.

Natalie broke the silence.

"So we can brainstorm any ideas to get to those goals? Anything that strikes us? And nobody's going to think we're crazy with imaginative ideas?"

"Correct."

"Well then, what's next?"

Jackson looked at each participant momentarily and when the scan was complete, he said, "Game on?"

With nods of approval, Jackson continued.

Vision/Mission discussion

The first thing I'd like to do is define our mission. Who are we? When I ask that question, let's just toss some words out that describe the Company. With that he uncapped a marker and was ready to start writing on the flip chart.

Who Are We?

small
scrappy | entrepreneurial
innovative | fashion
design based | textile
US based business | leather
ladies accessories | focus on US mdse
men's????? | artisan
soft goods | local
gift wrapped | ethical
custom | friendly
assembler | boutique
shipper | clever brand

Fashion Clicks is a boutique business selling unique, high quality, artisan sourced fashion accessories to men, women and children. The Company sells through traditional brick & mortar boutiques, major retailers and the internet. The Company will deal respectfully with employees, customers and suppliers.

"OK, now we have a rough draft of the Mission/Vision statement. Let me just talk for a few minutes. In this planning effort, we'll talk about People, Processes, Plant/Assets, Product and Market.

Just in general, when I think of people, I'm going to challenge each of us to think about any person, organization, company, agency etc. that we interact with, at any time during the year. And People can be either inside the Company or outside the Company."

Natalie cleared her throat and asked, "Can you be more specific. This is new territory for me."

"Sure thing. When I say people, I want us to challenge how we do business. Let me use an example. Let's say historically we receive two different components from two different companies in Vietnam. Let's say an accent silk scarf, and a matching pattern silk pouch. Sound familiar?

Today, they are both shipped to us separately, and we assemble the two components into a single unit, package the product in a gift-wrap, and send the package to the customer.

In this case, *people* would include each of the outside suppliers. The challenge that I'd like us to think about is perhaps having the items assembled into a single unit in Vietnam by Company A."

"But if you do that, won't we have to lay people off since we won't need the assembly labor."

"Good question, Natalie. Now let me add to the equation that we're going to increase our sales by 30%. Can we increase sales by 30% today?"

"No way."

"So, in this case, we won't need to lay anyone off. In this example, I want us to think about doing things differently so that we can increase sales. In this case, that puts pressure on our selling process. Any ideas how we could increase sales by 30%?"

"Let's add some new products."

"There you go."

"Sell through more distribution channels?"

"Such as?"

"How about expand sales through the internet."

Natalie suggested, "But we don't have any experts in selling on the web."

"So what do you think we need to do."

"Get a web-sales person?"

"But we can't afford a full-time web person."

"So what do you think we do?"

"Hire a part time person?"

"Or maybe hire a one-time consultant to create the system?"

"OK, I think you've got the People concept – inside and outside. Let's shuffle to the Process."

"Didn't you just give us an example of Process? Change how we assemble a product."

"Yes Ma'am. Exactly right. Now here's another question for you. What if we have this great documented process – for example, we clear inbound shipping daily, and get the stock on the shelves."

Again, Natalie offered, "Jackson, you know that orders come in and sometimes they may sit on the dock for days before we can check them and stock the shelves."

"OK. Are we happy with that? Or should we change something?"

"Maybe we could schedule shipments, or better coordinate our activities so that we clear the docks daily with part-timers, or maybe scheduled overtime?"

"Ah yes, a process change."

"Or what if we had the shipper package the products so that they could easily be unloaded, checked in, and properly stocked?"

"Again, a process change that involves *people*. So that could be a twofer – people and process."

Patricia interrupted. "Can you tell us a bit more about plant and assets?"

"Gladly. Now, we all know that I'm brainstorming, and you folks will create the answers, but what if we changed the layout of the warehouse – maybe had all the "A" items closest to the pick line… or maybe added a label printer that would eliminate walking around the facility once an item is picked?

And when we're talking about plant and assets, should we be expanding our trademarking and branding to make the asset more secure?"

Patricia questioned. "Do we have the money necessary to trademark some of these items? Doesn't that cost a lot of money?"

"That's what many people believe, but take a look at the trademark and copyright regs. You don't need to be an attorney to make the filings – just takes a few simple steps, and you establish a reasonable amount of protection. And if you really have a knockout design, you can do the full-Monty, and *register* the trademark, which costs a few dollars more. Check out the patent/trademark site to get a better understanding of the requirements.

So we've covered plant and assets – think differently!

And next, we have Product. Let's think about today. Our products are generally high-quality textiles. If we want to increase sales, are there any other materials that we might use for our accessory products?"

"Leather? Composites or carbon fiber for the high-tech look? Maybe for the outdoor person?"

"Now that's an interesting suggestion. Have we ever considered RFID – Radio Frequency Identification – protection in our products? Or the outdoorsperson. Have there been any changes in the millennial demographic hobbies?"

Patricia, somewhat excited, "And I noticed that in the mission you slipped in men and children that could change our market definition."

"And I thought that I would get away with that. But you're right, Patricia. Again we want to think differently… since that's the easiest way to grow profitably.

Any thought about *market*?"

Natalie offered, "Guessing that by changing the definition of our market, that may open up entirely new segments that can be properly served by our existing processes. Small packages, high-quality product, gift wrapped and sent to our customers."

"Yes ma'am. Right on target. So as we start this brainstorming, let's challenge every element of today's business, with the idea of growing the Company by 40-50% during the next 3-4 years. And when you think about that kind of growth – well, you'll see that we can afford investment that would not be possible growing at 3% a year.

Are we ready to launch this process with a new mindset?"

All nodded affirmative, and Natalie was first to shout, "Let's do this thing."

Jackson projected the rough P&L as a way to frame the future.

	2017	2018	2019	2020	2021	2022
Millions US $						
Inflation		2.0%	2.0%	2.0%	2.0%	2.0%
Price Increases		2.0%	2.0%	2.0%	2.0%	2.0%
Baseline	6.0					
Pricing Impact		6.1	6.2	6.4	6.5	6.6
New products						
Soft Goods		0.6	1.2	1.2	1.8	2.2
New product lines						
Sport			0.3	0.6	1.0	1.5
Hard Goods				0.2	0.2	0.2
	6.0	6.7	7.7	8.4	9.5	10.5
Market channels						
Baseline	6.0	4.5	4.5	4.4	4.3	4.5
Mass Market		1.5	1.0	1.3	1.7	2.0
Web (US)		0.5	1.3	1.9	2.4	2.5
International		0.2	0.5	0.8	1.1	1.5
Total	6.0	6.7	7.7	8.4	9.5	10.5
Geography						
National	6.0	6.5	6.8	7.6	8.4	9.0
International		0.2	0.5	0.8	1.1	1.5
Total	6.0	6.7	7.3	8.4	9.5	10.5
Gross Margin		4.0	4.4	5.0	5.7	6.3
SG&A		3.0	3.3	3.5	3.8	4.2
Pretax		1.0	1.1	1.5	1.9	2.1
Pretax % Sales		15%	15%	18%	20%	20%
GM %		60%	60%	60%	60%	60%
SG&A % Sales		45%	45%	42%	40%	40%

During the next hour each attendee described their responsibility, their organization and some initial thoughts about what would be required to grow by 50%.

Brainstorming

After the functional descriptions, Jackson directed the group to discussing competitors, and Company strengths and weaknesses.

The white board was filled with information:

Strengths/Weaknesses

Too small	new products
E-business	shipping costs
quick decisions	flexibility
No leverage	gift packaging
strong brands	packaging language
brand awareness	promotion within package
limited distribution	affiliations
Few channels	affinity groups
great suppliers	facebook
breadth of line	seasonality
women only	sponsorships
advertising $$	spokesperson
social media	community awareness
order processing	benefits
money to invest	training

"Now we have the master list of strengths and weaknesses. Let's rank the top 5 strengths and weaknesses. Rank #1 as the greatest strength or weakness, and 5 as the lowest."

Using post-its, the team ranked the top 5. Once the ranking was complete, Jackson summarized their rankings, grouping similar items.

Strengths/Weaknesses

Strengths	Weaknesses
	1 Too small
	15 money to invest
	4 No leverage
5 strong brands	14 order processing
6 brand awareness	17 shipping costs
9 great suppliers	PRODUCTS
11 women only	16 new products
3 quick decisions	10 breadth of line
18 flexibility	Marketing
19 gift packaging	7 limited distribution
23 affinity groups	8 Few channels
26 sponsorships	20 packaging language
28 community awareness	21 promotion within package
29 benefits	22 affiliations
	23 affinity groups
	24 facebook
	2 E-business
	12 advertising $$
	13 social media
	27 spokesperson
	25 seasonality
	30 training

Jackson continued, "And who are our competitors?"

Patricia offered, "We've got a few competitors locally. Stores like Nordstrom's and Saks – high end with a broad selection of products."

Dave mentioned, "And there are the craft fairs – some of them have some very nice accessory products."

Competitors

Nordstrom
Macy's
Saks
Express
Urban Outfitters
Dillards
Lord & Taylor
Talbott
Coach   **
Lauren   **
Brooks Brothers **
Collection 18   **
Hobo   **
Kate Spade   **
Marchon   **

"We compete with bricks & mortar, and some of the pop-up shops?" Jackson asked.

Natalie responded, "Well, our real competition is anyone who has high quality accessory product, that understands fashion."

"And are those products generally textiles?"

"Mostly."

"And will our reputation – our brand – carry over to other women's accessory products? Leather, for example? Maybe some wearable technology?"

"For our loyal customers, that shouldn't be a major issue."

"And would our brand extend to accessories for men and children?"

"That could be a bit of a stretch. But if we can get the right designs, and the high quality, why not?"

"What will it take to break through those barriers? Patricia? Natalie? Any thoughts?"

"Design challenges for non-traditional fabrics, and design for men and children."

"What do we need to overcome the hurdle? Should we expand materials for women's accessories first? Especially since we already have their patronage?"

Jackson continued the pursuit of obstacles to expanding the brand to new materials, and the broader market – men and children. During the discussion, he listed all the issues on the whiteboard – some highlighted as major obstacles.

Obstacles

Special mat'l designers
Materials resources
Qualified production sources
Fashion awareness:
  men
  children
Brand build in new segments
Add sales channel/outlets
Social media awareness
Sponsors/sponsorships
Warehouse space
Improve inventory control

After about 30 minutes of rapid brainstorming, he stepped back to observe the board. Now when I look at the board, I see a list of competitor's names – but are some of these also the distribution channel?"

"Yes, the Macy's of the world are a sales channel. The Talbot's are both sales channel and competitors, and the Lauren's are pure competitors."

So what do we do next? Are we really trying to compete with specific brands – like 'Kate Spade' – to enhance our reputation, and get distribution as a result of brand recognition?"

Patricia said, "That will work. And it seems to be the most effective way to grow. And if we build our reputation – PR, high quality, unique designs – we have a better chance of getting into the major retail channels."

"So let's talk about PR and our reputation."

Jackson facilitated the discussion about market presence, group affiliations and linkages within the existing and expanded target audience. As he discussed the market opportunities, he listed ways to gain market awareness, expand the product line to men and children, and broaden distribution. The list included specific activities, possible costs and timelines that would get them to the $10 million goal.

Fashion Clicks Open Items

		2019				2020	2021
		Q1	Q2	Q3	Q4		
Compensation							
Develop executive performance program	Patricia		X				
Assess long term incentive program	Patricia			X			
Develop a profit sharing program	Patricia			X			
Evaluate current benefits programs considering 'millenial' input	Patricia			X			
Identify training courses for supervisors & managers	Patricia		X				
Complete an organization assessment	Patricia		X				
Update job descriptions	Patricia	X					
Review compensation	Patricia			X			
Identify and engage web expert to improve selling, sourcing, research capabilities	Patricia		X				
Update website to improve sales & attract talent	Patricia				X		
Identify and engage a branding resource	Patricia			X			
Equipment Llist							
Laser printers	Dave	X					
Work table mods	Dave	X					
Flow racks	Dave	X					
Review & reorganize warehouse & pick system	Dave		X				
Products - target quarterly NPD launch		X	X	X	X	X	X
Women	Natalie						
Textile-Fashion	Natalie						
Evaluate Textile-Sport Line	Natalie	X					
Evaluate Leather Line	Natalie	X					
Evaluate Technology Line	Natalie		X				
Children - Evaluate Potential Market	Natalie		X				
Textile-Fashion	Natalie						
Textile-Sport	Natalie						
Technology	Natalie						
Men - Evaluate Potential Market	Natalie			X			
Textile-Fashion	Natalie						
Textile-Sport	Natalie						
Leather	Natalie						
Technology	Natalie						
Web focus							
Facebook	Dave	X					
Linkedin	Tonya	X					
YouTube	Dave	X					
Instagram	Tom						
Other	Tom						
PARKING LOT							
Product videos							
Celebrity endorsements							
Trade shows							
Interns							
Working moms: Part-time & seasonal help							
Office/warehouse space review							

Once the draft matrix was developed, Jackson encouraged them, "Folks, we know that this isn't complete, but we've developed a process that will help us think through the best way to approach the market. So, when we look at this matrix, we see product line expansion, rolled out over the next 12-18 months. Nervous Natalie?" Jackson smiled broadly while glancing at both Natalie and Patricia.

"And Natalie, every one of those $ indicates a new product launch. So during the next few years, we'll need – what is it 25+- new products, including the new categories? Excited?" Jackson paused for effect.

"Then we look at the Public Relations affiliations. As we talked, I've dropped names into the slots. The assignments could all be wrong, but we've developed a process to attack the opportunities.

So when we actually get into these PR activities, let's estimate the time required to manage them. So for example, if we are sponsoring an event, it will take more time than if we are just attending a monthly meeting.

 I've put a lot of information on the board. Any comments?"

Natalie politely raised her hand. "That's a lot of new product innovation. Will we be hiring two new people to accomplish those intros?"

"So what do you think? In our earlier discussions we determined that you discovered many of the new products. Patricia – any thoughts?"

"Sure thing. Natalie, you're the new product development engine. We're going to do some reorganizing, and get you some time to dedicate to new product research. When Jackson and I talked about our goals – growing to $10 million – it was clear that new products were the key. New products are a combination of activities. We have to find the product, understand the materials and production process, design the product and then find a source to produce the product."

Jackson interrupted. "It's even more complicated. If we only use foreign sources for production, we'll need to build in a 90-day sourcing pipeline, which means a lot of inventory on the water. And what happens if the product is a bust? We have a financial mess. Whew."

Jackson paused to let the team think about the challenges. She continued.

"How do we resolve that? Find a local source, do some smaller pilot runs so that we understand market acceptance, and if it looks like a great product, outsource to a less expensive vendor. That means we need to identify local sources along with foreign sources.

As we thought about that, it seems that we might need Dave to help Natalie research and source vendors."

Dave's head popped up from his note pad. "And how will I have the time for that, considering the production operation that I'm now working?"

"Trickle down, Dave. Earlier I said reorganize the operation. That means we'll evaluate everyone's responsibilities, evaluate and delegate down through the organization."

Jackson interrupted. "And we're not going to accomplish all that today. Patricia will have that assignment to complete within the next 2 weeks. Right Patricia?"

As she was laughing, Patricia responded, "C'mon, Jackson. I'm the boss – you can't keep me on that tight timeline."

Jackson scanned the room. "The beauty of the plan is that we know where we're going - $10 million annual sales – and we know the challenges that we need to overcome to get there. When we're done with the plan, we'll each have specific tasks to complete."

Natalie looked directly at Patricia. "So, I'm critical to the success of the strategy?"

Patricia knew the reason for Natalie's question. "Yes, Natalie. And when we look at the goals, it won't just be the jobs that we do that will change, but we're going to evaluate each role and align the compensation to the new responsibilities. And in some cases, we need to provide some additional training to make sure that each of us has the tools necessary to do an A+ job."

Natalie was wistfully doodling *DAP* in her notebook.

Jackson continued. "So we've covered People, Process, Product and Market, but haven't touched Plant/Assets. Any thoughts?"

"We'll never push $10 million through this operation. Too small."

"That could be right, Dave. But let's back up a bit. We can change anything we like. So maybe we'll move to another facility... could be. But what if we changed the production and shipping process? Perhaps outsource some of the packaging work... maybe get some additional equipment and change the way that we process orders.

Look, we're not going to identify all the issues during this plan session, but if we see the obstacles soon enough, we can adjust our business to achieve the goals.

And that's why we're meeting as a team today. What are the issues?"

Jackson started a listing on the board.

Tonya shouted, "M-O-N-E-Y. We don't have a lot of resources, Jackson."

"Agreed. But rather than say we can't move forward, let's make a list of all the spending required to reach $10 million."

Jackson listed all the comments on the board.

Wish List

Flow racks	space
fork lift	videos
laser printers	compensation
shrink wrap equip	connections
mods to work tables	LInkedin
linkage to FedEx,	facebook
UPS, USPS	instagram
Delivery van	celebrity endorsements
billing software	affiliations
constant contact	association dues
more headcount	trade shows
local sourcing	PR spending
t&e	sales reps
web expert	distributors
redesign website	
training	

"OK, now we have a complete list of the wish list. So let's do all of these in the next 6 months."

Patricia's head immediately popped up from her notes. "Hold on Jackson. Far too many activities and won't that cost a lot of money?"

"Great observation. So what should we do with this initial list?"

Natalie suggested, "Maybe we should prioritize those things that will help us most during the next year. "

"Great idea. So, team, you've all got a pad of post-its. Let's take 10 minutes and think about what we need most. Pick the top 3 things that you think we should do this year. No constraints – if we need it, Patricia can afford it."

Patricia silently grimaced

After a few minutes contemplation, the team ranked those items considered a priority as 1-2-3.

Jackson grabbed a marker, and summarized 7 items on the right side of the board. "Looks like we have three groups of activities. New Products, operational improvements, and E-business. Any thoughts about how we can make that happen?"

Wish List

Flow racks	space	Priorities in the next year!!!
fork lift	videos	
laser printers	compensation	1. New Products
shrink wrap equip	connections	2. training
mods to work tables	LInkedin	3. laser printers
linkage to FedEx, UPS, USPS	facebook	4. work table mods
Delivery van	instagram	5. flow racks
billing software	celebrity endorsements	6. web design & billing
constant contact	affiliations	7. social media
more headcount	association dues	
local sourcing	trade shows	
t&e	PR spending	
web expert	sales reps	
redesign website	distributors	
training		

Natalie enthusiastically answered, "Sign me up for some new products. But I'll have to shift some of my daily work down through the organization."

Dave offered, "Hey Natalie, I can pick up some of your duties if you can give me a bit of training. And I'll push some of my work down through the organization. I think a couple of the workers would like to learn some new skills.

And I might even be able to figure out some improvements in the ops – where to put the new laser printers, and maybe get some info about how to redesign the workflow."

"Sounds good. So all that's left is the "E" part of our business. Any thoughts?"

Tonya said, "We're all a bit Internet savvy. How can we all contribute to that effort? I don't know web design, but between Xavier University and University of Cincinnati we may be able to get some interns into the mix. If you like I can do some research."

Patricia smiled. So out of – what is it, 30 hot items - we're going to focus on 7 and make the business better? And if I were to guess, we're talking about less than – let's say $12,000 - to kick this business up a notch. Whattayathink folks?"

Smiles all around. The team focused their energy on solutions to improve the business, listed specific actions to complete, and each accepted responsibility to complete the task.

"OK team," Jackson continued, "I'll put this together this evening, and send a draft summary to you for your review. Once we finalize with your comments, it's up to you. Comments?"

After some brief discussion, Jackson adjourned the meeting.

The Three Amigos #4

The First Watch Restaurant was unusually quiet this morning as the three owners met.

John was first to speak. "Well Doug, how have you been? It's been nearly a month since our last meeting."

"It's been a very good month. Business is up by 3% compared to last year. How about you, John?"

"We're up about the same, but looking forward to some serious growth during the next few years."

"Wish-list from the strategic planning meetings?"

"I'll call it planning for the future. Let's grab a booth – you OK with that Patricia?"

"Sure, let's get one in the back where we can talk about business without prying ears."

The trio was silent as they moved to the back of the restaurant. As they settled into the booth, the server brought a carafe' of coffee and menus.

As the server started to leave, Doug suggested that they were ready to order, as this was a restaurant they visited frequently. Orders placed, they started to discuss business.

"So you sound very upbeat, John. Have you been drinking the strategic planning Kool-Aid?"

"Yes and it's delicious. I'm kind of enjoying your jabs, Doug. We've learned a lot in the past weeks. Said another way, I'm amazed at what we've been leaving on the table every year. And I don't mean spending a lot of money to execute a strategic plan."

Patricia added, "The Kool-Aid is just fine. I'm amazed at what I've learned during the few sessions that we've had so far."

"So talk to me… my guess is that Jackson asks a lot of questions, and prepares some great PowerPoint's. Consultants do that kind of thing."

Dave responded, "You're right about the questions. Many questions – about things that I've never considered. The first thing we did was frame the business into its basic elements – People, Process, Plant/Assets, Product and Market – and we launched planning from there.

Before Jackson asked the questions, I never considered the basic elements separately. I always just thought about the business. When we broke it down to the elements, and analyzed how things work in our competitive environment, we discovered how to improve the business, and plan for rapid growth.

Everyone has tasks to do that will make us a better Company."

Patricia added, "Ditto. I'm a small Company and before Jackson, I concentrated on serving the customers as the number 1 priority. Customers are still at the top of my priorities, but now I've also focused on new product development as a key to my future growth.

When we thought about the Company's growth goals, it was very clear that new products were the key. Jackson's questions got me to think about sourcing today and the future. When we thought about new products, he pushed me beyond what we do today – where we package products – to one where we don't always think of products that way. In the future, we may acquire products fully assembled. We challenged how we think."

"And let me add to that, Patricia. Jackson pushed me to think about today's business. Historically we've been satisfied with average performance. Virtually all my metrics were at industry standards, and average doesn't cut it. When we re-examined our processes, we literally found bags of money.

We've taken the leaders in each functional area and identified tasks that they can do to make us a more valuable Company. Things like scrap and rework are easy marks. And when we looked at New Product Development – well, we're going to change the process to launch up to 3 new products a year, instead of a weak single launch each year. And when we launch, it won't be an *average* launch, but one that is 1st class – one without glitches."

Doug was startled with their enthusiasm. "Whoa folks. These sound like exciting activities, but how much is it costing you to do them. I mean, you must really be spending some money to get that kind of improvement."

John smiled and leaned back in his chair. "Virtually no incremental net spending. With the process improvements, we expect projects to be self-funding initially, and then increase earnings, while also investing in future growth. It's really some kind of alchemy."

"I hate to say it, John, but Ditto. We're looking at almost unimaginable change using the people in the organization. We just have to think differently, and discard the non value-added activity. Have you heard of *Lean Business*, Doug?"

"Sure thing, but we are loyal to our employees. We've had a no-layoff policy for decades."

"Common misconception, Doug. Lean doesn't necessarily mean layoffs. It means getting rid of non-value activities. When we get rid of the non-value added, we dedicate the resource to growth. Hey, that's enough about hard business topics. Did you see that the Reds picked up a new pitcher?"

Once John changed topics the conversation lightened to baseball and international trade.

John Davidson Strategic Plan

John Davidson Co.

Executive Summary

The John Davidson Co. was originally established in 1998 as Metal FABS INC., a regional metal fabricator. During the past 20 years, the Company was acquired by John Davidson, renamed as The John Davidson Co. and reoriented to precision casting and premium value added metal fabrication.

During the past 5 years the Company has expanded distribution globally. This strategic plan will refocus the Company's resources exclusively on precision cast parts and high value-add metal fabrication, and trim product offerings by reducing electrical and chemical product lines.

Vision/Mission

John Davidson Co. is a highly ethical, industrial products Company that develops, manufactures and distributes complex, highly engineered and premium value, metal fabricated parts and castings serving the global markets. The Company will treat employees, suppliers and customers with respect. Our business will grow organically, and through acquisition, licensing, and joint ventures.

| Description | 2017 | 2018 | Plan | | | | | | |
| John Davidson | (Act) | (Est.) | 2019 | | | | Tot | 2020 | 2021 |
Total Company			1st	2nd	3rd	4th	Year		
Capital Spending	500.0	450.0	250.0	400.0	300.0	250.0	1,200.0	1,500.0	1,500.0
Number of New Products				1	1	2	4	6	6
New Product Sales							2,000	3,500	6,500
Variances as % of Sales	0.6%	2.0%	2.0%	2.0%	1.5%	1.5%	n/a	1.2%	1.2%
US New Customer Sales (000's)							2,000	4,000	5,000
# of Apprentices in training	n/a	n/a	1	3	5	6		12	15
Headcount	350	400	400	400	400	400	n/a	450	500
(000's US $)									
Revenue	27,770.0	29,960.0	7,500.0	8,500.0	9,000.0	9,800.0	34,800.0	41,300.0	50,020.0
Gross Profit	10,799.8	13,088.5	3,100.0	3,950.0	3,950.0	4,080.0	15,080.0	18,835.0	22,943.0
GP %	38.9%	43.7%	41.3%	46.5%	43.9%	41.6%	43.3%	45.6%	45.9%
SG&A	8,608.7	10,183.0	2,400.0	2,900.0	3,100.0	3,370.0	11,770.0	14,600.0	17,806.0
Profit Before Tax	2,191.1	2,905.5	700.0	1,050.0	850.0	710.0	3,310.0	4,235.0	5,137.0
PBT % Sales	7.9%	9.7%	9.3%	12.4%	9.4%	7.2%	9.5%	10.3%	10.3%
DSO	62	64	63	61	59	54	58	50	50
Inventory Turns	2.0	2.2	2.2	2.4	2.5	2.7	2.8	3.5	3.5

Key Programs

Keys to this strategic plan will be to accelerate successful new product launches, expand international sales, and improve manufacturing productivity. This will be completed by:
- Revise New Product Development processes, working with key functional areas - R&D, Sales, Marketing, Manufacturing and Finance.
- Reorganize sales operations to focus on growth of new "A" customers, while retaining existing customers.
- Review and modify the entire marketing mix to improve awareness of the Company in all channels.
- Expand international sales to new global operations through deeper penetration of major global companies, and greater sales to countries where we do not have sales today.
- Review manufacturing processes to reduce variances and scrap as % of sales.

Description	2017	2018	Plan							
Vito	(Act)	(Est.)	2019				Tot	2020	2021
International			1st	2nd	3rd	4th	Year		
Number of New Customers	1	1					2	4	5
(000's US $)									
Revenue	2,955.0	5,915.0	1,400.0	1,600.0	1,800.0	2,000.0	6,800	8,100.0	9,720.0
Gross Profit	1,625.0	3,549.0	840.0	960.0	1,080.0	1,200.0	4,080	4,860.0	5,832.0
GP %	55.0%	60.0%	60.0%	60.0%	60.0%	60.0%	60.0%	60.0%	60.0%
Direct Expense	200.0	250.0	150.0	150.0	200.0	200.0	700.0	750.0	750.0
Contribution Margin	1,425.0	3,299.0	690.0	810.0	880.0	1,000.0	3,380.0	4,110.0	5,082.0
DSO	65	65	63	63	60	60	60	55	55

Key Programs

International will be a growth engine for the Company through three main programs:
- Further penetration of existing global customers.
- New global customers, concentrating in existing countries.
- Expanded distribution to new countries using US Commercial Services resources.

NOTE: Incremental direct spending will increase by $50k/quarter in the first 2 quarters of 2019 to develop new markets. Additional direct spending will occur as sales goals are achieved. Provided the goals are achieved in the first 3 quarters, the Company will hire an additional sales resource in Q4.

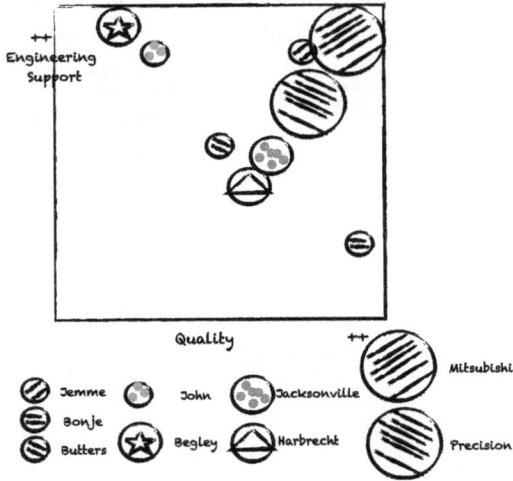

362

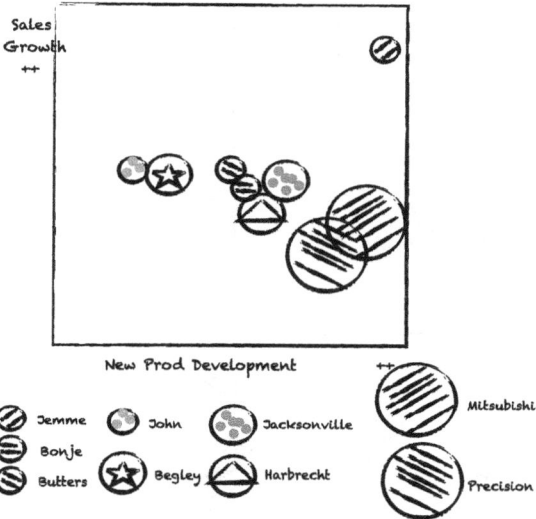

Sales Growth ++

New Prod Development ++

Legend:
- Jemme
- Bonje
- Butters
- John
- Begley
- Jacksonville
- Harbrecht
- Mitsubishi
- Precision

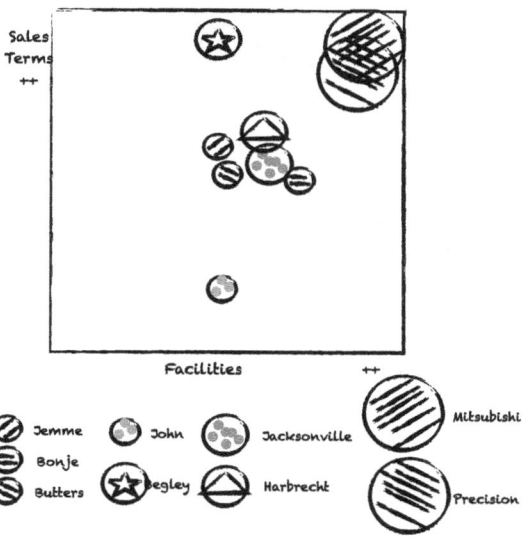

Sales Terms ++

Facilities ++

Legend:
- Jemme
- Bonje
- Butters
- John
- Begley
- Jacksonville
- Harbrecht
- Mitsubishi
- Precision

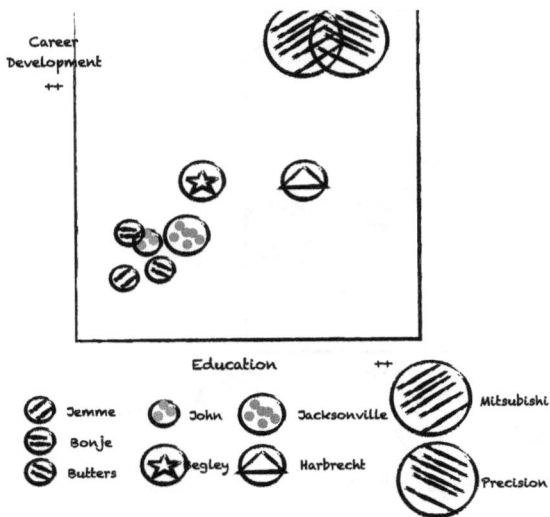

Career Development ++ / Education ++

Jemme
Bonje
Butters
John
Begley
Jacksonville
Harbrecht
Mitsubishi
Precision

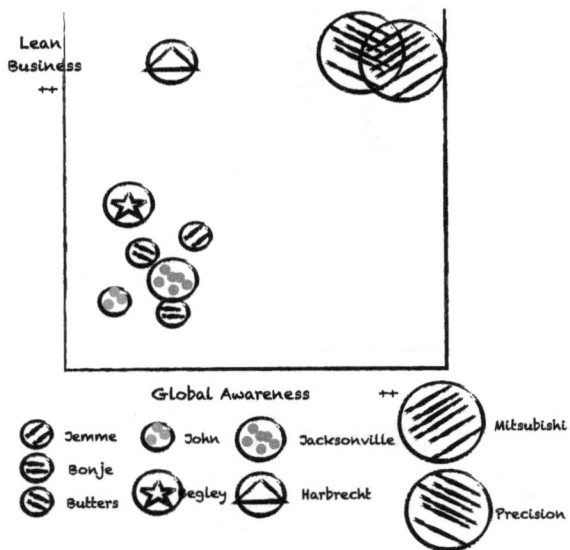

Lean Business ++ / Global Awareness ++

Jemme
Bonje
Butters
John
Begley
Jacksonville
Harbrecht
Mitsubishi
Precision

John Donaldson Co.

	Resp	2019				2020	2021	Est. Cost	
		Q1	Q2	Q3	Q4			Exp	Capex
								(000's $)	
Engage lean business consultant	Bill	X							
High-low mfg. standards review (top 50% of production)	Bill	X	X	X					
Review & change Purchase Price methodology	Bill		X	X					
Root cause analysis of scrap	Bill		X						
Engineering focus - cost reduction	Bill			X	X				
Production assessment - make vs. buy	Bill				X	X			
Inventory & logistics review	Bill					X			
Implement new sales call & management plan	Jason	X							
Western territory analysis	Jason		X						
Sales force evaluation	Jason			X					
Website upgrade	Jason					X			
International market research & market assessment	Vito			X					
Website upgrade for international	Vito				X				
Assess the need for translation of collateral material	Vito				X				
Add business development exec	Vito			X					
Expand tradeshow from 3/year to 4/year	Vito					X			
Establish a marketing intelligence committee	Janice	X							
Develop a company pricing strategy	Janice			X					
Develop a competitive intelligence process	Janice	X							
Develop an overall market strategy	Janice				X				
Improve basic finance procedures	Mitch								
- A/R detail & balancing	Mitch								
- Inventory reconciliation & routine procedures	Mitch	X							
- Expand manufacturing accounting analysis	Mitch	X							
- Review IT infrastructure & eliminate routine tech problems	Mitch		X						
Strategic imperatives	Mitch								
- Pricing analysis & strategy	Mitch			X					
- Product line profitability analysis	Mitch			X					
- Trade channel profitability analysis	Mitch			X					
- Implement formal forecasting process	Mitch		X						
- Implement improved budgeting process	Mitch			X					
Establish new product committee	Reg	X							
Develop NPD process	Reg			X	X				
Complete engineering time study	Reg	X							
Launch new products quarterly	Reg		X	X	X	X			
Workforce comp & benefits review	Bev	X							
Executive comp review	Bev			X					
Upgrade performance review process	Bev		X						
Conduct employee satisfaction survey	Bev	X							
Establish training & apprentice programs	Bev		X						
Establish community service & contribution committee	Bev		X						

Fashion Clicks Strategic Plan

Fashion Clicks

Executive Summary

Fashion Clicks started as a business in Patricia Sammons living room in 2011. This solo hobby with sales of several hundred thousand dollars developed into a fast growth Company fashion accessory business with annual sales of more than $6 million, employing nearly 3-dozen people who design, source and distribute products generally within a few hundred miles of its warehouse. The business recently started distribution using the Web, and expects rapid growth through expanded distribution.

Mission

Research, develop and source high-quality fashion accessories for women, men, and children. We will continue to serve the boutique retail segment, and expand sales to major retail outlets, and on the web. Our business will maintain the highest ethical standards when dealing with employees, customers, and suppliers. The business will grow through aggressive new product development.

Description Patricia Knudsen Total Company	2017 (Act)	2018 (Est.)	Plan						
			2019				Tot Year	2020	2021
			1st	2nd	3rd	4th			
Number of New Products	1	2	-	1	1	2	4	5	6
New Product Sales		0.3	-	-	0.3	0.5	0.8	0.8	1,200
Website Transactions (000's)		1.5	1.5	2.5	3.0	5.0	12.0	25.0	50.0
Average Order Size ($)	60	60					85	100	125
Headcount	n/a	n/a							
(000's US $)									
Revenue	6,000.0	6,700.0	1,600.0	2,100.0	1,700.0	1,900.0	7,300.0	8,400.0	9,500.0
Gross Profit	3,800.0	4,000.0	950.0	1,200.0	1,000.0	1,250.0	4,400.0	5,000.0	5,700.0
GP %	63.3%	59.7%	59.4%	57.1%	58.8%	65.8%	60.3%	59.5%	60.0%
SG&A	2,500.0	2,700.0	550.0	750.0	650.0	850.0	2,800.0	2,800.0	2,900.0
Profit Before Tax	1,300.0	1,300.0	400.0	450.0	350.0	400.0	1,600.0	2,200.0	2,800.0
PBT % Sales	21.7%	19.4%	25.0%	21.4%	20.6%	21.1%	21.9%	26.2%	29.5%
DSO	65	60	55	53	50	45	45	45	45
Inventory Turns	2.5	2.2	2.2	2.4	2.6	3.0	3.0	3.5	3.5

Key Programs

Keys to this strategic plan will be to accelerate successful new product launches, expand web sales, and upgrade the Company's culture. Specifically:
- Launch accessory products for Men (Q1-2020) and Children (Q3-2019)
- Launch new materials:
  - Leather (Q4-2019)
  - Tech Line (Q2-2020)
- Launch a sport line (Q3-2019)
- Develop a brand identity known worldwide (Q3-2019)
- Relaunch website to expand the internet sales channel (Q3-2019)

Fashion Clicks Open Items

		2019				2020	2021
		Q1	Q2	Q3	Q4		
Compensation							
Develop executive performance program	Patricia		X				
Assess long term incentive program	Patricia				X		
Develop a profit sharing program	Patricia				X		
Evaluate current benefits programs considering 'millenial' input	Patricia			X			
Identify training courses for supervisors & managers	Patricia		X				
Complete an organization assessment	Patricia		X				
Update job descriptions	Patricia	X					
Review compensation	Patricia			X			
Identify and engage web expert to improve selling, sourcing, research capabilities	Patricia		X				
Update website to improve sales & attract talent	Patricia				X		
Identify and engage a branding resource	Patricia			X			
Equipment List							
Laser printers	Dave	X					
Work table mods	Dave	X					
Flow racks	Dave	X					
Review & reorganize warehouse & pick system	Dave		X				
Products - target quarterly NPD launch		X	X	X	X	X	X
Women							
Textile-Fashion	Natalie						
Evaluate Textile-Sport Line	Natalie	X					
Evaluate Leather Line	Natalie	X					
Evaluate Technology Line	Natalie		X				
Children - Evaluate Potential Market	Natalie		X				
Textile-Fashion	Natalie						
Textile-Sport	Natalie						
Technology	Natalie						
Men - Evaluate Potential Market	Natalie			X			
Textile-Fashion	Natalie						
Textile-Sport	Natalie						
Leather	Natalie						
Technology	Natalie						
Web focus							
Facebook	Dave	X					
Linkedin	Tonya	X					
YouTube	Dave	X					
Instagram	Tom						
Other	Tom						
PARKING LOT							
Product videos							
Celebrity endorsements							
Trade shows							
Interns							
Working moms: Part-time & seasonal help							
Office/warehouse space review							

2019 – Three Amigos

John, Doug and Patricia continued their monthly meeting and agreed that they would not discuss strategic planning until the one-year anniversary. Doug reminded them that October was the 1-year anniversary of their first strategic plan.

Rather than just have a general discussion of their Company's results, he suggested that they each report how well their respective Company's performed during the past 12 months. They agreed to an optional template that highlighted the year's performance.

Doug was first to discuss the Company's results. "You know, '18 wasn't the greatest year, but we managed to bounce back a bit in '19. Several things happened during the year that somewhat surprised me. We had some unplanned replacement capital spending – nearly $1 million of machinery in the factory needed immediate replacement. It seems that the department manager's let the routine maintenance go on a few of the automated machines, and the machines crashed during peak season.

It was a real mess. That also hit our sales, and the customers were really angry –we lost several of our major customers. To avoid even more losses, we had to concede pricing adjustments to a few of the majors. That cost us a few million dollars of Gross Margin. Given those losses, we recovered very well, and were only about $1.6 million short of budget. The team did an extraordinary job of recovery.

Unfortunately, I had to demote several managers who had been with us a long time. Broke my heart, but they just didn't deliver.

John, how was your year? If I remember correctly, you had some very aggressive plans.

(000's $)	2017	2018	2019 Amt	2019 Fav (Unf) Bud/Strat Amt	%
Headcount					
# New Products	1	0	2	(2.0)	-2
Capital Spending	1,500.0	1,000.0	2,500.0	(750.0)	
DSO	67	64	68	(8.0)	
Inventory Turns	3.2	3.0	2.9	(1.0)	
% Return on Equity	5.9%	4.7%	4.0%		
Sales	91,000.0	90,000.0	91,500.0	(1,500.0)	
Gross Margin	41,000.0	40,000.0	39,900.0	(2,000.0)	
Margin %					
SG&A	13,200.0	14,100.0	14,500.0	350.0	
Pretax Profit	27,800.0	25,900.0	25,400.0	(1,650.0)	
Pretax % Sales					

Comments:

"Sorry to hear about your misses compared to the annual plan. We had a decent year. You'll recall that we concentrated on several areas to improve performance – quality, new product development, closer sales management, and management incentives and a few other areas.

While we barely exceeded our sales budget, sales increased a bit more than 15% over 2018. The keys on that – new product development and a better launch process, aggressive sales management and sharing the wealth.

During the past few years, I became complacent, and the strategic plan gave me the insight to open up to more modern management methods. By engaging the entire senior management team, we identified activities that we could do to improve the business without a lot of incremental spending. And when I say incremental spending, it was a combination of spending offset by true savings in the Company.

First of all, we streamlined the new product development process and fully engaged executives in sales, marketing, manufacturing, R&D and finance."

"Whoa, John. That sounds like an administrative boondoggle. How could you get anything done with such a diverse group?"

"Jackson aligned us to a common goal – profitable growth that we all bought into. Once we had a common goal, we worked together rather than in silos. In previous years, we were lucky to get one new product out the door. In 2019, we actually launched 3 new products – one short of plan.

Bill, the manufacturing VP completely changed his stripes. He virtually demanded improved reporting from the CFO. Once they started digging into the numbers, we identified the root cause of manufacturing failures, and scrap and rework are down by more than 50%. So my costs went down, but better yet, my customers were happier getting 1st quality products nearly every time.

And each executive had performance goals for their function that contributed to the success of the Company. For example, can you believe that Mitch, the CFO, volunteered to prepare come competitor analysis using the bean-counters analytical skillset?

Mitch really surprised me when he worked with the sales and manufacturing folks to improve the financial reporting. And he also ventured outside his historical boundaries and started insuring some of our foreign receivables – moved away from the Letter of Credit only to make us more competitive on the global scale.

And speaking of global, Vito was on fire. He met with the US Department of Commerce, and launched some analysis, defined a marketing program to enter some untouched countries, and voila, as Vito would say, sales increased.

Vito is on the way to increasing sales from the 2018 base by 50%.

You know, when I was putting this summary together, I was trying to figure out how we achieved so much. I think the answer was simple. I asked the team for their insight into the business, and from a planning point of view, removed all constraints. The magic happened.

One major cultural change for us was quarterly meetings to refocus on our objectives. In the past, the brief monthly meetings concentrated on day-to-day activities, and we never considered our long-term strategy. We still have the monthly meetings – better focused than before – but now, each executive knows they will report against their quarterly objectives every 90 days. Knowing that the team relied on their performance, each exec made sure that they got the tasks done.

Ninety days is a great time frame. It allows the execs to manage the daily requirements, and also fit the quarterly deliverables into the mix.

I don't want to paint too rosy a picture. We missed our budget targets in several areas. We spent about $150k more than budgeted for an opportunity; headcount was over budget by 5 heads, and my DSO only decreased by 9 days instead of the planned 10 days. Inventory turns were at budget – an improvement of nearly 50% over 2018, and between the DSO improvement and inventory turn improvement, overall borrowing declined from 2018.

While we increased SG&A spending by about $1.5 million dollars, we paced the increase so that we would always hit the profit targets.

Doug, I think it's fair to say, I couldn't be happier, and I think that the 2021 strategic goals are possible."

Throughout John's discussion, Doug remained silent. Begrudgingly he said, "Sounds like you had a good year, John. Patricia, how'd you do this year?"

				John			
(000's $)	2017	2018	2019 Amt	2019 Fav (Unf) Bud/Strat			
				Amt	%	%	
Headcount	350	400	405	-5			
# New Products			3	-1			
Capital Spending	500.0	450.0	1,200.0	(150.0)			
DSO	62	64	55	-1			
Inventory Turns	2.0	2.2	3.0	n/a			
% Return on Equity	11.0%	15.0%	21.0%	-2%			
Sales	27,770.0	29,960.0	34,550.0	250.0			
Gross Margin	10,799.8	13,088.5	15,150.0	(70.0)			
Margin %	38.9%	43.7%	43.8%	n/a			
SG&A	8,608.7	10,183.0	11,650.0	120.0			
Pretax Profit	2,191.1	2,905.5	3,500.0	50			
Pretax % Sales	7.9%	9.7%	10.1%	n/a			

Comments:

"Well, I don't have such outstanding results, but the strategic plan helped me focus on some critical changes, and we're well down the path to our 2021 goal.

We reorganized our workforce so that we could get more new products – promoted Natalie and focused her on new product development. We successfully launched 4 new products last year."

Doug seemed surprised. "But isn't that huge compared to prior years?"

"Yes, but they weren't launched on time. One was late in the season, so we only increased sales by about 9% compared to 2018. But since we launched 4 new products, our margins increased by 10% - NPD has a great impact on Gross Margins.

We were able to increase our average order size by more than 20% due to the newer premium products, so my shipping volume didn't stress us too much. I'm not sure if you remember, but we also planned to invest in website and web selling. By reviewing our organization, hiring interns and sourcing some web-based consultants, we were able to keep SG&A under tight control. It was a surprise how much talent we have internally when presented with a challenge.

When I saw the increased productivity, I couldn't resist providing some financial incentives to the team, and with the higher gross margins, it was easily affordable.

Profits were up nearly 25% over 2018. I don't have nearly the great performance as John, but we're early in our culture change.

Doug, while I missed some of my goals this year, I couldn't be happier about the transformation of the business. I'm optimistic that we can hit the $10 million of profitable sales within the next two years. A year ago, I questioned my common sense, actually believing that I could increase profitable sales by 50% in a three-year period. But we're going to do it."

While Doug was impressed with their results, his compliments were shallow and somewhat insincere. It seemed that he was questioning his judgment to dismiss strategic planning so quickly a year ago.

	Patricia				
(000's $)	**2017**	**2018**	**2019 Amt**	**2019 Fav (Unf) Bud/Strat**	
				Amt	**%**
# of New Products	1	2	4		
New Product 000 $		0.3	0.8		
Web Trans (000's)		1.5	12		
Avg Order Size ($)	60.0	60.0	85.0		
Headcount					
(000's US $)					
Revenue	6,000.0	6,700.0	7,300.0		
Gross Profit	3,800.0	4,000.0	4,400.0		
GP %					
SG&A	2,500.0	2,700.0	2,800.0	0	
Profit Before Tax	1,300.0	1,300.0	1,600.0		
PBT % Sales					
DSO	60	45	45		
Inventory Turns	2.2	3.0	3.5		

2020 – Three Amigos

On the one-year anniversary the 'Three Amigos' again met to review the results.

Again, Doug led the discussion, presenting his Company's results.

"Well, we survived another year. While we beat last year's results, why does it seem that the years are getting tougher?

Sales were up by about 2% - we expected this year would be minimal growth. And we were able to maintain profitability – but a bit below 2019. When I talked with the team, it seems that I need to invest more in NPD. With our existing older product lines, I can't get the historical premium pricing. That forced me to provide some extended terms to remain competitive, but we still managed to achieve profitability of about 25% of sales.

Inventories were up and DSO were up, so we cut back in capital spending and SG&A. We're developing some short term fixes to get back on track.

So while it wasn't a stellar year, banking more than $25 million feels pretty good. John, what's your year look like?"

(000's $)	2018	2019	Doug 2020 Amt	2019 Fav (Unf) Bud/Strat Amt	%
Headcount					
# New Products					
Capital Spending	1,000.0	2,500.0	950.0		
DSO	64	68	75		
Inventory Turns	3.0	2.9	2.5		
% Return on Equity	4.7%	4.0%	3.6%		
Sales	90,000.0	91,500.0	93,500.0		
Gross Margin	40,000.0	39,900.0	38,500.0		
Margin %	44.4%	43.6%	41.2%		
SG&A	14,100.0	14,500.0	13,900.0		
Pretax Profit	25,900.0	25,400.0	24,600.0	-	
Pretax % Sales	28.8%	27.8%	26.3%		

Comments:

"This year was a good year, Doug. Sales were up by nearly 28% due to accelerated new product introductions. Those new products carried some great margins, and this year we were first to market with two of our products. During the year we successfully launched 6 new products – right on budget. I was amazed at how the team worked together to get them out the door. And we also acquired several orphan products from Hitachi that added $4 million to revenue.

We acquired 6 new "A" customers in the US, opened 2 new countries with the help of the US Commerce Department resources, and started to align all our marketing mix to the targets we defined two years ago.

The team is working as a singe unit competing against the world. We've reduced DSO's and improved inventory turns. That funded our CapEx, while also reducing my borrowing. I couldn't ask for more from the team.

And this year, we created an incentive comp program to really make our success financially important to the execs.

While we did that, we've also established training programs for employees. We now make sure that tactical skills and supervisory skills are available for those qualified and interested employees. Initially we were concerned about training people so they could move on to other companies, but when they saw the Company growth and career opportunity, we were able to keep most of the people and better yet, we could attract some top-shelf talent. Just a very pleasant surprise.

I honestly think we can reach the $50 million sales target we set 2 years ago."

Doug was silent, while Patricia was bubbly.

"John, this has been an outstanding year for you. My gosh, two years ago you and I were concerned about this strategic planning project… but here we are today.

(000's $)	2018	2019	2020 Amt	2020 Fav (Unf) Bud/Strat		
				Amt	%	%
Headcount	400	405	435	15		
# New Products		3	6	0		
Capital Spending	459.0	1,200.0	1,150.0	-		
DSO	64	55	52	-2		
Inventory Turns	2.2	3.0	3.5	0		
% Return on Equity	15.0%	21.0%	22.0%			
Sales	29,960.0	34,550.0	44,500.0	3,200.0	7.7%	
Gross Margin	13,088.5	15,150.0	19,580.0	745.0	4.0%	
Margin %	43.7%	43.8%	44.0%	n/a		
SG&A	10,183.0	11,650.0	14,150.0	450.0	3.1%	
Pretax Profit	2,905.5	3,500.0	5,430.0	1,195.0	28.2%	
Pretax % Sales	9.7%	10.1%	12.2%	n/a		

John

Comments:
Comments:

- Acquired orphan products from Hitachi…$4 million annual sales

This was an excellent year for me as well. We continued with the same strategy – additional new products, expanded lines to men and children, broader distribution on the web, and firmly establishing the brand. We discovered an exceptional branding expert on the web. While our initial spend with them was limited – more of a trust thing – as she delivered results, we continued to spend.

My average order size is now $100 compared to $60 two years ago. My sales are up by 15% and profits are up by nearly 40%. You know, I've got so many things going, I didn't even fill out the entire worksheet. Sorry Doug.

We're paying for Natalie to get her DAP degree, and we're now planning to move to new facilities within the next year. I've started a phantom stock program so that the employees can actually feel the impact of the Company's success.

I'm about 99% certain that I'll meet the strategic plan we developed two years ago, and we revisit every October. I'm so happy about what's happened during the past two years, and it's all because I took a chance with Jackson."

(000's $)	2018	2019	Patricia 2020 Amt	2019 Fav (Unf) Bud/Strat Amt	%
# of New Products	2	4	5		
New Product 000 $	300.0	800.0	800.0		
Web Trans (000's)	1.5	12.0	25.0		
Avg Order Size ($)	60.0	85.0	100.0		
Headcount					
(000's US $)					
Revenue	6,700.0	7,300.0	8,400.0		
Gross Profit	4,000.0	4,400.0	5,000.0		
GP %					
SG&A	2,700.0	2,800.0	2,800.0	0	
Profit Before Tax	1,300.0	1,600.0			
PBT % Sales					
DSO					
Inventory Turns					

About the Author

Mike Gendron (CPA-Inactive) is the founding partner of CFO Insight LLC. He has extensive experience throughout Europe, Asia and Latin America in companies ranging in size from Business Week's 'Hottest Growth Companies in America' to billion-dollar companies. Industry experience includes high-tech electronics, telecom equipment, industrial instruments and FDA regulated operations.

During his career, he has been the CFO of global corporations – both public and private – and he has extensive experience in Fortune-500 corporations. He has participated in M&A transactions in France, Germany, China, Mexico, Canada and the US in industries such as high-tech electronics, telecom equipment, FDA regulated and industrial instruments.

He frequently speaks and writes about mergers & acquisitions, strategy, and high-growth operations, and he maintains a website (http://www.CFOInsight.net) dedicated to financial management and M&A.

In addition to flying high-performance airplanes as an instrument rated pilot, Mike enjoys backpacking, skiing and golf. Mike is Vice-Chairman of the Management & Entrepreneurship Advisory Board at Xavier University, and a member of numerous private company advisory boards.

Other Books by Michael P. Gendron

Preserve The Value: A Novel/Guide to
Successfully Integrate an Acquisition

Cashing Out @ Full Value: A Novel/Guide for
Boomers Selling the Family Business

Doing the M&A Deal: A Quick Access Field
Manual & Guide

Creating the New E-Business Company:
Innovative Strategies for Real-World
Applications

Integrating Newly Merged Organizations

A Practical Approach to International
Operations